LETTERS FROM THE PARIS PEACE CONFERENCE

CHARLES SEYMOUR
at his induction as president of Yale University, 1937

Behind him are Carl A. Lohmann (left), secretary of the university, and Edgar S.
Furniss, provost.

LETTERS FROM THE PARIS PEACE CONFERENCE

by Charles Seymour

Edited by Harold B. Whiteman, Jr.

New Haven and London, Yale University Press, 1965

CONTENTS

FOREWORD

THE PARIS PEACE CONFERENCE commanded the attention of the world in 1919. Since then the Treaty of Versailles—its framing, its purposes, its consequences, and its collapse—has commanded with unequaled intensity the study of participants at the Conference, observers, journalists, historians, contemporary and successor statesmen alike. "The treaty is the most abused and least perused document of history," was the observation of Lloyd George, one of its authors. "No document composed in the twentieth century has generated greater or more enduring controversy," correctly observes a later writer.[1] Monographs, memoirs, and minutes; biographies and autobiographies; diaries and reminiscences; histories of every description—the stream of publications about the Peace Conference continues to flow, having already produced more printed words than any other single historical event.

The explanation of this unabating interest involves several factors. First of all, the diplomatic assemblage summoned at the end of the Great War of 1914–18 faced tasks of such magnitude and complexity that it exceeded in importance any of its predecessors. The congresses of Vienna and Berlin had merely undone or minimized the effects of the Napoleonic Era and the Russo-Turkish War, respectively, but the Paris Conference had to remake the world—or so it seemed.[2] Then, too, if this attempt had been more successful, if the peace had been "won" as the war had been won, the extraordinary attention focused on the events of 1919 might not have emerged to the same degree. This was not the case, for the train of consequences stemming from the war and the Peace Conference has been swift and disastrous. History has sadly renamed the Great War as World War I, since World War II grew directly out of the same problems that confronted the peacemakers of 1919 and the solutions they

1. Theodore P. Greene, ed., *Wilson at Versailles*, Problems in American Civilization Series (Boston, 1957), p. 4.
2. See Charles Seymour, "Versailles in Perspective," *Virginia Quarterly Review*, 19 (Autumn 1943), 481–97.

devised. Interest in the Paris Conference has grown almost in proportion to the awareness of its failure.

On hand for the Conference were representatives of the 27 nations and 5 British Dominions which formed the victorious military coalition. Spokesmen for numerous minority groups were also present, but there were no representatives of Russia or the defeated Central Powers. The 70 delegates of the Allied and Associated Powers were led by the heads of government of the three great Western nations—President Wilson, Prime Minister Lloyd George, and Premier Clemenceau—and were assisted by staffs of general and special assistants who totaled several thousand, the Americans alone numbering approximately 1300. In effect, this extraordinary gathering faced problems at two distinct levels: first, the guiding principles and second, their application to the many specific questions stemming from the war and the vast political upheaval it produced.

Prior to the Conference, Woodrow Wilson had dramatically revived an old vision of a new and better world, a dream shared by war-weary peoples everywhere, when he proposed a new set of international principles to replace militarism, balance of power, imperialism, excessive nationalism—all the evils that seemed to have produced the war. His open commitment to open diplomacy, self-determination, impartial justice, disarmament—the substance of his famed "Fourteen Points" and subsequent pronouncements—reawakened old ambitions and released new and powerful forces throughout the world. Both vital to and symbolic of the Wilsonian program, of course, was a democratic world organization in the form of a League of Nations. Also implied by his program was a peace of moderation.

The Allies were formally committed to this program—though with important reservations—by the terms of Germany's surrender and the armistice of November 1918. Presumably it was to be the basis for the forthcoming peace. The military events of the war, which at the time was the most extensive of all global conflicts, did not, however, lay the groundwork for a settlement of true moderation. Other passions had been created among the European Allies who, with victory, thirsted for revenge against the Central Powers and sought means to convert their victory into territorial gains, economic advantages, reparations, and permanent military security. Moreover, they had other formal commitments, the so-called "secret treaties," which involved widespread territorial annexations on anything but Wilsonian principles. It proved unfortunate that these commitments, designed during the course of the war itself either to strengthen alliances or to induce neutral nations to take up arms on the Allied side, were not renounced at the time the Wilsonian principles were accepted. France made a proposal to this end, but the President ignored it since France simultaneously proposed separating the peace settlement and the creation of the League.

Against this background, the actual course of the Conference became a series of struggles between the victors—struggles over principles, commitments, and applications. The vanquished were virtually ignored, as were the formal conditions of surrender. Germany's inevitable protests of betrayal were also ignored, though at a later date the revived military and political power of Hitler's Reich gave new substance to the protests, especially when he denounced the treaty by action and by word. This development, in turn, also helps explain the continuing fascination of Versailles.

Perhaps it is axiomatic that victors always quarrel over the spoils of war and over the principles which are to guide their subsequent actions, and that original causes and purposes seemingly disappear in new, angry, and agitated dynamisms. It is undoubtedly true that lingering problems, such as sporadic flare-ups of fighting and immense human suffering, especially in Central Europe, could have been anticipated at Paris as a normal consequence of the prolonged and widespread conflict of 1914–18. But the peacemakers faced yet another situation which was far from normal and added greatly to their problems, and which also provides another partial answer to the interest generated by the Paris Conference; they faced the end of an age.

Four of the great dynasties of Europe and Asia—Russian, German, Austro-Hungarian, and Turkish—were in varying stages of dissolution. The geographical center of world power and influence was moving from Western Europe, although not without resistance and uncertainty as to the direction of the move. Moreover, the ideological basis of international politics was under direct revolutionary assault from one quarter, while from another an almost equally revolutionary attempt was being made to submit the relations among nations to the control of democratic objectives and processes. In the East, Bolshevism was already exercising a precarious rule in parts of the domain of one of the fallen dynasties and was striving to fill the vacua left by the others. From across the Atlantic, Wilson's program gave promise of a radically different approach to problems of law and order, peace and security, for the first time in modern history.

Revolutionary movements were not new to the European statesmen at
Paris, who were accustomed to upheavals in the name of nationalism.
Bolshevism, however, assumed an intraclass, international base, and the
resurgence of democratic idealism sparked by Wilson also transcended
national boundaries. It seemed that the year 1919 might well mark the
beginning of an international age unless older nationalisms and power
structures were revived and reinvigorated.

Lenin's revolution was largely ignored by the peacemakers, who
rationalized that military operations still dominated the Russian scene and
that the revolution would soon be quashed. But as the agreed basis of the
peace, Wilson's plan could not be ignored, even though the results of the
1918 elections in the United States raised serious questions as to the support the President commanded at home. The pivotal issue of the League
became the dominant theme at Paris and in some way or to some extent
influenced all other considerations: the military and economic terms imposed upon Germany, the character of the successor states carved from
the former empires, boundary readjustments, provisions for French security, disposition of distant colonies, reparations. The particular solutions
reached in each case usually reflected the degree to which the Wilsonian
program was accepted by the statesmen at Paris or by their governments,
for in the end both levels of Conference problems were settled by a series of uneasy compromises. On the one hand, the European Allies got
many of their materialistic objectives—but not all of them, nor as openly
as they would have chosen. On the other hand, Wilson obtained his
League, but at a high price in terms of his other objectives and principles.
Moreover, his very principles had proven upon occasion to be contradictory in application.

The result was that the new world at birth seemed to suffer many of the
ills of the old. This fact, added to the President's unwillingness to make
further compromises with his domestic opponents, led to the eventual rejection of the Treaty and the League by the United States Senate. That
Wilson had earlier made compromises at the Conference in order to preserve the League was a frank recognition that forces of history, geography,
economics, and politics could not be modified easily or rapidly even by
such high principles as justice and equality and self-determination.

Given the many powerful ingredients that made up the Paris Conference, and given the difficulty of a final evaluation of diplomacy in operation under the best of circumstances, it is no wonder that history's verdict
on the Treaty of Versailles has been mixed and the conflict of opinion

sharp.[3] The failure to secure peace, of course, has generated a decidedly critical tone, but the range of criticism has been extreme: the treaty was harsh and reactionary, or soft and idealistic, or an ineffective combination of both—one or the other would have been preferable. Wilson has been criticized as being a political idealist and an economic reactionary, or, worst of all, for being inconsistent. Other attacks on Wilson allege a lack of preparation for the Conference, a tactical error by personal participation, and an intellectual and moral breakdown in the face of criticism and illness. More friendly interpretations defend Wilson as being in advance of his time and propose two general theses: the fault lay not in the Treaty, but in the later failure to capitalize on it and in subsequent events in both Europe and the United States; or, the Treaty was the best possible under the circumstances, and the President, fully aware of its shortcomings, depended upon full American participation in an effective League to set aright the legacy of unsolved or badly solved issues.[4]

The scope and intensity of this debate reveal another aspect of the prolonged study of the Conference. Wilson epitomized an even more significant quarrel over the basic guiding principle of American foreign policy and national security. Had world conditions so changed that political isolationism should be abandoned for political involvement? The Senate answered—for reasons of principle, but also for personal and partisan reasons—in the negative, but the question continued to be asked during the two decades between world wars. There then occurred a great diplomatic revolution when the United States undertook the leadership of international organization and a system of military and political alliances.

One further and final measure of understanding of the attention attracted by the Treaty comes from the realization that some 500 newsmen and journalists came to the French capital to observe and report. They arrived with an expectation created by Wilson's promise of "open covenants openly arrived at," a response to the popular conception of evil secret diplomacy. The President was quickly to discover that this aspect

3. In his "Refighting the War on Paper," *Yale Review, 18* (June 1929), 625–45, Seymour predicted unanimity of judgment would probably never be possible. For a summary of the arguments see Ivo J. Lederer, ed., *The Versailles Settlement,* Problems in European Civilization Series (Boston, 1960). The same author's *Yugoslavia at the Paris Peace Conference* (New Haven, 1963) is a detailed study of one of Seymour's major preoccupations at the Conference.

4. This was Seymour's conclusion. See "Versailles in Perspective" and his "Woodrow Wilson in Perspective," *Foreign Affairs, 34* (January 1956), 175–86. See also Greene, *Wilson at Versailles,* pp. v–x.

of his moralistic idealism could not withstand the less disinterested demands of his European associates, to say nothing of the sheer impossibility of achieving any accommodation of conflicting purposes in the glare of publicity. The waiting world learned very little of what was going on as the conferees became more and more secretive in their deliberations. Rumor, conjecture, and immediate criticism were the inevitable results and laid the groundwork for prolonged examination by later historians whose sources and techniques for study and restudy have steadily improved. During the Conference itself records of every kind, official and personal, accumulated rapidly but were not released. They have been made available only slowly and intermittently over the years.

When the Conference convened in January 1919, Charles Seymour had just celebrated his thirty-fourth birthday. During the previous year he had also celebrated his promotion to a full professorship in the History Department of Yale University. Since he had been a faculty member for less than seven years, his ascent up the academic ladder had been both swift and a faithful augury of the distinguished twin career as historian and university administrator which was to follow. His participation in the work of the Paris Conference as chief of the Austro-Hungarian Division of the American Commission to Negotiate Peace marked a turning point in his own professional career and placed him in the forefront of the ranks of American scholars who contributed much to the subsequent understanding of the dramatic and agonizing years between 1914 and 1919.

Born in New Haven on the first day of 1885, he was the son of another illustrious Yale scholar and professor of Greek, Thomas Day Seymour. His forebears included a great-great-great-grandfather given an honorary degree at Yale's first graduation in 1702 and two Yale presidents. His birthplace is today the site of one of the university's residential colleges, and he was never to be absent from Yale for long. Upon completing high school in 1901 he traveled to King's College, Cambridge, where three years later he received his first B.A. degree. He then returned to Yale as an undergraduate and earned a second baccalaureate degree as a member of the class of 1908. Resolved to continue graduate work in history, he studied at the University of Freiburg in Germany in the summer of 1908 and at l'École des Hautes Études of the University of Paris during the following winter; he then qualified for the M.A. degree from Cambridge in 1909. Once more he returned to Yale, this time to the Graduate School, where he received the doctorate in 1911. Simultaneously he was appointed instructor in history and married Gladys Marion Watkins of Scranton, Pennsylvania.

Seymour's early teaching concentrated on European history and especially France, his major interest at the time. Within the short span of seven years he wrote two books—*Electoral Reform in England and Wales* (New Haven, 1915)[5] and *The Diplomatic Background of the War, 1870–1914* (New Haven, 1916)—co-edited a selected collection of the writings of Thomas Carlyle, co-authored a study of democratic development in elections, and joined with several other scholars in a revision of a twelve-volume historical reference series.[6] During the same period his first two children, Charles, Jr., and Elizabeth, were born. The third, Sarah, came after the war in 1920.

Seymour's demonstrated competence within a department noted for its excellence, and his association with one of its older members, led in mid-1917 to his being asked to serve on "The Inquiry," the details of which he himself outlined in the introduction he wrote for this volume.[7] The existence of this group of 150 scholars and the wide range of their studies provide ample refutation of the allegation that President Wilson's only purpose was the creation of the League of Nations. On the other hand, the League was central to his thinking. As he encountered at Paris successive difficulties and setbacks to his more comprehensive program he became increasingly convinced of its absolute necessity.

Before the Conference met, Wilson foresaw difficulties ahead for his program. This realization and the fear that spokesmen for the old regime of power alliances might sweep aside his cherished concept led to one of the many debatable decisions the President made. He resolved to go to Paris himself. He also decided to take with him certain members of the Inquiry—eventually 23 in all—to serve as the Division of Territorial, Economic, and Political Intelligence. Somewhat to the chagrin of the State Department and the Military Intelligence Division, which were also represented within the American Commission as were other branches of the government, this group became Wilson's primary source of information and advice.

5. A revision of his doctoral dissertation.

6. Samuel B. Hemingway and Charles Seymour, eds., *Selections from Carlyle* (Springfield, Mass., 1915); Seymour and Donald Paige Frary, *How the World Votes* (2 vols. Springfield, Mass., 1918); Donald E. Smith, Seymour, et al., eds., *The New Larned History for Ready Reference, Reading and Research* (12 vols. Springfield, Mass., 1922–24).

7. See also Lawrence E. Gelfand, *The Inquiry* (New Haven, 1963).

Although Seymour had left the Inquiry in mid-1918 to serve as a special assistant in the State Department, he was included in the small contingent of scholars that sailed for France with the President aboard the S.S. *George Washington*. A very young member of a delegation whose characteristic was youth, he responded to the excitement of the mission and to its sense of high purpose. He shared with another young man, the British diplomat and author Harold Nicolson, the feeling that, "we were to journey to Paris, not merely to liquidate the war, but to found a new order in Europe. We were preparing not Peace only, but Eternal Peace. There was about us the halo of some divine mission. We must be stern, righteous, and ascetic. For we were bent on doing great, permanent, and noble things."[8]

In Paris the eager young historian found himself rubbing shoulders with many of the great and near-great from the intricate world of European politics. He also found, in addition to the scores of specific problems which demanded the attention of the assembled statesmen, an underlying clash of philosophy and method between those who wanted to push ahead boldly into the uncertain areas of a new order and those who preferred to look to the past, repair its mistakes, and restore the old order. For a personal record of the events of the Conference he undertook a series of letters, first to his wife until she was able to join him and then to her family, in which he set down many of his impressions and preoccupations—and his frequent encounters with Yale classmates or associates, including some former students—during the hectic six months of the Conference. At the same time he was conscious of the need for discretion in discussing some of the thorny issues, and the reader of his letters may well occasionally regret that complete candor was impossible since his correspondence did not enjoy diplomatic immunity.

The experience at Paris changed the course of his professional life as an historian. Although he continued to teach European history for some years, he eventually shifted to American diplomatic history, and the five major works he published after the war dealt with this subject and the wartime period. In 1921 he wrote *Woodrow Wilson and the World War* (New Haven), and in the same year he and Colonel Edward Mandell House co-edited, under the title *What Really Happened at Paris* (New York), a set of papers written by members of the American delegation. This association, initiated through the Inquiry and continued in Paris where House served as Wilson's chief lieutenant, proved most significant.

Charles Seymour developed a close friendship with the Colonel. When

8. Quoted by Seymour, "Versailles in Perspective," p. 482.

the latter retired from public life to the inner councils of the Democratic Party, he entrusted his invaluable diary and papers to Seymour for study and safekeeping at the Yale Library. The result was the publication between 1926 and 1928 of the four volumes of *The Intimate Papers of Colonel House* (Boston). Just as the Colonel's gift established Yale as a leading center for the study of American diplomatic history, the appearance of these volumes made Seymour a foremost authority in the field. Early recognition of his ability as an historian came with the award of honorary degrees from Western Reserve University, where his maternal grandfather had once served as president, and from Trinity College, and by his designation in 1922 as a Sterling Professor, Yale's most distinguished faculty appointment, and in 1923 as departmental chairman. Two years later he was sponsored by the Belgian-American Educational Foundation as a visiting professor at the universities of Brussels, Ghent, Liège, and Louvain.

Seymour's two later books, *American Diplomacy During the World War* (Baltimore, 1934) and *American Neutrality, 1914–1917* (New Haven, 1935), products of his mature and energetic scholarship, confirmed his reputation and also spelled out one of the major interpretive answers to the question of why the United States had entered the war, a question born of American guilt feelings and disillusionment. His conclusion—the submarine policy of Germany—provided a rather unpopular antidote to more sensational theories of the moment, which centered on allegations concerning profit-thirsty munitions makers and Wall Street bankers who manipulated American policy, and also, in effect, attacked the isolationist neutrality legislation of the 1930s.[9]

Seymour's career as an administrator also flourished after the war. He became provost of Yale in 1927 and played a major role in an immense building program, including the establishment of nine of the colleges that comprise the undergraduate part of the university. By serving also as the first master of Berkeley College he helped put into operation in 1933 a program designed to reintroduce personality as a basic and indispensable

9. Seymour's thesis developed in such articles as "Secrets of British Diplomacy: Earl Grey's Revelations," *Current History, 23* (December 1925), 328–34 (a review of Grey's *Twenty-Five Years, 1892–1916*); "Diplomatic Background of America's Entry Into the War," *Current History, 33* (January 1931), 540–44; "American Neutrality: The Experience of 1914–1917," *Foreign Affairs, 14* (October 1935), 26–36. He also wrote a brief, lucid synthesis of historical interpretations of the outbreak of hostilities: "How the War Came," *Virginia Quarterly Review, 7* (October 1931), 599–606 (a review of Bernadotte E. Schmitt's *The Coming of the War*). A vigorous exception to Seymour's views came from R. L. Buell, "Neutrality, Then and Now," *Saturday Review of Literature, 13* (December 21, 1935), 5.

element in education.[10] Four years later—at a moment when his historical interpretations and his opposition to the neutrality legislation based on opposing views were subjects of public controversy—he was selected to become Yale's fifteenth president, a position he held until his retirement in 1950.[11] It was his responsibility to guide the destinies of his university during the difficult and chaotic years of World War II, during which the university was dedicated to the dual role of carrying on the regular curriculum for civilians and training specialists for the armed services while still fulfilling the basic objectives of undergraduate education, both on an accelerated year-round basis.[12] Despite these extraordinary strains, his administration produced important and lasting innovations in the undergraduate curriculum aimed at strengthening the relationships among various disciplines and encouraging independent study, the establishment of a number of research and teaching institutes, and the flourishing of an alumni organization unmatched by any other American university. During his presidency a tenth undergraduate college was built, the student body almost doubled, and the university's endowment increased substantially.

Associates found the president's warm, easy, and wise demeanor of old to be unchanged and unchanging. He continued to relax with a corncob pipe and his collection of mystery novels, or with an informal group of fellow songsters, but simultaneously he spoke out vigorously and with increasing authority on contemporary questions: he stressed the intellectual and moral responsibility of the individual as the basis of freedom; he accepted the classic and liberal definition of the university's role as "the unhindered search for truth" with which to clarify issues and on which to build rational opinion and wisdom, but he also insisted upon a university creed that there is a difference between right and wrong and upon a university obligation "to make the distinction and to give effect to it"; he described himself as a conservative in that he put emphasis upon the established values; frequently he spoke of the need for the university to maintain an atmosphere characterized by a spiritual tone, but at the same time he warned against academic isolation from the main currents of national thought; and he anticipated the necessity of applying the liberal arts to

10. Charles Seymour, "The New Yale," *Review of Reviews, 83* (June 1931), 44–45.

11. A small measure of excitement was added to the moment of his election by divinity students picketing the trustee's meeting in protest against the failure of a popular professor to obtain academic tenure.

12. Seymour described Yale's pioneering wartime program in several articles in the *New York Times Magazine.* See issues of September 29, 1940; April 12, 1942; September 6, 1942; December 27, 1942; also *Life, 12* (June 1, 1942), 55 ff.

new, vital uses in a changing world, and the need for improved non-Western studies, expanded adult education, and increased educational opportunities for the disadvantaged everywhere. His gracious and responsible leadership and his stature as a scholar of distinction were both recognized by many of Yale's sister institutions, ten of which awarded him honorary degrees—including Princeton, Harvard, the University of Lyon, and the University of Hawaii. He also became an Honorary Fellow of both King's College and Stanford University, and a Commander in the French Legion of Honor.

The demands of his administrative duties temporarily removed President Seymour from his activities as an historian, although he did write his article on "Versailles in Perspective" in 1943 as a guide and a warning to a new group of peacemakers who would have to settle the even wider-ranging problems and suffering created by World War II. Significantly he urged against any attempt to legislate a comprehensive world settlement in any one conference. Chaos and suffering should be eliminated first; economic issues should be given full attention; then a more deliberate approach to political problems and international organization should follow. Persuaded that American public opinion in the period of World War I and its immediate aftermath unfortunately did not realize how our security would have been threatened by a German victory, and unshaken in his original faith in the League of Nations,[13] he saw clearly that any new league must be built on a public consensus and must be aimed at removing causes of war, rather than attempting merely to prevent war.

After his retirement in 1950 President Seymour returned to history and to the House Papers, to which had been added several other contemporary collections, including those of Gordon Auchincloss, Vance C. McCormick, and Frank L. Polk—all Yale men who were involved with the Conference—and of Sir William Wiseman, the chief of British Military Intelligence in the United States during the war.[14]

Seymour's studies and frequent consultations with Wilsonian scholars fully occupied his final years, especially after the dramatic shift in Ameri-

13. In dismay over the reaction in the United States to the Treaty of Versailles, Seymour wrote a strong defense of the League, based on duty and self-interest, soon after his return from Paris: "The League of Nations," Yale Review, 9 (October 1919), 28–43. The signing of the Locarno Pacts in 1925 greatly encouraged him. See "The Beginning of the Peace," Yale Review, 15 (January 1926), 209–25, and "Imaginative Courage," Outlook, 153 (October 9, 1929), 221 ff. But the resurgence of American isolationism in the 1930s came as a blow to his belief in internationalism and especially in Anglo-American cooperation. See "A Stay-at-Home Policy for America" (a critical review of Charles A. Beard's Open Door at Home), Current History, 41 (March 1935), 675–80.

14. Gelfand, The Inquiry, p. 116.

can foreign policy released a new wave of sympathetic interest in the chief architect of the unsuccessful League, whom he now termed "the greatest of all prophets in the cause of international justice and freedom."[15] During this period he also wrote a summary of his own conclusions about certain aspects of the Paris Conference, which he delivered in 1951 at the first Isaiah Bowman Memorial Lecture at The Johns Hopkins University.[16] On that occasion he said:

> The Peace Conference, representing the democracies, reflected the mind of the age; it could not rise measurably above its source. That mind was dominated by a reactionary nostalgia and a traditional nationalism . . .

> So long as there are nations, selfish national interests are bound to exist. We must take account of them. We must learn to define exactly our own political interest; we must understand clearly and objectively the interests of our allies and of our enemies. No ultimate and permanent adjustment can be made that disregards political interest.

> But in that adjustment the principle of justice must play a major and, in the end we may hope, a determining role . . . The idealistic vision of Woodrow Wilson must always be before our eyes, not merely a vision of justice in the abstract, but one that shall be administered with even hand through the organized co-operation of all the nations of the world. Only thus can there be a permanent assurance of bridging the gap between national self-interest and human justice.

Another project dealt with the abrupt and rather mysterious ending of the friendship between Wilson and House. This human drama, part of the larger personal tragedy of Wilson's illness and defeat, pricked the curiosity of many historical students. Speculation centered on House's apparent willingness to compromise on the League question, on his assumption of too much authority, and on Mrs. Wilson's zealous protection of

15. Illustrative of Seymour's many contributions are the preface to John W. Davidson, ed., *A Crossroads of Freedom: The 1912 Campaign Speeches of Woodrow Wilson* (New Haven, 1956), and "The Role of Colonel House in Wilson's Diplomacy" in E. H. Buehrig, *Wilson's Foreign Policy in Perspective* (Bloomington, Ind., 1957), pp. 11–33. See also Arthur C. Walworth, *Woodrow Wilson* (New York, 1958).

16. *Geography, Justice, and Politics at the Paris Conference of 1919* (New York, American Geographical Society, 1951), reprinted in Lederer, *The Versailles Settlement*, pp. 106–14.

her husband's position. The two principals remained silent and shed no public light on the cause of the rupture.

Colonel House did, however, entrust Seymour with his version of the break, but enjoined him to maintain 25 years of silence following his death, which occurred in 1938. House's memorandum, completed and elucidated by Seymour, was published in August 1963.[17] Very quickly it produced a posthumous "rebuttal" from Wilson's personal physician, Admiral Cary T. Grayson, actually written in 1926 but also withheld until 1964.[18]

With the encouragement of his university press, Seymour also undertook to edit the letters he wrote while in Paris. He commenced this undertaking the year of his death (1963), but was unable to complete it. The task has now been finished with the publication of this volume. Both in general design and in detail, the author's original plan has been preserved. Happily he finished an introduction and a few of the identifications of the many names that appear in the letters. The latter are followed by the initials "C.S."; others have been supplied by the editor. Aware that the meaning and significance of a unilateral correspondence can be enhanced by some background explanation, the author compiled a partial list of topics and events for annotation. This served as a basis for the chapter prefaces and the expository footnotes that have been added to his work. An original outline for chapters, apparently made with an eye chiefly on evenly balanced pagination, has been altered slightly to correlate with the various phases of the Conference.

The integrity of the original letters, the fresh and vivid impressions of a younger man required to take a stand on many controversial questions have been carefully preserved. He occasionally commented on his own naïveté, dogmatism, inconsistency, or inaccurate prophecy—and these comments are included—but the original observations have not been changed. In a sense this volume is a diary, unfinished but essentially unaltered. In the course of his rereading of the letters, the author made a few stylistic corrections and a few deletions of family or personal references that would not interest the general reader. With the assistance of Mrs.

17. Seymour, "End of a Friendship," *American Heritage, 14* (August 1963), 5–9.
18. Grayson, "The Colonel's Folly and the President's Distress," *American Heritage, 15* (October 1964), 4–7. The publication of the House Papers, in process at the time Grayson wrote, displeased Mrs. Wilson and the Admiral, the only two persons who had access to the President during the critical months of his illness in 1919–20. They felt that the Colonel assumed more credit and responsibility for Wilson's program than was his due.

Seymour, Miss Elizabeth Seymour, Charles Seymour, Jr., named in his father's will as literary executor, and of Clarence W. Mendell, Sterling Professor Emeritus at Yale and himself a participant at the Conference, another similar review has been made.

The completion of the editing and annotation has involved many persons in addition to members of the Seymour family. For most, including myself, this has been a task of love and respect for a friend, mentor, or associate; in particular Ivo J. Lederer, formerly associate professor of history at Yale, Howard Gotlieb, formerly Yale University Archivist, Judith Schiff, Librarian of the Historical Manuscripts Collection in the Yale Library, and Marian Neal Ash and Ruth L. Davis of the Yale University Press have all contributed greatly to the completion of the work. Robert L. Williams and Dorothy deFontaine prepared the two special maps. Others not fortunate enough to know Charles Seymour attended to many details, including the copying of all the original letters by Ellen Patterson of the Historical Manuscripts Collection. All of us have enjoyed the experience of viewing the Paris Conference through his eyes, and through this experience have come to know more of the man himself and of the great meeting he attended. It is this experience we want to share.

H. B. WHITEMAN, JR.

New York
March 1965

INTRODUCTION

by Charles Seymour

HALF A CENTURY AGO, during the First World War, the habit of drafting college professors en masse for the public service of the United States had not yet seized upon Washington. There still lingered from the nineteenth century a suspicion, not entirely unwarranted by valid evidence, that the life of a scholar, uncompromising in its search for the truth, is not the best preparation for the rough realism of politics. The nation was trying hard to get used to the surprising fact that a professor in the White House could actually put through Congress a tough and contentious legislative program. It would have been further shocked had it known that President Wilson, in preparation for the most critical peace conference of history, had been minded to select as advisers not the elegant and experienced diplomatists of tradition, but a group of pedagogues, who were doubtless well equipped to write scholarly books but who could hardly be expected to understand the facts of international life. Fortunately for the popular sense of national security, the functions of this recently appointed group of presidential advisers and the names of those selected were carefully kept secret.

It was in the summer of 1917, after some three months of American participation in the European war, that President Wilson became sharply aware of the acute difference in war aims that divided the United States from our European associates in the struggle against Germany. "England and France," he wrote to his intimate adviser Colonel House, "have not by any means the same purpose as ours." He recognized also the need of careful preparation of the case which he planned to argue before the final peace conference and the necessity of authoritative determination of the facts upon which it would rest. Talk of peace was in the air that summer, stirred by the Pope's proposal of a negotiated compromise. The British and French had already set up study groups and were beginning to draft specific proposals which might serve as bases for a comprehensive peace settlement. In September 1917 Wilson wrote to House asking him to organize a corresponding study group so that our own "pipes would be laid" and our national policy in problems of the peace clarified and implemented for argument.

It was entirely in character that Colonel House should proceed in this undertaking without publicity ("privately" as he expressed it, "secretly" as his later critics termed it). As always, he secured complete cooperation from news correspondents, so that it was not until the very eve of the Peace Conference that any public notice was taken of the studies under his direction. As cover, an innocuous and rather nondescriptive title was assigned to the organization—*The Inquiry* it was called. (Later historians have liked to accent the first syllable of the word; this would have sounded strange to the ears of members of the group, who invariably pronounced it In*qui*ry). It seemed to House important to avoid any public reference to peace studies lest it appear that the end of the war was regarded as imminent. He desired also to escape importunate applications for appointment to the staff, for the work promised to be exciting and might prove important. The organization of studies was decentralized; much of the research was carried on in the library of the American Geographical Society in New York, but with significant research going forward in the New York Public Library, the Library of Congress, or in the university libraries of the various scholars attached to the staff. Members of the Inquiry remained as far as possible anonymous, and their appointment went unnoticed by the public press.

The functions of the Inquiry in actual operation have been later described, and properly so, as falling within the general field of "intelligence." Later at the Peace Conference in Paris the organization was formally given the name of "Division of Territorial, Economic, and Political Intelligence." Our papers and reports were kept under lock and key; the nature of our investigations was never discussed with outsiders. But it was far from resembling a cloak and dagger affair. We had little to do with secret documents; a large part of the material gathered was from encyclopedias, open to the wide world. We did not deal in ciphers and codes. In my own case the major sources of information were found in the current volumes of the census for Austria and for Hungary. There was little material essential to my reports that could not be found in the Library of Congress. The special demographic authorities necessary to research in problems of the frontier were secured by the American Geographical Society. Extraordinary demands for esoteric materials were invariably met through the magical influence of Colonel House.

It was characteristic of the latter that after laying down the broad lines which the Inquiry was expected to follow he disappeared into the background. The details of administration relative to personnel and to program he delegated to his brother-in-law Sidney Mezes, president of the College of the City of New York, who was named director of the organization. Mezes, a genial but retiring philosopher, exercised a very loose control, scarcely more than indicating to the individual scholars concerned the area or the specific problem for which they would be regarded as responsible and the general nature of the reports which would be called for from time to time.[1]

The problem areas to be studied were for the most part obvious: territories covered by the "secret treaties"; traditional frontier issues such as those touching Schleswig, the Tyrol, Trieste, and the Adriatic coast and islands; Belgium; the Saar; nascent national entities taking form in Austria-Hungary, the Balkans, and the Near East; the "liberated" German colonies. Problems of finance, of economics, and of general international organization were not attacked by the Inquiry on a large scale and were left for subsequent study by other advisers. The selection of the "experts" who would direct the studies in this area and that was apparently haphazard, and not always related to the special field of the scholar's interest. In my own case I was invited to join the Inquiry, I supposed, by reason of my friendship with Isaiah Bowman, who had recently left the Yale faculty to become director of the American Geographical Society.[2] Notwithstanding his relative youth Bowman was already recognized as an outstanding demographical authority; the wisdom of his decisions on policy and the vigor of his personality enabled him shortly to assume a position of determining influence in the Inquiry. He assigned to me responsibility for the territorial problems in the Austro-Hungarian area.[3] When I protested

1. Mezes (1863–1931), California born and educated, married Mrs. House's sister. He served successively as professor, dean, and then president at the University of Texas from 1894 until 1914, and he headed City College from 1914 until 1927.

2. Bowman (1878–1950), a scholar in the geological sciences and geography, took advanced training at Harvard and Yale, and served on the Yale faculty until 1915. As executive officer of the Inquiry he assumed a leading role in its organization and the appointments to its staff. At the Peace Conference he served as chief territorial specialist for the American Commission and on various territorial commissions. After his return to the United States he rejoined the American Geographical Society until 1935 when he became president of The Johns Hopkins University. During World War II he filled numerous advisory posts within the State Department. A dynamo of energy, to his enthusiasm and unflagging drive the Inquiry owed its increasing influence as much as to the invaluable support of Colonel House. (C.S.)

3. Serving under Seymour in this division were Robert J. Kerner, age 30, William E. Lunt, 35, and Austin P. Evans, 34.

that I knew them only as a tourist and merely from headlines he bade me "get down to work and become an authority." In drafting my reports I was comfortably left to my own devices as to the material I would include and the conclusions I was permitted to draw. One of my colleagues remarked that in the organization of our research he was reminded of the comment of the Biblical chronicler: "And every man did that which seemed right in his own eyes."[4]

Nevertheless the papers accumulated over a period of 18 months by the Inquiry, and now deposited in the National Archives, represent a vast amount of research and brought together a wealth of erudition. And as the investigators gained experience, a surprising proportion of the material thus gathered ultimately appeared pertinent to the negotiations and decisions of the Conference in Paris. Aside from Bowman, I think, great credit for the work of those early days should go to Walter Lippmann, who for a period of nine months acted as secretary of the Inquiry, to which he brought his editorial talent and especially the genius of his clarity of expression and his judgment in the isolation of and emphasis upon vital issues.[5] He and Bowman were primarily responsible for the final form of the report which Colonel House took with him to Washing-

4. Later Seymour wrote that members of the Inquiry were chosen, "almost invariably" by Bowman, on the basis of "general capacity and scholarship." Regional experts were scarce. "Lunt and I myself had not special knowledge of the regions to which we were assigned . . . We were kept on because Bowman liked our reports." Letter from Seymour to Gelfand, cited in *The Inquiry*, pp. 314–15.

5. Lippmann (b. 1890), Harvard '10, journalist and author on political science, was a special assistant to Secretary of War Newton Baker. Among the original appointees to the Inquiry, he served on the research and executive committees, one of the inner five (Mezes, Bowman, Lippmann, James T. Shotwell, and David Hunter Miller). Early in 1918, he became fed up with the idea of meticulous research. "We've skimmed the cream of the adventure of Inquiry," he said and accepted a captain's commission in the Military Intelligence Division. Mezes and House never forgave him; they refused to let him come back at the time of the Peace Conference. If he had been given the post that went to R. S. Baker, he might have been of infinite service. His genius for clarification would have been invaluable for writing communiqués. His lively critical sense was controlled by a poise that estopped exaggeration. The clarity of his mental processes qualified him for drafting programs more than for effective administration or handling of subordinates. After World War I he returned to journalism and has established himself as the "dean" of political commentators. (C.S.) Ray Stannard Baker (1870–1946), journalist and author, served as a special commissioner of the State Department in Europe and then as chief of the Press Bureau of the Commission. Later he wrote two studies of the Conference, *Woodrow Wilson and World Settlement* (3 vols. New York, 1922), and *The Versailles Treaty and After* (New York, 1924). Then as the "authorized" biographer he compiled *Woodrow Wilson, Life and Letters* (8 vols. New York, 1927–37).

ton for discussion with Woodrow Wilson in January 1918 and which
served as the basis of the speech of the Fourteen Points. In later crises
the Inquiry was able to produce at short notice documented recommendations which won the respect and the approbation of President Wilson.

It was generally taken for granted during the final months of the war
that from the ranks of the Inquiry a small group would be chosen to
serve as an advisory board of some sort to the President and the United
States delegation at the Peace Conference. But how many and who would
be selected remained a matter of speculation up to the signing of the armistice and for some days after. There were at that time no formal chiefs
of division in the very loose organization that constituted the Inquiry, and
no hint was given as to who might be needed at Paris. Colonel House
had left in mid-October to sit with the European chiefs of state in settling
the terms of the armistice, and with no indication to any of us who was to
be picked for service with the Peace Commission. Actually, although
nothing had been said, selections had been virtually made by the time of
his departure, to be announced by Dr. Mezes a week or so after the
signing of the armistice.

From the early summer of 1918 I had been detached temporarily from
the work of the Inquiry in New York and appointed a special assistant in
the Department of State, stationed in Washington. This appointment I
owed to my friendship with William Bullitt, a former history pupil of
mine during his undergraduate days at Yale.[6] An active and pervasive
news correspondent in Germany and Austria during early war days, when
the United States became a belligerent Bullitt was given a post in the
State Department where he was responsible for current intelligence relating to the Central Powers. He found himself overloaded with reports
from Berlin and Vienna and persuaded William Phillips, Assistant Secretary of State,[7] to secure me on loan from the Inquiry to take over responsibility for current despatches relating to Austria-Hungary. My ap-

6. Bullitt (b. 1896), Yale '12, worked for the Philadelphia *Public Ledger* until
he entered government service. At the Peace Conference he was in charge of current intelligence and undertook a special mission to Russia which led to disagreement with Wilson over Allied policy toward the Bolsheviks and to Bullitt's angry resignation. Later he
returned to serve as ambassador to Russia (1933–36), and to France (1936–40). During World War II he became special assistant to the Secretary of the Navy for a year,
then enlisted in the French Army. (C.S.)

7. Phillips (1878–1957), Harvard '00, career diplomat and statesman, served in
numerous foreign posts including that of ambassador to Belgium and Italy (1936–41)
and also as Under Secretary of State (1922–24 and 1933–36).

pointment in the Department of State proved a fortunate chance for me: it brought me into close contact with Bullitt, who knew everyone who had anything to do with the war from the President down; and it gave me an intimate picture of political developments in the special field to which I had been assigned by the Inquiry. It also put me into a preferred position when the time came for appointments at the Peace Conference.

At the moment of the signing of the armistice, November 11, I was still working in Washington and wondering what would happen. But shortly I was ordered to report back in New York at Inquiry headquarters and warned to be ready for departure for Paris at an early date. It was not until Thanksgiving that, together with the others selected, I was definitely informed that we would be included in President Wilson's staff when he sailed for France on the *George Washington* early in December. Even then it was only by the merest good luck that I was spared a cruel, last-moment disappointment. We were under strict orders not to disclose the fact of our appointment or the approximate date of the ship's sailing until it was officially announced by the President's office. But the wife of one of the appointees could not resist a little boastful gossip in the family, and her cousin, a resourceful newspaperman, was not one to resist the temptation of a minor scoop. His paper announced that Professor Clive Day and Professor Seymour would "accompany" the President to the conference in Paris. The notice was printed in the New York papers. Had this premature announcement caught the eye of President Wilson the two thus named would certainly have been struck from the rolls forthwith. But we were protected by our inconspicuous political unimportance and the incident passed without further notice.

My personal good fortune was further enhanced by the circumstance that Day and I were assigned to the same cabin on the *George Washington* as later, in Paris, we came to share the same suite in the Hotel Crillon. He was my father's first cousin, but despite the difference in our age he treated me always as friend rather than junior relative. For 35 years an outstanding member of the Yale faculty,[8] and its secretary for most of that time, his poise and shrewdness assured him a position of distinctive influence in his collegiate life; these qualities, combined with his authoritative scholarship, brought him similar distinction in the Inquiry and among the division chiefs assigned to the American Peace Commission. His special scholarly field was economic history; but by the rather curious

8. Day (1871–1951), Yale '92, studied at the universities of Berlin and Paris before joining the Yale faculty.

logic that determined appointment as "specialists" in the United States delegation, he was made chief of the Balkan Division and later served on the Rumanian and Greek territorial commissions, although he had no previous intensive knowledge of those areas. His intellectual qualities and working habits were such that he very soon acquired an impressive mastery of the fields to which he was assigned. His control of facts were matched by the judicial care with which he weighed them. At Paris there was no American to whom the European delegates listened more readily.

To our cabin on the ship was also assigned William Linn Westermann, classical archaeologist, at this time professor at Wisconsin and shortly after the Peace Conference appointed to the Columbia faculty.[9] Like that of Day his temperament inclined toward the realistic and not infrequently verged upon the cynical. His estimate of the honesty of European statesmen was pessimistic. Completely loyal to the idealistic objectives of President Wilson's program he was not to be diverted by a starry-eyed idealism from the recognition of unpleasant facts. Like Day he began each morning with a grey scepticism. Of the latter it was said that if on waking his companion should report from the window, "It's a fine sunny day," his comment would be, "I find it hard to believe." Such pessimistic and critical attributes were not without value when it came to the analysis of expansive programs such as were fathered by Venizelos of Greece and Bratianu of Rumania.[10] By and large the "idealistic" college professors of the Inquiry turned out to be rather hard-boiled. They regarded with a cold

9. Westermann (1873–1954) was trained at the universities of Nebraska, Berlin, and Missouri. At Paris he was chief of the Division of Western Asia of the American Commission and delegate, with Clive Day, on the Greek Commission. After the Peace Conference he was a member of the Commission on the Armenian Boundary (1920). (C.S.)

10. Eleutherios Venizelos (1864–1936), Cretan revolutionary, helped effect the union of Greece and Crete in 1908. He became leader of the pro-Allied Progressive Liberal Party and six-time Prime Minister of Greece between 1910 and 1933. In 1935 he was accused of inspiring the republican revolt against the royalist government of President Zaimis and fled to Italy. He was tried in absentia for high treason and condemned to exile, but was later pardoned when King George II returned to Greece. Ion Bratianu (1864–1927) was the nationalistic and authoritarian leader of the Liberal Party and five-time Prime Minister of his country between 1909 and 1927, when he prevented the accession of Carol III. His government was in power throughout the war period, and he concluded the secret treaty in 1916 which brought Rumania into the war on the side of the Allies. Chief Rumanian delegate to the Paris Conference, he alienated Wilson and refused to sign the Treaty of Versailles as a protest against the division of the Banat of Temesvar between Rumania and Yugoslavia. Bratianu claimed the province was promised to Rumania in 1916.

eye both the enthusiasms of the newly freed nationalities and the equally self-interested calculations of traditional imperialism.

Such comment would apply to all the more influential members of the Inquiry who found themselves on the *George Washington* and who were destined shortly for responsibility as specialists on the American Commission. In many respects Charles Homer Haskins stood out as the most impressive of the entire group.[11] Professor of history at Harvard, he had known President Wilson since the latter's student days at Johns Hopkins, where Haskins also took his advanced degree. His scholarly field was the history of Western Europe, especially in the Middle Ages; but his range of knowledge was so extensive that he was to be called on for a variety of jobs, particularly in devising practicable solutions to the knotty problem of the Saar and those of the Danish and Belgian frontiers. We younger historians trembled somewhat to find ourselves in such august academic company, but we soon perceived not merely the depth of his wisdom but the richness of his genial benevolence. President Wilson, who greatly admired Haskins, once remarked to me that he was one of the "rare New England historians who did not regard the westward march of the American frontier as an aspect of the expansion of greater Boston."

Of comparable influence in the group on the *George Washington* must be counted the historian of the old British colonial system, George Louis Beer.[12] Born and brought up in a banking milieu and always the man of the world, Beer's authoritative historical studies had placed him among the most distinguished of American scholars. He bore the manner as well as the garb of the traditional career diplomatist and we greatly admired both, looking forward to the day when we also would appear with equal aplomb in the approved striped trousers and short black jacket. (Paren-

---

11. Haskins (1870–1937), trained at Johns Hopkins and Harvard, started his teaching career at his first alma mater and then moved to Harvard in 1902 by way of Wisconsin. He served as dean of the Graduate School of Arts and Science at Harvard (1908–24) and also as chairman of the American Council of Learned Societies. He was a co-author with Robert H. Lord of *Some Problems of the Peace Conference* (Cambridge, Mass., 1920).

12. Beer (1872–1920), a graduate of Columbia, was for a decade interested in Cuban commercial activities. He joined the Columbia faculty and devoted his great talent to the study of English colonial policy, chiefly in the seventeenth and eighteenth centuries. He was chief of the Colonial Division of the Inquiry and of the Peace Commission. With the acceptance of the mandates system he found himself forced to intervene in other issues outside his special field as, for example, Fiume and the Adriatic. He was appointed to the Secretariat of the League of Nations, director of the Section on Mandates. What promised to be a brilliant career was cut short by his untimely death the following March. (C.S.)

thetically the officials of the State Department had been a trifle worried
lest our accustomed professorial attire should seem less than adequate in
the diplomatic corridors of Paris; to each of us there had been advanced
in addition to our December salary a check for $150 which we were told
must be expended on new and appropriate clothing. Hence we became
somewhat clothes-minded and eyed Beer with admiration. He was the
Beau Brummel of the ship, yielding nothing to any genuine career man.)

But Beer's position in history is one of greater significance. It was he who
picked up the ideas of General Smuts[13] on colonial mandates and adjusted
them to fit the mental processes of Woodrow Wilson. In this respect
Beer made one of the most vital of all contributions to the Covenant of
the League and to the work of the Peace Conference. He was able to
bring to the attention of the President those aspects of the old colonial
system which could be fitted into Wilson's personal philosophy in the light
of twentieth-century conditions. His presentation of the mandates system
and the possibilities of its development opened Wilson's eyes to the opportunities that lay before the League of Nations, not merely as an instru-
ment of pacific conciliation but as one of significant international organization.

Adequate analysis of the complete roster of Inquiry members gathered
on the ship would require a full-scale independent study. In general terms
it should be noted that their subsequent academic careers as well as their
service at the Peace Conference went far to vindicate their selection. The
eminence which they later achieved was impressive, whether as scholars,
teachers, or university administrators from coast to coast. This fact is the
more notable in view of their youth at the time of their appointment to the
Peace Commission; the oldest were barely in their fifties, the younger in
their early thirties. Youth and inexperience brought certain disadvan-
tages; but they were happily free from the academic stuffiness that sometimes characterizes elderly professors. The members of the Inquiry were
destined, however, to suffer in their Paris experience from two outstanding
defects. They were conscious always of their amateur status and hesitant to

13. Jan Christian Smuts (1870–1950), Boer hero in the War of 1899, was Minister of Defense of the Union of South Africa in 1914, later served in Lloyd George's
War Cabinet and worked actively for establishment of the League of Nations. He also
served twice as Prime Minister of South Africa, the second time during World War II
(1939–48). The mandate system he proposed was accepted by Wilson as a compromise to any outright division among the victors of former enemy colonies. The former
colonies were administered, in varying degrees of control, by designated powers who, in
turn, were responsible to the League of Nations.

stand up to their European opposites with determination. Harold Nicolson later complained that we did not call down fire from Heaven in defense of Wilsonian principles: this was what the British liberals were waiting for.[14] But in a dozen spots along the Czech or the Rumanian border the Americans were too polite or too timid to quarrel. The Americans were also unorganized as a group, so that their judgment was never effectively concentrated or forcefully exercised. Responsibility for failure in this respect may be attributed to lack of leadership in the Inquiry itself, where the authority of Mezes was rarely if ever exerted; even more unfortunate was President Wilson's inability to organize and utilize the brains which were offered him.

When the *George Washington* sailed it was generally expected that there would be ample opportunity on the voyage for discussing the larger aspects of the peace program: perhaps the drafting of a time schedule for the meetings in Paris; a recognition of priorities in the topics to be discussed and decided by the Conference. Perhaps President Wilson's dislike of a formal, hard-and-fast program interfered with the hopes of the French and Italian ambassadors, Jusserand and Macchi di Cellere, that a definite program might be achieved.[15]

The Americans, apart from the officers in charge of the ship, comprised three groups: the Inquiry members, whose status was as yet entirely uncertain; representatives of the State Department, evidently more concerned with the conditions under which the American Commission would work than with items of the peace settlement; thirdly, officers of the Military Intelligence Division under General Marlborough Churchill.[16] These last had secured control of the large forward saloon on the upper deck of the ship and transformed it into a handsome and impressive map room; they obviously took it for granted that they would be the technical advisers of the President and Commissioners on all territorial aspects of the settle-

---

14. Nicolson, *Peacemaking, 1919* (London, 1933), p. 177. "A master of diplomatic technique," in Seymour's words, Nicolson (b. 1886) was a member of the British delegation at the Peace Conference. Disenchanted with Wilson's failure to preserve intact his program for peace, he became one of the President's most outspoken critics.

15. Jules Jean Jusserand (1855–1932), diplomat and author, served as French ambassador to the United States from 1902 until 1925. Macchi di Cellere (1866–1919), lifelong Italian diplomat, served in Washington as secretary of the legation (1902–04) and later as ambassador (1913–19). Both men were Wilson's guests aboard the *George Washington*.

16. Churchill (1878–1942) served as Assistant Chief of Staff, Military Intelligence Division.

ment. Secretary of State Lansing was not happy over the prospect;[17] he regarded the M.I.D. with even more suspicion than he did the Inquiry. President Wilson visited the map room more than once, but it was reasonably clear that he did not intend that the M.I.D. should exert serious influence then or later. The important conferences he held during the voyage were with the representatives of the press and, as the ship approached the shores of France, with members of the Inquiry.

To the latter at the close of the voyage, and to their great satisfaction, President Wilson gave clear indication that he regarded the group with a benevolent eye; furthermore that he planned to make of it a board of technical advisers, to whom he would turn for assistance in fashioning the peace, and upon whose learning he would count in disputes with European governments. But such a situation was as yet merely a promised prospect. Of the peace itself and how it would be accomplished, and the role of the Inquiry in achieving it, he spoke only in the most vague generalities. This was true even of his comment on the League of Nations.

The "higher-ups" themselves were not much better informed of the President's purposes. The *George Washington* carried a number of persons who in one capacity or another were to be in the service of the Peace Conference at Paris. None of them seemed to have a clear conception of what that service was to be or what would be the relations of one individual to another in carrying out the President's program. The two Peace Commissioners on board, Robert Lansing and Henry White, career diplomat of long service,[18] told us frankly that they knew of no plan of organization nor schedule of procedure. Years later I asked John W. Davis, who was on the ship en route to his post as ambassador to St. James,[19]

17. Robert Lansing (1864–1928), Amherst '86, lawyer and author, specialized in international law. Once Counselor for the Department of State, he served as Secretary from 1915 until 1920, when he resumed his law practice and wrote three books on his government service. Much later his papers were published, *Papers Relating to the Foreign Relations of the United States: the Lansing Papers* (2 vols. Washington, GPO, 1939) and evoked a commentary by Seymour in *Foreign Affairs, 19* (January 1941), 414–25, in which the absence of any influence from Wall Street and "the close relation between European turmoil and American interests" were stressed. Lansing came closer to viewing the war in security terms than did most of his contemporaries.

18. White (1850–1927) was a Baltimorean with a European education. He was the senior American delegate at the Algeciras Conference in 1906 and also served as ambassador to Italy and later to France during the years 1905 to 1909.

19. Davis (1873–1955) was a West Virginia lawyer and congressman, named Solicitor General by Wilson in 1913. He was appointed ambassador to Great Britain in 1918, replacing Walter Hines Page and serving until 1921 and the return of the Republican Party to power. Davis joined with Frank Polk to form the law firm of Davis,

what instructions he had received from Wilson that would enable him to correlate his diplomatic duties with the work of the American Peace Commission. "None whatever," he replied. "No instructions from first to last." Thus the President's crusade began to get under way—a magnificent improvisation.

It was not likely that members of the Inquiry would be better informed. They received only a single instruction: they must be on board at Hoboken by 10:15 of the evening of December 3, 1918. The President would embark the following morning at 9:00 and the ship would sail immediately.

New Haven, Conn.
Winter 1963

Polk, Wardwell, Gardiner, and Reed in 1921, ultimately perhaps the most distinguished law partnership in New York. After a long-drawn-out struggle in the Democratic convention of 1924, Davis received the nomination for the presidency, but he was soundly defeated by President Calvin Coolidge. He returned to law, specializing in constitutional questions. (C.S.)

LETTERS FROM THE PARIS PEACE CONFERENCE

CROSSING THE ATLANTIC

December 4–13, 1918

WAR'S END IN 1918 had been preceded by diplomatic events of a dramatic nature. The Allied and Associated Powers had turned back the final German offensive and during September were successfully advancing all along the western front, but still on French soil. Then the Central Powers began to dissolve. Rumania reentered the war and Austria-Hungary proposed a discussion of peace. Next, on September 29, Bulgaria signed a separate armistice. German military leaders, foreseeing a military collapse, urged a peace petition based on Wilsonian principles.

The Kaiser's government appealed to Wilson for an armistice on October 6, as did Austria-Hungary the next day. Now that time was on his side, Wilson acted carefully and wisely. He insisted on assurances that the German people stood behind the government. Since the Austro-Hungarian Empire was dissolving, he added the principle of self-determination for the Czechoslovaks and Yugoslavs and sent Colonel House to conduct negotiations.

Time would not wait for leisurely diplomacy. Turkey signed an armistice with Great Britain on October 31 and Austria-Hungary with Italy on November 3, two days after a revolt took place in Austria. A socialist republic was proclaimed in Berlin, and on November 9 the Kaiser abdicated and fled. Meanwhile, in conferences with Colonel House, Prime Minister Lloyd George indicated Great Britain's continuing unwillingness to surrender its historic supremacy over the seas to the equally historic American contention that neutral shipping was immune from belligerent control save under certain specified and limited conditions. This was the doctrine of "freedom of the seas" which Wilson had reiterated. Simultaneously Premier Clemenceau entered a reservation specifying France's determination to recover compensation for damages done to the civilian population of the Allies. Premier Orlando of Italy also entered a reservation on the settlement of the territorial question of Fiume, which was occupied by the Italians within a fortnight of the armistice. This last reservation was never officially recognized. Moreover, the armistice with Austria-Hungary, as well as that with Turkey, was made prior to acceptance by all the belligerents of Wilson's program as the basis for peace, which cast additional doubt on the validity of Orlando's position.

President Wilson also secured approval of military terms from Marshal Ferdinand Foch, Commander in Chief of the Allied Armies. On November 11 a one-month armistice, later to be renewed, was signed. Meanwhile the President suffered a repudiation at the polls when the American electorate rejected his appeal to elect a Democratic majority in both houses of Congress and instead returned Republican majorities. Wilson was determined not to lose the objectives of his program, but he knew it would not be easy. Notwithstanding the election results he considered himself the only leader who possessed a full mandate from the people, a somewhat debatable contention when, a few weeks later, Lloyd George received a popular vote more overwhelming than any yet recorded in English history, and when Clemenceau received a three-to-one vote of confidence in the French Chamber of Deputies.

Wilson had long felt that he himself should go to the Peace Conference in order to use his personal influence and moral leadership at the scene. He saw himself as the only disinterested arbiter and despite many arguments raised in opposition, including some reluctance from Lloyd George and Clemenceau to associate with a "head of state" as opposed to a "head of government," he announced on November 18 that he would attend and then on November 29 that he would be one of the five American Commissioners.[1] Five days later he boarded the S.S. *George Washington* in Hoboken. A former German liner, the ship was disabled at the outbreak of war but had been repaired and converted into an American military transport. Under the command of Captain Edward McCauley, Jr., U.S.N., she had ferried over 50,000 American troops.

Just before he sailed Wilson spoke before Congress and said, "I shall count upon your friendly countenance and encouragement." Here he found, however, more than mere reluctance. Pricked by the omission of

1. Thomas A. Bailey, *Woodrow Wilson and the Lost Peace* (New York, 1944), pp. 71–86, summarizes the debate on Wilson's decision to go to Paris.

any senators from the list of the American Commissioners, and also by the President's procedure of by-passing legislative confirmation by appointing the Commissioners as executive agents, Senator William E. Borah of Idaho introduced a resolution on December 5 calling for the forthcoming peace treaty to be made public immediately upon its receipt by the Senate and for all consequent deliberations to be conducted in public sessions. The following day a resolution calling for the appointment of eight senators to attend the Peace Conference was killed by the Senate Foreign Relations Committee. There could be no mistaking, however, the rising tenor of Republican sentiment in anticipation of March 1919 when control of Congress would shift.

As the convoy steamed across the Atlantic there were other indications that undoubtedly gave Wilson concern. On December 7 Lloyd George publicly demanded the punishment of the Kaiser and other war criminals and underscored the French claim for reparations, while omitting any mention of a League. The Allied blockade was still in effect, and after an unreasonably long delay General John J. Pershing's Army of Occupation was nearing Coblenz, but on December 10 street fighting between government troops and Sparticus communists broke out in the streets of Berlin and Munich. A week later a republic was declared in Hungary, additional evidence that history might not await the deliberations of the peacemakers.

Against this background, at once tumultuous and uncertain, the events of the passage, including the high point of Wilson's first meeting with members of the Inquiry, were intensely absorbing to the young historian whose first serialized letter commences.

❧

S.S. *George Washington*

Wednesday, December 4, 1918

I have just come in from an hour's walk on the upper glass-enclosed deck, with Clive Day, enlivened by the passing and repassing of Mrs. Wilson who paces up and down *toute seule,* and feel that the trip is fairly started. Apart from the motion of the propeller there is little to shake one up as yet, although one member of the Inquiry has taken to his berth, and the destroyers around us are rolling and pitching violently. I am writing in what was the officers' lounge which has been assigned to us as a sort of club room, while the regular smoking room evidently belongs to the military and State Department crowd, and the library is given over to the President and secretaries as a conference room.

There is, you see, a certain amount of social segregation, which is keenly felt by the more aristocratic of the Inquiry such as Haskins and Beer. I have made free use of the State Department room, however, and shall continue to do so although as yet I have not been invited into the President's conference room.

"His Nibs" has been walking the deck this afternoon like an ordinary mortal and talking with Bowman, Young,[2] and Haskins. I didn't happen to be with them when he came up and didn't join them. He looks tired and worried. Mrs. Wilson, whom we passed a dozen times on the deck, is certainly not good-looking—an enormous mouth and teeth! I have met several of the ladies—Mrs. Auchincloss, Mrs. Mezes, and Mrs. Miller who all belong to the House family outfit.[3]

---

2. Allyn Abbott Young (1876–1929), scholar in the field of economics and finance, achieved a distinguished teaching record at Wisconsin, Stanford, and Cornell. After the Peace Conference, he became professor of economics at Harvard. At Paris he served as chief of the Division of Economics and Statistics of the American Commission. Principal author of the Young Plan of 1929, which was the last concerted effort to produce an effective schedule for reparations payments, he was a man of impressive conviction in discussion and overpowering force of argument. (C.S.)

3. Gordon Auchincloss (1886–1943), Yale '08, Seymour's classmate, married Colonel House's daughter. A lawyer and an active member of the Democratic Party, he served in the legal branch of the State Department and then became secretary to the American War Mission to England and France in 1917 and secretary to his father-in-law during the armistice negotiations and at the Conference, where he kept a copious diary. After the war he returned to law practice in New York. David Hunter Miller (1875–1961) was Auchincloss' law partner and served in the Department of State from 1917 to 1919. He was with the Inquiry from its inception as treasurer in charge of accounts and contributor in the field of international law. At Paris he was Colonel House's chief assistant on the question of the League of Nations, possessing an "uncommon ability to draft legal memoranda with artful polish" (Gelfand, *The Inquiry*, p. 51). With Bowman he represented the dynamic qualities of the Inquiry in comparison with Lippmann, Mezes, and James T. Shotwell. After the Conference he continued to work in support of the League. Miller published *My Diary at the Conference of Paris* (20 vols. Privately printed, 1928). James Thomson Shotwell (1874–1965), Canadian-born historian and university professor, served the Commission as librarian. Later he wrote *At the Paris Peace Conference* (New York, 1937).

The ladies eat in a private dining room with the presidential party, which leaves the others in the main dining saloon.

On arriving last night we were somewhat shocked to discover that practically no changes had been made in the ship since she had been used as a plain transport. Hence there are very few rooms that can be used and a large amount of herding together is necessary. The President and the ambassadors and Secretary of State and Commissioners fill up the suites with baths. Most of the single rooms have been combined into large cabins with four or five berths. I am in the most desirable of these with Clive and Westermann. Lord was to have been with us but was slipped into another room.[4] The room is very large, with five berths and two washstands, and the three of us manage very comfortably though we have to go outside for our baths. We get plenty of good but very cold air through the porthole. I think I shall be glad to use my fur coat as a bed puff. The berths are very comfortable, and if there is much rolling they are likely to prove better than the presidential beds. Fortunately Westermann is one of the nicest of the whole party—I took to him when I first met him in New York—he is a Princeton man, originally from the West, specialist on Turkey.

I had a first-rate sleep last night after getting our luggage arranged and was wakened at 7:30 by a sergeant of marines who announced that "His Nibs" would be on board shortly. We got up leisurely and without bothering much about the President went up to a good breakfast. We rose from the table to the strains of "The Star Spangled Banner" to find Mr. and Mrs. Wilson crossing the gangplank. Secretary Baker was already on board—in fact had the next table to me.[5] We

4. Robert H. Lord (1885–1954) was a Harvard professor of modern European history and a protégé of Archibald Coolidge. He served the American Commission as a technical expert on Polish affairs. He collaborated with Haskins in writing *Some Problems of the Peace Conference.* He was ordained a priest of the Roman Catholic Church in 1929 and became a Monsignor and papal domestic prelate in 1950.
5. Secretary of War Newton D. Baker did not attend the early part of the Conference and was not listed on the ship's passenger list. Either he simply came to see the President's departure, or Seymour meant to say Secretary Lansing. Baker (1871–1937) became Secretary of War in 1916 following a successful political career in Cleveland,

didn't sail until 10:20. It was quite thrilling as we backed out, with a warship firing a salute of nineteen guns and opening up her big siren; then all the ferryboats and tugs tied their whistle ropes down and there was such a blare it was impossible to talk as we went down the river. In every window of the big buildings handkerchiefs were waving and the air was full of paper fluttering down.

We had two destroyers in front, one on each side, and two behind, with four or five aeroplanes circling around overhead—sometimes very low. It was the first time that I had ever looked at an aeroplane very close to and on *a level*. When we got into the bay the *Pennsylvania* fell in in front of us just behind the two first destroyers and more aeroplanes joined in. We spent all the morning on the upper front deck watching the aircraft which did all manner of tricks flying far closer to us than they did at Chatham.[6] As we got further flying-boats took the place of the aeroplanes and finally a big dirigible circled around. They stayed with us until the middle of the afternoon, long after we lost sight of land.

Thursday, December 5, 1918

I was stopped in my writing yesterday afternoon by Bullitt who came up to walk and talk with me. We are having fine weather and I am feeling very fit, though I feel that *you* would question the desirability of sitting up. It is not rough but there is something of a sea on and the ship rolls so that for a period of many seconds there is nothing but sea visible and then for the following seconds nothing but sky. But the ship is steady and the roll very slow and there is no pitch at all. But I am glad not to be on the de-

---

Ohio, capped by two outstanding terms as reform mayor. He served until the close of Wilson's administration in March 1921, despite critical sniping based upon charges of sentimentality and wasteful idealism. President Coolidge appointed him a member of the Permanent Court of Arbitration at the Hague in 1928 and President Hoover appointed him a member of the Law Enforcement Commission in 1929. (C.S.)

6. The Seymour family maintained a summer cottage at Chatham on Cape Cod.

stroyers—their masts go over until they seem to be almost flat in the water and the waves are breaking over their decks all the time. They are a wonderfully pretty sight with the bright sunlight on their blue and white camouflage. When the sun is out and the waves blue it is very difficult to distinguish them at half a mile's distance and the camouflage deceives absolutely as to their direction and speed. Sometimes they stand in quite close so that we can see the men on board. There are always two far ahead of us; then the *Pennsylvania* about half a mile ahead; two destroyers on the starboard and three on the port side, and two astern. Last night looking out at their lights it seemed almost as if we were in harbor especially as there was then very little motion. They flash over signals to us which Clive maintains he *can* read, though he doesn't feel it fair to the country to worry his brain with mechanical details!

The ship is entirely manned by the Navy, whose guests we are. The waiters are all Jackies; a Jacky wakes us in the morning and brings our hot water and tidies the room. We see a gunner's mate about our baths. Evidently the Navy does not like water, for yesterday the bathrooms were all locked and it was only when we protested that they were made ready. All the meal calls are sounded on bugles. At first we feared that being late to meals would mean losing the meal, but we find that we can eat as late as nine in the morning and this morning I did. Apart from the rooms where we eat and sleep and smoke all the fittings have been torn out of the ship, which is as bare as a barn. One great advantage of the Navy regime and the absence of ladies is that one can smoke anywhere, although a sign in our cabin urges us not to smoke a pipe in bed as the "blankets are apt to catch fire easily." The food is very good. Plain with no choice but well cooked.

We have an orchestra of Jackies for our meals, and at dinner a very elaborate quartet singing swipes and solos—"Mandalay," etc. Last night at 8:15 came the movies. You will not believe me—I could not believe my eyes—but it was true—the title of the feature:

"The Second Marriage." The plot of the play follows the emotions of
the lady who only discovers the virtues of her first husband after some
months of marriage to her second. Imagine the effect on board. As it
happened, I don't know why, although the ambassadors and Mrs.
White and Mrs. Lansing came in, Mr. and Mrs. Wilson at the last
moment decided not to.[7]

Thus far the only great personage I have played with is Mr. White.
I talked and sat with him this morning for some time. He is an "old
dear," just as nice as he can be but he is certainly doddering. I fear
from his talk that he is not going to count at all except in a purely
social way. He spoke pleasantly of my book, which lies on the President's desk in his conference room.[8] I spoke good morning to Mr.
Lansing and Bullitt introduced me to Macchi di Cellere, and I bow to
the President and Mrs. Wilson when we walk on deck. I take back
part of what I said of the latter; she is attractive when she talks and
smiles and she has fine eyes. The President looks drawn, the corners
of his mouth are down. No one knows what kind of a policy he has
in mind and Bullitt is much worried. He says that Baker is the only
man in power with a brain and he simply adores the President and
questions nothing that he says or thinks. House may not be able to
count for much over there because of his health which is bad. What
I fear is that Wilson will go to Lloyd George holding an American
greater navy and mercantile marine as a club to enforce his interpretations of the "freedom of the seas." Then if Lloyd George does not
back down, and I don't think that he will, we shall be driven by the
President to unlimited naval expansion. And the worst of it is that the
spirit of cooperation will disappear at once and be replaced by competition and jealousy.[9] I think the next five weeks are going to be criti-

7. President Wilson's first wife, the former Elly Lou Axson, died in 1914. In December 1915 he married Mrs. Edith Bolling Galt, a widow.
8. *The Diplomatic Background of the War, 1870–1914.*
9. Seymour's prediction came true, but not precisely as expected. Wilson used
naval expansion as a club to force the Senate to ratify the Treaty of Versailles. When he
failed, the United States did enter a naval building race, terminated by the Washington Conference of 1921–22. Seymour later characterized this letter as "an example of
youthful naïveté."

cal, in that they will test whether or not Wilson's speeches are merely verbiage or whether they really mean something.

One of the pleasantest men I have met on board is Raymond Fosdick, the younger, who has charge of morale in our camps and is going over to get into cooperation with the French and British.[10] Fling, of Nebraska, is on board; he is a major in the M.I.D. and sits near me at table.[11] He is rather heavy. Beer, who is in charge of colonial matters for the Inquiry and, so far as I can see, is the only one who dresses better than I do, has been very interesting. He has had a career in business with the Seligmans,[12] then a traveler in Africa and Asia, then a gentleman of leisure who spends it all working very hard and writing very good books on British colonial policy. He admires G. B. Adams, considers Andrews overrated.[13] He is a snob—with perfect manners toward those whom he snubs, but has been very friendly with me.

Apart from the stenographers, clerks, and draughtsmen there are very few civilians aboard. The dining room is filled with the naval officers who run the ship and military men going over on one excuse or another. Hence there seems little need of dressing for dinner and even Beer and Haskins appeared last night in dark sack suits. My only regret is that I did not get the Norfolk suit I looked at, for it would have been just the thing. Boat drill comes in five minutes and I must find out where my "Abandon Ship Station" is.

10. Raymond Blaine Fosdick (b. 1883), a lawyer with lively interest in social welfare, was chairman of the committee on training camp activities, 1917–18. He became Under-Secretary of the League of Nations in 1919 and later president of the Rockefeller Foundation (1936–48). (C.S.)

11. Fred M. Fling (1860–1938), Bowdoin '83, received the Ph.D. from the University of Liepzig in 1890 and became professor of history at the University of Nebraska in 1891. A writer on historical method, he was attached to the historical branch of the General Staff as a major. In Paris his mission was to collect material for a history of the Peace Conference. (C.S.)

12. A banking firm with strong international connections.

13. Adams (1851–1925) was a noted historian, editor of the *American Historical Review*, and author. He was involved in neither the Inquiry nor the Conference. Charles McLean Andrews (1863–1943) trained at Trinity College and Johns Hopkins for a teaching career in history which took him, in order, to Bryn Mawr, Johns Hopkins, and then Yale (1910–31). He specialized in British colonial policy in America.

Friday, December 6, 1918

We certainly are having a comfortable trip and discovered the reason for it this afternoon when we were shown our position on the chart, for we are taking an extreme southerly course; the first day we sailed southeast of New York and since then due east; if we keep on this course we shall come to the Azores some time Monday morning. There is a great question as to whether President Wilson will want to stop. Probably we shall cut northeast first in order to avoid the rough weather in the Bay of Biscay. Although we are due south of Newfoundland there has not been a hint of fog and it is warm as spring. The first day I was glad for my fur coat, but today we have been standing around on the deck without any coat at all, and the glass-enclosed deck is almost oppressive. We have had the electric fan going in our stateroom.

Last night we ran into a fairly heavy swell so that crockery tumbled off the tables and one rolled around a little in one's berth; but the roll is very slow and rather soothing than otherwise. It is beautiful to watch the destroyers in this swell, especially the ones close to us. They go absolutely out of sight in the trough of the sea, and then ride way up on the top of the wave. They are wonderfully trim and almost graceful in their rolling and pitching. Late yesterday afternoon I went up to the extreme bow with some men and had a clear view of our convoy, the *Pennsylvania* about half a mile ahead but looking very near and very impressive with her enormous beam and great guns. We counted ten destroyers altogether.

Our social relations with the President's family are not close (a masterly understatement). He has been in his cabin all morning; said to be indisposed with a cold, but I met him a few minutes ago on the deck looking very genial and brisk. We noted with pleasure at boat drill yesterday afternoon that we had the same "Abandon Ship Station" as he and Mrs. Wilson, standing cheek by jowl with them. They are in Boat 12 and we in 12A, which comes down after theirs. Boat drill is amusing—loud trumpet calls and orders "Ready to abandon ship." One rushes to one's stateroom and dons life preserver, then up to the station on deck. We have not been able to spot Mrs. Bolling and suspect that she is not on board, and we don't dare ask the high muck-a-mucks who would know.[14] I walk and talk a little with Mr. White who is charming on the war of 1871 and the Algeciras Conference but who does not seem to be thinking very hard about the coming conference. He is nice as can be but quite simple. I met Mr. Davis, the new ambassador to England, and M. Jusserand but only formally and did not get a chance to talk with them. After all, they probably would not talk about things I should really like to know.

Far more interesting was a long talk with Col. Ayres who was on Pershing's staff and is said to know far more about the strategy and tactics of the war than any other American officer.[15] He said that the man really responsible for the success of the American army organization and the speeding up of affairs was General March, whom he regarded as the greatest organizing genius of the war.[16] The practical Chief of Naval Operations was a Captain Pratt, who is on this ship but whom I have not met.[17] Daniels, he thinks, deserves great credit for keeping his hands off and leaving the organization to Roosevelt.[18] Daniels is reported as saying, "If the Navy wins the admirals will

14. Mrs. Wilson's mother, Mrs. William H. Bolling, was not aboard.

15. Leonard P. Ayres (1879–1946) was a statistician and an educational and industrial counselor. He became director of the Division of Statistics of the War Industries Board, then chief statistician of the American Expeditionary Forces (General Staff with rank of colonel). He also served as chief statistical officer of the American Commission and set up a military advisory center in Paris, rivaling that of the M.I.D. In 1924 he became the economic adviser to the Dawes Plan Commissioner. A scholar in uniform, he was avid in collection of facts, eager to share their significance, unpleasantly intolerant of factual error. (C.S.)

16. General Payton Conway March (1864–1955) was Chief of Staff, U.S. Army.

17. Captain William Veazie Pratt (1869–1957) was Assistant Chief of Naval Operations (1917–19) and became Commander in Chief, U.S. Fleet (1929–30) and Chief of Naval Operations (1930–33). He also served as a delegate at the Washington and London Naval Limitation Conferences in 1921–22 and 1930, respectively.

18. Josephus Daniels (1862–1948), editor and author, served as Secretary of the Navy during Wilson's two terms, later became ambassador to Mexico (1933–42). Franklin Delano Roosevelt (1882–1945) was then Assistant Secretary of the Navy (1913–20). He was in charge of inspection of U.S. naval forces in European waters in 1918 and of demobilization in Europe in early 1919, during which period he came to the Conference. In 1920 he resigned to run, unsuccessfully, for the vice presidency.

get the credit; if it loses I shall get the blame. I would rather the admirals get the credit."

Ayres explained the strategy of the St.-Mihiel and Argonne drives at great length. He confirmed all the stories which we have heard as to the effect of Château-Thierry upon the turn of events. He said it was impossible to overestimate the extent to which French and British morale had been crushed—they were simply dead beat. They had no confidence in the Americans, no matter how numerous, believing that we were simply raw levies. Then after we had received permission to attack, the marines got out of hand and refused to stop and fairly smeared the Germans opposite. In a day the news had gone from mouth to mouth all along the French lines: "These men will fight." After that there was no stopping the French. He also confirmed the story of Foch ordering Haig to send him American units to be replaced by French, and Haig saying he preferred the Americans; to which Foch replied, "So do I." He explained that the diversion of the big German offensive from Amiens to the Marne was due to political factors behind the German Crown Prince, which tallies with my own information. Part of the credit of the second victory of the Marne should go to the Portuguese because they crumpled up so completely before the German division attacking that it went way through, too far, and got cut off![19]

19. This account apparently concerns three separate military actions:

(a) General Erich Ludendorff launched Germany's third major offensive of 1918 in late May and drove as far as Château-Thierry, only 50 miles from Paris. The U.S. 3rd Division blunted the attack at the Marne River; the U.S. 2nd Division stopped it at Belleau Wood. The latter victory was probably more significant, but the action at Château-Thierry was more widely publicized. From this sector the Germans tried to launch their final "peace offensive" in mid-July.

In August General John J. Pershing (1860–1948), Commander of the American Expeditionary Forces and later Chief of Staff, organized the U.S. First Army. Previously American units had been scattered under British or French commands, despite Wilson's insistence on American command. Marshal Foch, Commander in Chief of the Allied Armies, finally agreed to this principle, although General Henri Philippe Pétain, the French Commander in Chief, had misgivings because of American inexperience. Wilson thus created the legend that Americans did not serve under foreign commands. Actually the British, under Field Marshal Sir Douglas Haig, preserved a greater integrity of command.

The initial operation of the First Army was to eliminate the St. Mihiel salient,

Sunday, December 8, 1918

Yesterday was a lost day so far as writing was concerned, partly because I seemed to be in conversation all day long, partly because there is a sense of laziness and relaxation in the air which precludes even such activity as wielding a pen. It is impossible to be anything but lazy in this tropical atmosphere—blue skies and bluer water, and a slow swell which is lulling rather than disturbing. I have been walking with Westermann for an hour and then watching the white spray on the blue rollers and the destroyer off our port side. It is so warm that last night I wore my summer pajamas and although the porthole was open slept without a blanket for a large part of the night. It is the hottest day today imaginable; I am in my lightest blue suit and still find myself warm. Imagine sitting on the open deck without a rug on December 8!

I take great pleasure in my complete equipment, having appeared in all my different suits, while my shirts and neckties have drawn warm admiration and envy from my roommates. I hope that you will tell your father how much pleasure and convenience I get from the wristwatch. I shall certainly never wear anything else traveling. I am using Mr. Hemingway's cigars as tips for our Jacky, since we are not supposed to give money.[20] Now that we have settled down we are very luxurious in our habits, calling for various things from our

---

which had resisted Allied attacks for four years. It then shifted to the area of the Meuse River and the Argonne Forest and opened the final Allied offensive which led to the armistice.

(b) Much earlier, in 1914, Crown Prince Wilhelm, a controversial and propagandized figure, commanded the Fifth German Army, the pivot of the German strike into Belgium and France. The First German Army under General Alexander von Kluck, at the extreme right (west) of the attack, reached Amiens and seemed ready to encircle Paris. Then unexpectedly it wheeled to the southeast toward the Marne, by-passing the city. Fear of overextending his forces, the prospect of trapping the fleeing French forces, and the timidity of General Karl von Bulow on his flank led to von Kluck's decision.

(c) The locale of the account of the Portuguese troops seems mistaken. They collapsed in the face of General Ludendorff's second offensive of 1918, which occurred in the Lys sector of Belgium.

20. Samuel Hemingway of New Haven, father of Samuel B., Louis, and Donald.

Jacky. We simply didn't understand how to use him at first. He wakes us in the morning with "first *chow call*, gentlemen."

Our closest approximation to the great persons comes at the movies, which the last two nights have been extremely good. We have had Charlie Chaplin and Douglas Fairbanks, who are evidently favorites of the President. Last night I sat next to M. Jusserand, and the night before about ten feet from the Wilsons. Jusserand is very affable but I have not had any private conversation with him. He is a little iron-grey-headed man, lively in manner. Ambassador Davis is typically American, grey hair, clean shaven, tall, alert, with more of the lawyer than the diplomatist in his appearance. Cellere is the obvious diplomat—a light-haired Italian, English clothes, and a very polite bow on deck but inaccessible (to the lower echelons). Creel looks common, flashy, with loud clothes.[21] I was in a group talking with him yesterday in the M.I.D. room and can assert that although he may be clever he is a man of unlimited conceit.

Lansing I see very rarely—he is expressionless and mute. Of the big men Fosdick interests me most. He is friendly with a charming smile and manner and talks delightfully. He thinks Mr. Wilson uses words without any idea of the effect they have on other people. Of the women, Mrs. Lansing seems the nicest—I have only just been introduced to her—and Mme. Jusserand the most distinguished; they both seem plain simple folk. Mrs. Wilson dresses without much style it seems to me; but as one watches her she certainly has a personal magnetism. She is not *grande dame*. Mrs. Auchincloss, who is said to be charming, has been in her stateroom constantly. The President is guarded closely—there is a strong-arm man always sitting in front of his stateroom, while marines patrol the deck outside his windows.

21. George Creel (1876–1953) was a journalist appointed by Wilson to be chairman of the Committee on Public Information. With superb and tawdry advertising talent he popularized Wilson's leadership in the war, but he lacked the mental capacity to grasp and explain the issues which the President faced at the Peace Conference. (C.S.)

Monday, December 9, 1918

Our perfect weather continues—it's almost inconceivable on a winter trip to Europe. This morning after my cold saltwater plunge I stood in front of the open port drying myself and the wind coming in felt balmy and tropical. It is too hot to stand in the sun, even with the lightest clothes on. The sea is almost without a ripple, but with long rollers so that there is a slow long roll to the boat. All but two of our destroyers have left us, but the *Pennsylvania* is always its thousand yards ahead.

The morning has been spent in taking pictures. We have at our table the signal corps officer who is responsible for all the pictures to go into the war records and who is to make all the pictures of the Conference.[22] He took still pictures of the Inquiry group all together, then individual pictures of each of us; then moving pictures of groups of three of us at a time, talking and smoking; then pictures of the specialists (division chiefs) of the Inquiry combined with the six officers of the M.I.D. who are on board. All these movies go into the war records and copies are sent back to the Committee on Public Information to be shown at home. So keep a watch for movies of the President's party. The President himself and the ambassadors, I regret to say, are being photographed separately.

Yesterday most of the afternoon and evening was spent in going over the ship. We were shown around by the Chief Petty Officer and it was intensely interesting, since apart from our living and eating quarters no change has been made since the boat was a transport and it was easy to visualize conditions as they were when the war was on. He was a very frank man and didn't attempt to gloss over unpleasant features. The old main smoking room of the boat was and still is a hospital; beautifully light and airy with room for about 90. There were some dozen men in it when we went through. At the time of the influenza epidemic they had 400 cases on board; there were 80

22. Major F. J. Griffin.

deaths on a trip and a regular morgue was established in the refrig-
erating plant below. We were told of officers brought back because
of treachery and cowardice. There is a fine operating room; a man
was to have had his appendix out yesterday, but refused the operation.
But on a very rough trip the surgeon took out two inches of bone from
the head of a sailor who had fallen from the rigging. The C.P.O.
explained the method of getting the life rafts overboard. There are
scores of them on the top deck, some large, some small. In case of
torpedoing the boats are pushed some ten feet away from the ship,
the passengers going down rope ladders into the water and *swimming*
to the boats or rafts in their life-jackets. This is considered safer
than lowering boats already filled. He said the *Lincoln* went down in
eight minutes. He was only 300 yards from the *Covington* when she
was torpedoed, and said they were all very angry with her crew for
deserting her; her captain was court-martialed.

The old main dining saloon of the boat has been turned into a
sort of recreation hall for the crew—they had movies coming back
from France but the poor troops going over had nothing of the kind.
We went through three or four decks where the troops slept. They
carried 5000 at a time in addition to the crew; the limit was the number of men they could crowd on deck at abandon-ship drill. The troop
beds in three tiers are made of iron piping with a two-foot, six-inch
strip of canvas. My respect for the troops went up when I imaged
being cooped up for ten or twelve days down below the water line,
unable to go from one deck to another and only allowed in the fresh
air for a few hours per day, with the only light at night coming from
a single blue light. We went through the kitchens, where they had
seven 80-gallon aluminum tanks for making coffee, and very good
coffee it is, and the bakeries with the temperature at 160° where
they made 5000 loaves of bread a day. The C.P.O. said that many
of the troops were pitifully scared—especially those who had never
seen the sea. Lots of them wouldn't take their clothes off or sleep and
even if they weren't sea-sick could hardly eat.

In the evening we went through the present crew's quarters and
saw the stokers, machinists, electricians, gunners, tailors, and cooks

either working or loafing or sleeping. They are supposed to sleep in hammocks but a large proportion of them had simply thrown themselves on the steel floor and were sleeping without even taking off their shoes to make a pillow. I expressed sympathy for their weariness but the C.P.O. said it was simply because they were too lazy to take their hammocks down or their clothes off; as he expressed it, "they don't give a damn." He has a liking for the sunny side of things and was unwilling that we should regard the men as dear innocent Jackies and took pleasure in showing us his sheet with the record of the men's misdoings and their punishments—anything from smoking below decks or intoxication to stealing. He took us to the cells—narrow little coops way below the waterline. One man was in there for 20 days on bread and water! Several on his sheets of punishment had had as much as 40 days.

Altogether the Jacky's life does not seem easy. But we asked some of them separately whether discipline was bad and they said, "Oh no —nothing like so strict as on a battleship." They are not impressed at the idea of carrying the President and complain of the monotony. Before, they said, they would fire at anything they saw in the water and always had the chance of running into a submarine and on the whole enjoyed the life pretty well. All of them seem anxious to get out of the navy, now that the war is over, and get more money. Several of them are college boys and want to go back. Those in the wireless room were particularly attractive. They were communicating with the *Pennsylvania* both by telegraph and telephone, with Paris, and with Washington all at the same time. We have mimeographed sheets of wireless news given to us every morning, which tell us more about events at home and abroad than the daily evening paper—"The Hatchet"—which appears at dinner time.

Off the Azores

Tuesday, December 10, 1918

Our convoy met us this morning. Just as I got on deck at 8 o'clock four destroyers came steaming up on both sides of us, turned and are now running abreast. Half an hour later we sighted land and since then have been running along the coast. It looks good to see land again after six days. The top of the mountain is in clouds. This is St. Miguel, the largest of the islands where Columbus landed on his return from his first voyage. It is pretty country with green fields laid out like a patchwork quilt. We turn northeast now and keep on that course until we reach the latitude of Brest, when we turn due east. It looks as if we should not reach Brest before Friday night. We have been receiving and giving gun salutes—very trying to the ears! We are going in close formation, hardly more than 500 yards behind the *Pennsylvania* and it must be a pretty sight for the islanders.

I have been working hard for an hour or so to get some materials in usable form. It seems that the Italian Ambassador does not like some of the maps shown by the M.I.D. (and they are awfully bad). He has made some sort of a diplomatic protest and the President is anxious to smooth things over and get at the exact facts of the situation in the Adriatic which lie at the bottom of the Italian-Jugoslav trouble.[23] This grows rather worse than better. So I am told to hold myself in readiness for a conference with him this morning or tomorrow. I had an interesting talk with Bullitt last night, who has been much exercised that no one had any idea as to what the President had in mind or wanted to do. Creel has been unable to tell him anything and said he couldn't use his propaganda because the President wouldn't give him a hint as to which way to jump. Jusserand told him that the President had intimated that he meant by a League of Nations only an agreement between the powers signatory to the peace treaty not to make war and to combine against any nation threatening the peace. This would not provide for any council or executive machinery and would be hardly more than they did in 1815. Jusserand expressed himself as in favor of rather more organization.

23. The secret Treaty of London of 1915 brought Italy into the war in return for the Allied promise of Austrian territory at the head of the Adriatic and on its eastern shores, by which Italy would gain strategic control of the sea. Unfortunately this area was occupied mainly by Slavs, who gained their independence in 1918. They opposed the transfer, especially of the city of Fiume.

Well, Bullitt finally went to the President and told him that everyone was much up in the air because of his silence; "His Nibs" was
very nice it seems, said he was grateful for having his attention called
to the matter, and promised to say something. While I was talking to
Bullitt, Clive had a chat with White and Lansing, the latter apparently talking very freely. The former said that he didn't expect to be of
much use in deciding questions, but hoped because of his wide ac-
quaintanceship to be able to bring the right sort of men together. I
think he is quite right and will help enormously in a social sense.
White is evidently prepared for a loose sort of League with a council, but is opposed to Taft's complicated machinery.[24]

I had a very interesting talk with Fosdick yesterday afternoon. He
said that he had seen my book on Pershing's desk! He is a cheerful
soul by nature, but says that he is appalled by the insight into social
conditions which his work has given him. He is a sane soul but so
utterly desperate as to how the working classes can get decent living
conditions that he is becoming quite revolutionary on the theory that
every country needs a thorough purging out.

Yesterday afternoon we had all kinds of entertainments for our
benefit. On the aft hatch the sailors had constructed a ring and gave
us three boxing bouts and a wrestling match followed by a pie-eating
contest, three men to a side, who ate big cranberry pies from a table
with their hands tied behind their backs. Then at four a destroyer
came abeam of us about half a mile off and dropped five depth
bombs. The first was exploded about 50 feet beneath the surface and
made a tremendous geyser of water; the others, exploded about 100
feet under the surface, made very little commotion on top.

I was stopped writing this morning by a call to a conference with
the President. He explained that the particular subject he wanted to
discuss with me he was going to leave until later, but he wanted to go

24. Former President William Howard Taft (1857–1930) had endorsed a plan
sponsored by the League to Enforce Peace, along with other important personages such
as Harvard President A. Lawrence Lowell. Essentially the plan involved three branches
of international government—a parallel drawn from the American government. See
Ruhl J. Bartlett, *The League to Enforce Peace* (Chapel Hill, N.C., 1914).

over the whole situation with the Inquiry specialists. The others came in—Clive, Westermann, Haskins, Lord, Bowman, Beer, Mezes, and Bullitt, who is acting as the liaison officer between us and the State Department. The President said that he wanted to go over the situation with us and make absolutely clear his position and his policy. He talked for an hour and a quarter and at the end of that time asked and answered questions. I can't put on paper what he said—he asked us to keep it confidential and I should be afraid of my letter's being opened. I shan't even put it in a memorandum book. Much of it will doubtless come out anyway during the next month. Much I can probably remember. I can say that he is on what seems to me the right track exactly as regards general policy, and you know pretty well how I feel. You will remember how your father felt on the matter of a probationary period for Germany before she enters the League of Nations. He will be interested to know the President agrees with him, although I did not and do not.

The whole talk was very intimate and in one respect it was really a historic occasion because it is absolutely the first time the President has let anyone know what his ideas are and what his policy is. His manner was very friendly. He explained that he could not know the details of all the questions that were coming up, but would be forced to rely on the information we gave him; that he wanted us to come to him freely and that we must expect him to call on us. One phrase sticks in my head—"You tell me what's right and I'll fight for it."

His talk was impromptu and colloquial, but very fluent, with a literary flavor and constant allusions or quotations; what interested me and surprised me most was the constant humor running through everything. Equally interesting was his unconscious use of phrases—epigrams such as, "When certain men applaud me, I know I am wrong." And others with regard to the current situation which I don't dare quote. Such usage seem to have become second nature to him. Everyone agreed that the personal impression made was very favorable. There was no touch of egotism—he spoke with extreme modesty and twice laughingly apologized for his ideas saying that they weren't very good but he thought them better than anything else that he had heard. At times he showed great vigor—saying in regard to a certain point that "his back was up and very stiff"; another time he was semi-humorous in regard to a point which he considered vital saying that if it were not secured "the conference wouldn't be worth either your or my attendance, and I wouldn't come home, but would go some place to hide my head, perhaps to Guam."

I sat about three feet from him and in talking he fixed each one of us with a very direct look of several seconds. Standing, he is short, as you know, but sitting he looked large. His personal magnetism is very strong—I realized it as I had years ago in college. Several points he made seemed better then than afterwards. But I am enormously relieved; I think tremendous difficulties and dangers are ahead of us, and complete success impossible; but I do think that he has a policy and that in its broad lines it is the right policy. Naturally we are pleased that he is going to use us.

·   ·   ·

Despite his disavowals, Seymour did make some incomplete notes of the meeting of December 10 immediately after it ended. Later he added an explanatory preface:

These notes were made by Charles Seymour on returning to his cabin. They were read to Clive Day and their accuracy attested. On arrival in Paris they were written out in typewritten form. They are not as detailed as those made by Isaiah Bowman or William C. Bullitt; there is no essential conflict apparent in the three drafts of the conversation.[25]

25. All told there were seven records made of the meeting. Bowman's version is printed in Seymour, *The Intimate Papers of Colonel House, 4,* 280–83. Bullitt, who prompted the President to call the meeting, left his in his diary in the Yale Library. A fourth record, that of William Westermann, is contained in his personal diary in the Columbia University Library. Seymour also noted that "the conference virtually took the form of a monologue by the President." See Gelfand, *The Inquiry,* pp. 170–75. Seymour was initially more enthusiastic and optimistic about the President's program than were

The President after greeting us cordially and shaking hands indi-
vidually with us, sat down at his desk and motioned us to sit in an
open semicircle around him. His manner was informal, almost casual. The general tone was that of a friendly faculty committee.

He began by insisting that in a certain sense we Americans held a
supremely advantageous position and were the only one of the powers so placed; we alone, of all the nations at the peace table, could
claim to be entirely disinterested. This resulted in our achieving
something of a position of a referee. But only if we met our responsibilities with our traditional devotion to justice and international gen-
erosity could he capitalize on our position.

He looked back, he went on, with the deepest satisfaction at the
course of United States foreign policy: We had gone to war with
Spain not for annexation but to provide the helpless colony with the
opportunity of freedom. When it came to collecting a Chinese indemnity for Boxer outrages, the other powers based their demands
not upon a fair evaluation of damages but upon their estimate of
the utmost that could be squeezed out of China; but the United States
had raised our demands to the limit, not to enrich ourselves but to
pay the indemnity back to the Chinese for education of their youth.

·   ·   ·

The foregoing view of American policy by Woodrow Wilson throws it
into more rosy moral light than is generally admitted by foreign historians. The original version of Seymour's notes continues.

Difficulties confronted us—selfishness of each of other powers.
Anxious to find out what Germany could afford to pay and make her
pay it. Not a question of restitution. Direct evidence that this [is]

---

his associates. Gelfand writes that Wilson's "inspiring words" failed to cheer Beer, Haskins, Young, and Westermann, all of whom considered the program "too vague and
inadequate." In retrospect, Seymour had to agree. He concluded that the program was
"impromptu," just as were the President's remarks aboard ship. Still, Seymour never
changed his view that Wilson, although failing to represent American political forces,
did represent the hopes of the American people and that he became more realistic as the
Conference progressed. See "Policy and Personality at the Paris Peace Conference,"
Virginia Quarterly Review, 21 (October 1945), 517–34.

contemplated. Official representatives did not really represent. If curious poison of Bolshevism to be avoided necessary to get in touch with real masses of people. Existing statesmen too weatherwise to see weather. If coming peace based on anything but justice and comprehension of opinion of masses, next catastrophe would not be a war but a cataclysm.

Difficulty also from demands of new nascent nationalities—not satisfied with free port of Danzig and guarantees of free access to it. Must be understood the new states should include only persons who want to be included. Criterion not who are intellectual or social or economic leaders but who form mass of people. Must have liberty— that is the kind of government they want.

Lasting settlement necessitates League of Nations. Not cynical— but old system of powers, balance of powers, had failed too often— couldn't trust a nation because no one to speak for it. League to have a council made up of ambassadors to smaller, neutral power[s]. When trouble threatened, council to 'butt in'—propose settlement after reference to their own governments. If unsuccessful the offending nation to be outlawed—"And outlaws are not popular now." Commercial boycott—all postal and telegraphic communication to cease.

League through a small power—Scandinavian or Swiss—to administer German colonies which should be property of League. Property always stabilizes an institution. Also Constantinople. Did not favor acquisitions of colonies by Great Britain. Colonies themselves jealous of further accessions by mother country.

Opposed to machinery of League to Enforce Peace. Such machinery under discussion would break down conference in a day.

Reemphasizes necessity of absolute justice, without which peace could not be permanent—"wouldn't be worth attending—I should not go home, but to Guam—world would not be worth living in."

·   ·   ·

President Wilson apparently then alluded to theories of the historian Albert Bushnell Hart concerning Southern loyalty during the Civil War and New England's influence on historical interpretation, but Seymour's notes are too fragmentary for full comprehension.

American victory at Château-Thierry. Carlyle on how to make honest men out of world of knaves—not impossible provided only minority of knaves have special interests. Always enjoyed passage in Acts: "All with one voice for about the space of two hours cried out ... Great is Diana of the Ephesians"—in the interests of the silver-smiths.[26]

Wednesday, December 11, 1918

I have just been one of a group talking with Ambassador Jusserand. He is naturally cautious and gives nothing new, although even the platitude is interesting coming from him. I asked him about the armistice and whether the French would have preferred to fight on. He said that it would have been impossible to sacrifice more lives when the Germans were willing to surrender but that he believed that most of the French felt that it would have been better to go on for three or four weeks so as to destroy forever the tradition of German military supremacy. He said that without any question the German armies were shattered, that in a very short time they would have been made prisoners of war. This, he felt, would be good for the Germans.

He spoke appreciatively of what the Americans had done, emphasizing the fact that because of the immense American reserves Foch could take chances in his offensive and run the risk of local defeat. I have, however, testimony on unimpeachable authority, that the Americans did very much more. "The Americans at Château-Thierry saved Europe and the world. And they did it contrary to orders. There was a gap of thirty miles. The French and British were all in. The

26. In Acts 19: 24–40, there is related the account of Demetrius and the angry silversmiths of Ephesus. Threatened by the loss of their lucrative business should Paul persuade the people to cease their worship of Diana and to destroy her temple, they caused a disturbance in the town assembly.

Americans against orders filled the gap, advanced, and for the first time the tide definitely set against Germany. Furthermore we have it in writing from the French and British that this is true. Pershing has got them signed up." This is largely only what we have guessed before. The importance of it is that this confirms the truth of it absolutely. The source cannot be questioned.[27]

I have had long and very interesting talks with Haskins, Beer, and Bullitt on big issues, especially the League of Nations. The two latter feel that Taft's and Lowell's scheme is the only adequate one, and that a mere council of ambassadors at a neutral capital would be wholly academic. They believe in an executive, a legislature, and a court—this largely on economic grounds. Their point is that without some continued organization of force and raw materials, there will be such want and famine and high prices in certain sections, even England, that social revolution will be likely. As to the disposition of German colonies, Beer does not believe that the African colonies can be administered by the League, particularly if one of the smaller powers should act as the mandatory of the League. On the other hand, he thinks that Turkey could be administered by the League. But Westermann, who is a specialist on Turkey, does not think that the League could administer Turkey, although it might manage Constantinople. All this is probably not very interesting for you, but I send it along to keep a note of it, in lieu of keeping a diary. Possibly when I get to Paris I won't burden you with so much detail.

The weather continues so warm and the sea so blue that one has to think hard for the date. I found myself starting to write "June." We turned northeast yesterday noon and are now about in the latitude of northern Spain. We expect to get in Friday afternoon or evening, possibly taking a night train and getting to Paris Saturday morning. We hear that our baggage will have diplomatic privileges and will go through to the hotel unopened. We also hear that the Allied fleet is coming out to meet us. (Another historical note—I am sit-

27. The source probably was Colonel Ayers.

ting next to Jusserand as I write and he has just said that in 1830 "the French upset the misrule of the Deys in Algiers, it was upon the very decided representations and requests of Washington diplomats."[28]

Tomorrow I expect to be laid up, for this morning, in company with the others of the Inquiry, I was filled full of typhoid and paratyphoid germs. There is only one inoculation and they say that the effects are violent but comparatively brief.

Our evening entertainments continue to be elaborate. The orchestra is really very good and plays *Bohème* and *Butterfly*! Quartets do swipes between the movie films. Last night was another Charlie Chaplin and Fairbanks night while the night before we had William S. Hart in a western spy play, and so I have been on hand. The ambassadors never miss it, and roar with laughter.

Thursday, December 12, 1918

This has been a very full day. I expected it to be one of extreme rest because of my inoculation but fate willed otherwise. As a matter of fact I have come off very easily; I began to feel feverish in the afternoon and by evening felt as though I had a good honest case of grippe. I put on heavy pajamas and blankets and tossed about a good deal, but slept fairly well, although in the morning Clive and Westermann complained bitterly of my mutterings. However I felt quite decent in the morning, and although my arm is sore and my legs shaky I have been getting better all day.

Clive and I were called into conference with the President about 10 o'clock and were with him for the rest of the morning. He is going to Italy next week and wants to have certain general points established. It was extremely interesting both as giving us further in-

28. Long troubled by Barbary pirates on the northern coast of Africa, the United States forced a treaty in 1815 by a show of naval force. The Dey renounced ransom and tribute and agreed to a $10,000 reparation. For the next 15 years relations between the United States and Algiers were reasonably good, but the Algerians continued to maraud European trade, which led to a French occupation in 1830.

formation on the points toward which we should work and as indica-
tive of his attitude, which is that he wants to know the facts and wants
to have our opinion on the policy which he ought to adopt. This means
that if we know how we can exercise far greater influence than
seemed probable. He said several times—"Tell me what I ought to
do in this connection," or "What means, Mr. Seymour, can be uti-
lized to bring pressure upon these people in the interests of justice?"
He finally asked me to write a memorandum upon policy to be
adopted in a certain case. Moral factors appeal to him strongly, but
he shows himself distinctly a practical politician—an idealist, but
thoroughly aware of the foibles of human nature and willing to utilize them.[29]

He puts one at ease. I found myself arguing and opposing some of
his points freely, quite as I would in talking with your father, and
saying, "If you do this, it is absolutely vital that this other should be
done." His whole attitude is the reverse of omniscience. He began for
example by saying, "Am I right in those assumptions, which I suppose are true but which you gentlemen are capable of judging?" And
always a strain of humor, which, strangely enough, reminded me of
Mr. Taft. Talking about the union of Montenegro and Serbia he said
that he had been receiving various congratulatory and polite letters
from the King of Montenegro[30] which had rather mystified him, but
to which he had replied courteously in the spirit of the Irishman who
wrote: "Not that I give a damn—but how's your mother?" He

29. Seymour's observations on Wilson's requests for advice at this point seem to
differ from his later conclusions, as expressed in his introduction to this book. Perhaps
the dilemma is best explained by Nicolson in *Peacemaking, 1919*, pp. 197–200. "Mr.
Wilson was fully practical, admirably informed, perfectly precise . . . He was very willing to apply to his own admirable experts for information: he was seldom prepared to
listen to them when they ventured to render advice."

30. Exiled King Nicholas I (1841–1921) ruled as prince, then king, from 1860 to
1918. He attempted the modernization of a backward state and economy but pursued
an inconsistent course in European politics. Forced to flee by the Austrian invasion of
1916, he opposed union with Serbia, led by his son-in-law Peter I, but hoped for a
federation. Deposed by his parliament in 1918, the last of the Petrovich-Njegosh dynasty, he told the Paris press that he was relying on Wilson for a safe and independent future for Montenegro.

also showed much dry humor in telling of the extreme demands of the Poles.

Mrs. Wilson came in twice while we were talking and chatted briefly. She had mislaid the copy of the President's reply to the greeting which Poincaré is going to make to him on Saturday.[31] The President said: "This business of writing the answer to a speech which has never been delivered is rather complicated." (Poincaré's address came in by wireless yesterday).

In conversation Mrs. Wilson is simple—quite unaffected—making a pleasant but not a striking impression.

The points covered in our talk with Mr. Wilson were of such importance that I spent two hours with Bowman, Young, and Haskins talking them over and discussing the means by which we can present our facts to him most satisfactorily. He wants matters put at first in certain broad lines, and does not wish to be bothered by details. He is interested in simplifying everything as far as possible.

Then as I came out from this conference I met Fosdick and Mr. White and we spent an hour discussing the League of Nations. White expresses himself very strongly against anything that would restrict the sovereignty of the individual nations. He says that the U.S. would never stand for it—he would not sign it—and the Senate would never ratify it. He wants the simplest sort of mechanism with an economic boycott as the final and desperate last resort to prevent war. Fosdick on the other hand believes that a real League with surrender of wide powers by each state is necessary to control food and raw materials and forestall social revolution. Clive and Bullitt joined us later, Bullitt the most radical of all, hoping that the President would put up a bitter fight for a strong League based on the principle of radical social reform. Clive stands between White and

---

31. Raymond Poincaré (1860–1934), French statesman, was President of the Republic from 1913 until 1920. He also served three terms as premier, both before the war and during the 1920's. No friend of Clemenceau, he and Marshal Foch were leaders of the French demand to dismember Germany.

Fosdick, favoring a declaration in the treaty which would satisfy the labor classes and a promise to develop the League as soon as possible.

White told us very interesting things about the beginning of the war. He said that in 1912 a German general told him that the Kaiser wanted peace but that the officers were going to force him to make war—that the German army was at its top notch and wouldn't be any good without war. Then on August 16, 1914, he had a long talk with Falkenhayn,[32] who told him that he realized that the Germans were in for a serious business—they were prepared to fight France and Russia, but the entrance of England which was unexpected altered matters entirely. People talked of a three months' war, but he thought it would be a three years' war or longer. He had great respect for the French military organization. But he said to White that they would have smeared the French if it had not been for "the peace crowd up at the Palace" which had delayed the mobilization four days and given time to the Belgians to mobilize and defend Liège. White said further that he had never believed the Germans could be defeated until we came into it; that he had written to Germany that our entrance into the war meant Germany's defeat and that his letter had been shown to the Kaiser. White confirms a good many of my surmises in my book and speaks in very complimentary terms of the book.[33]

I am deserting the movies (Farrar and Wallace Reid at that) in order to finish this long letter. We are due in at Brest at 1 o'clock tomorrow and I suspect that there may not be much time for writing. If I get another call from the President I shall have no time whatever and in any event shall have to be working on my memorandum. I suppose we may run into rough water tonight, but thus far it is as smooth as ever and while not warm it is by no means cold. I just took a stroll on the open deck without a coat. I shall mail this from Brest,

32. General Erich von Falkenhayn (1861–1922) was Chief of the General Staff from 1914 to 1916. Mainly involved in the fighting on the eastern front, he opposed the strategy of Field Marshal Paul von Hindenburg, the Supreme Commander, and General Erich Ludendorff, First Quartermaster General and the political manipulator behind Hindenburg. Falkenhayn resigned in 1916.

33. *The Diplomatic Background of the War, 1870–1914.*

hoping that the boat will sail back at once. If any faster boat sails first they will transfer our mail to it.

I certainly can't express my thanks to Providence sufficiently that Clive has been on the boat and in the room with me. He is an ideal traveling companion—even-tempered, humorous; tell Elsie,[34] if you get a chance, how much it has meant to me. Altogether the trip has been far more pleasant and interesting than I had expected. Physically we have been absolutely comfortable and I did not think that we should have been brought in such close touch with the President, and be able to discuss matters so freely with Mr. White or Raymond Fosdick. Curiously enough the Italian Ambassador is the only notable I have not come into touch with (apart from Lansing) and I have just received a note from him asking me to look him up tomorrow morning. He seems to have heard of my interest in the Adriatic question (possibly through C. U. Clark)[35] and maybe wants to grill me. Now I must go and pack, as our heavy baggage has to be ready early tomorrow morning.

Friday, December 13, 1918

I must finish this up because the mail is about to be called for. We expect to get into Brest in three hours. Blue skies and perfectly calm seas. An hour ago the American battle fleet came out to meet us—it was a wonderful sight. The battleships are painted grey—enormous creatures. They fired presidential salutes, wheeled around slowly, and are now sailing alongside of us. I never expect to have such good naval protection again in my life. There are 23 warships around us! The battleships are quite close—on one side the *New York*, *Nevada*, *Wyoming*, and *Texas*—on the other side four dreadnoughts of the

34. Mrs. Clive Day.
35. Charles Upson Clark (1875–1962) was a teacher of Latin at Yale who became an acknowledged authority on contemporary Italian and Rumanian culture and politics. (C.S.)

Oklahoma type. Now French aeroplanes are coming out and wheeling around over our heads.

We evidently spend the afternoon in Brest and go on to Paris by the night train. I should be glad to pass through the country by daylight, but I suppose that it would show no signs of war. If we can go over the American [port] construction at Brest this afternoon I shall be glad of the opportunity to see it.

Well I must close this and wish all of you the merriest possible Christmas—the last that we are not all together. Goodbye until I write from Paris.

THE PARIS SCENE IN DECEMBER

December 14–29, 1918

PRESIDENT WILSON may have suffered a reversal at home in the November elections, but he was at the apogee of his prestige in the world. "He arrived in Europe as a true friend of mankind, closer to the principles of Christian charity and justice than any statesman in history."[1] He fully expected his program to overcome any obstacles presented by the Allies' secret treaties or by their growing demands for revenge against Germany, just as he then expected to utilize public opinion at home to overcome Republican opposition.

He received an unprecedentedly joyous reception in Paris, then journeyed to London hard on the heels of a triumphal visit by Clemenceau and Foch. Here the crowds were notably cooler than in France, but at the end of the month he went to Rome. The Italian reaction, despite the pending clash over Fiume, was hysterically emotional, even though the Italian leaders tried to prevent Wilson from making too close an impression upon the masses. They feared his great personal influence might offset their own plans for obtaining all of the promises of the Treaty of London.

These ceremonial visits, parades, and other primarily social or festive events in Paris prevented the President from making any serious effort to open the work of the Conference. Delay might have served a purpose in allowing passions to subside and in letting the Allies reach a clearer understanding of the situation in Germany. The delegates also needed time to prepare, and to attempt a reconciliation of their dissimilar purposes. Unfortunately tensions seemed to grow rather than subside. A general elec-

---

1. S. F. Bemis, *A Diplomatic History of the United States* (4th ed. New York, 1955), p. 631.

tion in Britain and an historic vote of confidence in the French Chamber of Deputies provoked added measures of anti-German feeling. Wilson's failure to visit the battlefields or devastated areas seemed an oversight to some; it also gave Clemenceau added reason to belittle the President's program. American troops, unable to secure adequate shipping to accommodate the plan of moving divisions home intact, became restive with the result that both military training and general educational programs were revived. Influenza was rampant. President Sidonio Paes of Portugal was assassinated in Lisbon. Further street fighting occurred in Berlin.

These were the external and visible problems. Although there were no immediate crises within the American Commission itself, the continued disorganization and failure of communication—characteristics of much of the preliminary work—undermined individual efforts and eventually weakened existing strengths. Wilson persisted in the idea that peacemaking was his personal crusade and heaven-blessed mission. He gave few further hints or guidance on his thinking about the overall settlement.

This is not to say that certain major questions—and tentative answers—were not taking form. What was to be the basis of reparations? Civilian costs or total costs? Germany's capacity to pay or the Allies' ability to receive without disruption of the European economy? Or, how long and for what purpose should economic controls be imposed on Germany? Was German military strength still a threat? And, again, how could principles of nationality, self-determination, security, strategic frontiers, and economic viability be reconciled? Or had new military technology rendered obsolete old concepts of security and strategy? Finally, what was the future to hold for the newly created states of Central Europe?

Some of the Commissioners were attempting to produce American positions on these perplexing questions. The members of the Inquiry, having established themselves as the principle agents for political advice, were again being called upon for scholarly memoranda and reports, now with the added insights provided by frequent discussions with colleagues from other nations. Unfortunately the results lacked coordination and direction.

Meanwhile certain other events, particularly within the former Austro-Hungarian Empire, were moving independently and rapidly into new situations which rendered obsolete many of the Inquiry's previous bases of consideration. Upon meeting Wilson at Brest General Pershing had observed, "He has been a good President to me but his hands are full now." Only in retrospect was the full significance of his observation evident.

At the moment, however, the situation did not look so bleak to Seymour.

He responded to the excitement and warmth of the French reception as he moved into the famed Hôtel Crillon, with its view of the Seine to the south, of the Champs Elysées to the west, and the gardens of the Tuilleries and the Louvre Palace across the Place de la Concorde—the finest of the Parisian squares, steeped in revolutionary history. Although the official American headquarters was No. 78 rue de l'Université, Seymour was pleased—and a bit amused—to discover that the Inquiry offices would be adjacent to the Crillon at No. 4 Place de la Concorde, directly above Maxim's, the old restaurant and cabaret of colorful reputation. Almost at once he found himself deeply involved in the intricate question of Yugoslavia, its boundaries and its future, and he also found somewhat to his surprise that he was working more for General Bliss than any of the other Commissioners. Simultaneously he confirmed his positive and favorable impression of Colonel House and his role as the man behind President Wilson.

Seymour's personal excitement had a special measure of happy recollection. Not only had he studied in Paris, but he had also spent part of his honeymoon here. As he set about his new tasks and became acquainted with the gathering statesmen of the world, he still found time to revisit many favorite spots, including churches, restaurants, clubs, and several libraries which he found useful once again. And everywhere, it seemed, he encountered familiar faces from the large Yale family—classmates, faculty associates, and former students—several of whom would become closely connected with his future administration of the University.

Hôtel Crillon, Paris

Saturday, December 14, 1918

I want to put on paper my impressions of the last hour before they get cold, hence I am sitting with Clive in our room and scratching an old paper without going over to our offices where there is sure to be confusion. I am quite unable to express, however, the really soul-shocking character of what I saw. We were in a balcony on the Place de la Concorde—first floor up—before us the whole Place with the city statues and the Strasbourg covered with triumphant flags; across the river the Palais Bourbon; to our right the Champs Elyseés. It was one mass of people—at least a hundred thousand, possibly more—all fighting to get a view of President Wilson. They had climbed upon the statues and had brought high stepladders on which they sat. It was a regular Parisian crowd—students and gamins mixed in with poilus and Turcos and Annamites,[2] more self-contained than the old crowds and thus giving evidence of the war.

Then, far across the Pont de la Concorde, came a squadron of cuirassiers galloping down the lane formed by the sky-blue poilus drawn up on both sides to keep the crowd back. We could hear the cheers across the Seine and American flags waving in the distance in front of the Chamber of Deputies. Aeroplanes were overhead and enormous guns going off. Then behind the second squadron of cuirassiers in an open carriage with Poincaré came Wilson, and the crowd lost its self-restraint. The noise was not American in volume but the enthusiasm was unmistakable and you couldn't question the fact that the mass of the people think Wilson is the savior.

I was reminded of a workman at Brest yesterday, who admitted that things had been pretty bad but pointed to the *George Washington* and said, "That man is going to make it all right." And the newspapers of yesterday had on their front sheets in large letters: *"Travailleurs, prenez note:* Wilson arrive Samedi." They have made today a general holiday here. After the President came Mrs. Wilson in a carriage heaped with flowers and I must say looking very well indeed. She seemed well dressed and at a short distance very good-looking. Then followed carriages with the chief French dignitaries, Pichon, Tardieu, and Pershing and Bliss.[3] It was a very brief cavalcade, but the people seemed anything but disappointed. After it had passed

2. Turcos (*tirailleurs algériens*) were infantrymen of the colorful Zouave regiments recruited in the French colony of Algeria. The Annamese, or Vietnamese as they were later called, were from the Indochina colony.

3. Clemenceau, Pichon, and Tardieu were three of the five French Peace Commissioners. Stéphen Jean Marie Pichon (1857–1933), French politician, statesman, and journalist, was Minister of Foreign Affairs in 1906 and again from 1917 until 1920. André Tardieu (1876–1945)—politician, educator, journalist, and recipient of an honorary doctor of laws degree from Yale in 1917—was Minister of Liberated Regions under Clemenceau. Leader of the Republican group (later Centre Republican), Tardieu was to serve three times as Premier. He also wrote *The Truth About the Treaty* (Indianapolis, 1921). Lieutenant General Tasker Howard Bliss (1853–1930), the fifth American Peace Commissioner, became Chief of Staff, U.S. Army, in 1917, and served on the Allied Supreme War Council. After retirement he was active in developing and discussing practicable means of peaceful international conciliation. (C.S.)

up the rue Royale all the poilus and people joined in a vast manifesta-
tion of the kind you know, forming ranks and marching around the
Place, people came down from the statues and off the enormous
German guns, which are arranged all over the Place, and fell in,
while the men who had rented their stepladders took them down and
went off. Seats in windows were said to be rented for 300 francs, but
I should say that ours was the best place of all. We learned later
that it was specially reserved for Mr. Lansing, who, however, was in
the procession and didn't need it.

Our arrival in Brest yesterday was impressive. I wrote you about
the great battleships meeting us early; more American destroyers
fell in later in the morning (30 of them), then French and British
warships. I counted 50 ships of war in the convoy and there may have
been more. As we approached the harbor they steamed ahead and
formed a narrow lane through which we passed. The President was
on the upper bridge, most of us on the lower bridge. The destroyers
formed a big outer circle—the battleships the lane. As we passed
each battleship the entire crew of it was manned at attention at the
rail—a wonderful sight! Each ship's band played "the Star Spangled
Banner" as we went by and each crew gave "three rousing cheers."
The magnificence of the ships—their perfect alignment—the cheers
—the music—and the guns brought tears of excitement to one's
eyes. We came to anchor at the end of the lane and then each of the
battleships sent over its launch with its commanding officer to pay respects to the President. The launch of the *New York*—the flagship of
the battle squadron—was a boatload of admirals. The first on board
was Admiral Sims—very tall, slim, well set up with close-cropped
pointed white beard, very ruddy cheeks and free and easy manners
—ideal sea-dog in appearance, but with thin piping voice.[4] Then arrived the boat with the French dignitaries, Pichon at their head, and

4. William Lowden Sims (1858–1936) graduated from the U.S. Naval Academy
in 1880. He advanced through the grades to permanent rear admiral. His service was
varied and he was appointed to command American naval operations in European waters in 1917. After the war he became president of the Naval War College. A critic of
the Navy's handling of war operations, he declined a Distinguished Service Medal.
(C.S.)

with them who but Pershing and Bliss. Pershing is, I think, the grandest man I ever saw—very tall, enormous in breadth but still not a hint of excessive weight. He walks with a touch of a swagger. I stood close to him when he met Sims who had not seen him since the armistice, and who was congratulating him—"How the hell did you do it?" he said to Pershing. They both of them look the part better than any celebrities I have ever seen.

Westermann knows Pershing and had quite a chat with him, and I was vexed not to be there at the moment. Bliss is tall, heavy, and has big white moustaches. It is a sight to see him and Pershing together with the four stars of a full general on one and three of a lieutenant general on the other. The President and the French dignitaries with the generals left in one boat, Ambassador Davis left in a launch for a battleship which is to take him to England, and the foreign ambassadors and the others left in another boat. We reached the town too late to see the reception for the President, but were interested in going through the crowd which was *en fête*, the women in thin white crinoline hats and the men in thin broad sailors with ribbons hanging down behind. Clive and Westermann slipped away from me and had a Dubonnet, which seemed hard!

We found a train deluxe all ready for us—about eight wagon-lits with diner. The compartments were of the kind you and I had coming from Italy to Paris seven years ago. Going out of Brest the railway skirts the road and we ran slowly, so that we could exchange greetings with the French and the American doughboys coming through the mud. The former cried: "Vivent les Américans" to which we replied suitably. The latter were much surprised to see people at the American port in civil dress—"Well I'll be blamed" cried one, "if they ain't real honest-to-God Americans." Another yelled: "How do you like it?" "Fine," said we. "You ain't been here as long as we have," he responded. Another yelled: "You ain't going in the right direction —America for me—I saw too much of Paris." All along the line French crowds yelled enthusiastically, doubtlessly not realizing that the President was in the first train.

We were called into the dining car and had as good a meal as I ever had in France; soup, fish, chicken and salad, camembert; to drink for four of us—a quart of red wine, one of white wine, one of champagne, chartreuse, and coffee, with a large and very good cigar. All this furnished by the French government. I have not paid a cent or sou for anything but tips and stamps from the time I got on the boat; since arriving in France I have not had to show a ticket or even my passport. Under the influence of the cigars and champagne we all agreed that we were disposed to be very friendly toward all French territorial claims, the left bank of the Rhine or even the incorporation of Berlin if they wished it.

Our luxurious berths proved very comfortable and I had difficulty in getting up at seven when we were warned that we would soon be in Paris. We were met at the station by 50 orderlies and a dozen U.S. Army automobiles which brought us on here.

I must stop to go over to the office—will tell more about our arrival and life here in my next. Our quarters are very luxurious and the meals served would make any outsider turn Bolshevik.

Monday, December 16, 1918

Yesterday, Sunday, was for everyone else a day of rest, but early in the morning came in a call from the president for the memorandum he had asked of me on the ship. So Clive, who was interested in the economic side of the question, and Lunt, who has studied frontier problems, got together and with the geographer Jefferson worked most of the day and into the night getting to bed at 1:30.[5] We were at it again this morning and finished up everything by lunch time. Now

5. William Edward Lunt (1882–1956), Bowdoin '04, Harvard Ph.D., '08, was professor of medieval history at Cornell (1912–17) and at Haverford in 1917. He then became chief of the Italian Section of the Inquiry and of the Italian Division of the American Peace Commission, but sat on none of the territorial commissions. In personality he was reserved and positive. He later served on numerous faculties, including Chicago, Wisconsin, and Temple. (C.S.). Mark Sylvester William Jefferson (1863–1949), Harvard-trained astronomer and educator, served as chief cartographer for the American Commission. Later he returned to the Harvard faculty.

it is in the hands of the stenographer and should be in the President's hands when he returns from the Hôtel de Ville and finishes benig made a citizen of Paris.

Tuesday, December 17, 1918

I got just so far yesterday when I was interrupted by a call to a conference and was unable to get back to my letter. Now I have the chance of a clear half hour and will go back to Saturday. We were brought from the Gare Montparnesse here in automobiles—Rue de Rennes, Bvd. St. Germain, Pont de la Concorde. If you remember the Parisian taxi driver you will recall that he is not noted for his caution, but he has nothing on the American Army driver—twice we were on the sidewalk and once skidded halfway around. (The streets were wet.) His idea of making a turn where the street came to an end, as they frequently do on the Rive Gauche, was to approach the corner at 35 miles per hour and not decide which way to turn until he saw which way was the most empty. Paris was very natural—unchanged outwardly—the same smell—the only obvious indication of war being the long queues of persons waiting outside an épicerie or a tobacco shop, or a confectioner who had put up a placard saying that he would have a limited amount of chocolate at such and such an hour. Long lines of poilus marched down the streets to form the Guard of Honor for the President, and cavalrymen all in steel helmets clattered along; sometimes a troop of the cuirassiers in their old uniform with long horsehair brass helmets trotted down. We had a puncture on the road and soon collected a moderate-sized mob around us of some 12 poilus, 15 students, and 30 gamins, which seemed natural. Some attempted to assist in the American as well as the French sense, which vexed our doughboy who said he had never seen folks so "God damn curyus" as the French.

At the hotel we were received in a blaze of glory making our way through a crowd which showed disappointment at not seeing "Vilson" but a mild interest in "his délégués," which was whispered about. My fur coat stood me in good stead and won great respect. Conditions here are of the most luxurious. We entered the breakfast room immediately, having slept too late to get coffee on the train. Almost to our horror the breakfast turned out to be about the best in our experience—bread very nearly white and with the finest crust, the most perfectly fried sole I ever tasted, plenty of delicious butter and all the sugar we wanted. The coffee has a good deal of chicory in it (after-dinner coffee is perfect—made separately in a drip pot for each guest, *café filtre*). The Crillon is said to be the only hotel which serves butter and sugar. The other meals are even more grand. We simply sign for all meals and tipping is forbidden. To give an idea of prices and our luxury if we have guests to meals we are charged 5 francs for petit dejeuner, 10 francs for dejeuner and 15 francs for dinner.[6]

Our rooms are equally splendid. I was assigned an enormous room *à deux lits,* high ceiling, white paneling, fireplace, enormous bathroom, very comfortable bed all done in rich old rose. Clive's room is smaller and less desirable and as the place is crowded he has come up with me. I think we both prefer it, for it discourages loneliness at morning and night and is much more convenient as we have very frequent conferences on business.

So you see we have no complaint with our position except that we are liable to get indigestion. But I am glad to have the various medicines on hand in case of minor ailments, which thus far have not appeared. The hotel gives us matches and shines our shoes. As to clothes I may have to get a top hat and morning coat for state occasions—such as the Hôtel de Ville function which I missed. But I think that there is going to be more fun and interest in getting in touch with the men behind the scenes than in going to outside events. Saturday night we dressed for dinner, but discovered later that there is free liberty to appear in our dining room undressed, although one must forego the pleasure of sitting next to the high diplomats.

I have seen so many people that I can't give any record of the

6. The exchange value of the franc in early 1919 fluctuated around 18 cents.

conversations which were generally of rather technical or a decidedly confidential character. I don't know whether letters are censored carefully; if I send mine through the diplomatic pouch of course they would not be censored at all, but they would be longer en route, probably resting in Washington for some time.

It goes without saying that there is wide difference of opinion between the diplomats of the various countries which does not appear on the surface. The Italians are incorrigible—their claims are utterly absurd, and they are in the wrong all along the line.[7] They are nasty about it and threaten a general blow-up in Italy if they don't get what they want. But they won't. The French are fine. There is a strong movement for the annexation of the Saar coal district (in addition to Alsace-Lorraine);[8] it is German in character, but small and could reasonably be regarded as a part payment by Germany for damage inflicted. There is a movement, not so strong, for the annexation of the whole west bank of the Rhine; but the Socialists are strongly opposed to this.

Clemenceau is for the moment the most popular man in France— one sees his picture everywhere, and not unflattering caricatures of his silhouette with that of a tiger beside it. They tell the story that when the Italians wired for help saying: "The Germans are attacking with full force and they fight like lions," he replied: "Yesterday we captured 18,000 lions. (Signed) Le tigre."

But if he and Wilson disagree on a point of principle I think the latter will find enormous support among the French masses. It is difficult to overstate his prestige here. People came in thousands from all parts of Paris on Saturday to see him—so that Philbin coming up had to stand for five hours in a train.[9]

7. Italian claims were based on the secret Treaty of London of 1915.

8. French claims for the Saar were based on a demand for compensation for Germany's destruction of mines in northern France during the final phases of the war. Alsace-Lorraine, a richly endowed and strategic district on the Rhine, had long been a military prize. Annexed by Germany during the Franco-Prussian War, its return became France's chief objective of the war.

9. Stephen Holladay Philbin (b. 1888), Yale '10, was a lieutenant in the Air Service assigned to the Peace Commission. In later years he became a leading patent lawyer in New York.

The French are popular with us, except with the accounting officers and treasury officials, for we certainly have to pay for everything we get. We didn't, it seems, actually pay rent for our front-line trenches, but we pay good rent for every inch of French soil which we occupy behind the lines. The British got most of their money from us on transportation. They wouldn't bring our men to Brest, but took them to England, which cost us an extra 50 dollars, per man, and they have charged 150 dollars per man for transportation from America to England. You can see that they are getting something to pay back the loans we have made. Their feeling is, I think, that they suffered so long in the war without us that we can afford to pay something. I heard of an American sailor who complained of the quality of the beer he got in England and was told: "Well it *is* a little stale; it's been waiting for you for three years."

The British trading classes are anxious to continue interallied food and shipping control and make this the basis for the League of Nations. Before I arrived I was inclined to believe this plan might strengthen the League. But since discovering the economic quarrels we have had, which had been settled only because we had to win the war, I am inclined to believe that it would split the League in a year. Hoover is opposed to the continuation of interallied control for more than another six months at longest.[10] The British want a five- or ten-year period of control, which would enable them to get a long start on Germany and break the advantage of the neutrals and the United States.

10. Herbert Hoover (1874–1964) engaged in many engineering projects scattered throughout five continents during the two decades prior to World War I. In 1914 he was named chairman of the American Relief Commission in London, and in the following year chairman of the Commission for Relief in Belgium. He was also the United States Food Administrator from 1917 until 1919 and a member of numerous economic and commodity commissions. At the end of the war he became chairman of the American Relief Administration. Blunt and outspoken in his more humanitarian concepts, Hoover frequently clashed with his European counterparts who saw relief operations as a political means of advancing national objectives. Twenty-five years later, after a career that took him to the White House, Hoover returned to the problems of relief when, at the request of President Truman in 1946, he undertook the coordination of food supplies for the war-devastated areas.

The question of indemnities is to the front now, but we are trying to keep it in the background. If only the British and the French won't commit themselves there will be no disagreement. The only way in which Germany can pay is by exporting goods. She has got to be allowed to make money to pay over to the Allies. If a man owed you a million the last thing you would do would be to stick a knife in him, especially if his estate was bankrupt. The utmost Germany *can* pay will not exceed the amount of damage caused, and we are in absolute agreement that she shall pay for that. I am giving the opinion of statistical experts. (It's very late and I must go to bed.)

Wednesday, December 18, 1918

It is a strange feeling to have spare time after breakfast but our offices are being reorganized and as a result it is impossible to do any work and I have escaped from the knot of persons retelling the news they picked up last night. So I will go back to where I stopped telling about our doings. Saturday afternoon we spent in unpacking and locating the more important material—maps and papers—sent over ahead of us. Our offices are right on the corner of the rue Royale and the Place—a large portion of them over Maxim's. They are extensive but cut up. I imagine that many of them used to be the gambling rooms of Maxim's. So it is going to be difficult to get them into working order. But they are most convenient and connected with our hotel by a covered arcade. We are apparently very fortunate both in our hotel and offices. House told me that the French were very unwilling to let them go, partly because of their central position, largely because the Crillon has been the social center of the Allied high command. It was here that the Supreme War Council lived, had all of their informal discussions, and their social gatherings.

We went out to see the crowds celebrating the arrival of Wilson. They were enormous—no traffic of vehicles on the boulevards or the main highways—packed like a Mardi Gras crowd. But, as I said be-

fore, it was very self-contained—the noise was muffled—and there
was no spontaneous outburst. Students had confetti and streamers and
a few horns and the midinettes walked with their arms about each
other or soldiers and stole the doughboys' caps as souvenirs. But most
of the people looked *tired*. It is foolish to say that Paris is not
changed. It goes about its business, whether work or play mechani-
cally. The poilus' faces are set and the women's largely expressionless. I was told that it was the same after the recapture of Lille and
the armistice. People gathered in front of the statues on the Place
but the crowds were entirely silent.

We stopped in at the University Union but Sam and Clare were
not there[11]—probably out seeing the crowds. So I could get no news
of anyone I was interested in. Sunday morning early came the call
for a memorandum—on Italian vs. Yugoslav claims, and we started
right to work. Day took charge of the economic questions involved,
Lunt handled Italian statistics, I took the Austrian statistics and the
general formation of the report.

We went out late Sunday afternoon over to the Union for an
hour and found both Clare and Sam. Both looked thin and tired—
older. I talked over Clare's work with him and hope to get him
transferred. Although he has not got his commission he does not want
to leave the M.I.D. so long as they want to use him. And if he should
leave it, he thinks that George Nettleton is counting on him and that
he ought to go back to the Union. If I can get him attached to the

11. The American University Union in Europe maintained a building in Paris for
social and cultural gatherings. Its director (1917–19) was George Nettleton (1874–
1959), Yale '96, who previously headed the Yale Bureau in Paris. After the war he
and the two men Seymour was seeking all returned to Yale and were intimately involved with the University for many years. Nettleton became Lampson Professor of English. In 1937 he temporarily served as dean of Yale College during Seymour's first year
as president. Earlier he edited the two memorial volumes, *Yale in the World War* (New
Haven, 1925). Samuel B. Hemingway (1883–1958), Yale '04, came from a large New
Haven family and was then an assistant professor of English. He served in Paris as a
Y.M.C.A. official. Later he became professor of English and master of Yale's Berkeley
College, succeeding Seymour. Clarence W. Mendell (b. 1883), Yale '04, was a
classicist who later served on the Yale faculty as Sterling Professor of Latin Language
and Literature and dean of the college (1926–37). In Paris he was first with the
M.I.D., then became an assistant to the territorial experts of the Commission.

Peace Commission I think this may help to break off relations with the Union. I think he has enjoyed the year and found it very interesting.

Sam, I think, has not been so happy. He hasn't been well physically I guess, and he has never come to like the French as well as the English. It was a mistake his going into the Y.M.C.A. The men don't seem to like it over well and they don't understand Sam's being in it. He says it has been very interesting and yet a good deal of a strain—more than they realized at the time. They reported that they had had a wonderful dinner with Law and that he was in fine form.[12] I got his military address and sent the letters on to him and hope for an answer soon. Lester Perrin had been in several times, just about a week ago, but has been sent to St. Nazaire to do routine work and goodness knows when he will get off again. He and Walter Davis and Biglow were all here together. Thornton was actually in Paris at the moment I was in the Bureau but characteristically had not left any address so could not be discovered. I could learn nothing of Jim Townsend, except that he is in some depot brigade.[13]

We worked late Sunday night and broke the back of the memorandum. At it again Monday morning and practically finished it by noon —embodying some few suggestions and corrections made by powers higher up.

12. Charles Law Watkins (1886–1945), Yale '08, was Seymour's classmate and brother-in-law. He enlisted in the French Army Artillery in 1917, and Seymour hoped to see him in Paris. After the war he with two other classmates organized the Watkins Coal Co.; later he became Associate Director of the Phillips Gallery and helped to start the Phillips Gallery School in Washington.

13. Lester William Perrin (b. 1886), captain, became secretary of the Austro-Hungarian Division of the American Commission and worked with the author, and later became a partner of Lazard Frères and mayor of Bernardsville, N.J.; Walter Goodwin Davis (b. 1885), captain, assigned to the American Legation in Berne and later to the Peace Commission's Mission in Vienna, turned to business and the law in Portland and also served as the president of the Maine Historical Society; Lucius Horatio Biglow, Jr. (1885–1961), captain, took up law and business in Deep River, Conn.; James Carlton Thornton (1884–1949), captain in the Field Artillery, later entered the brokerage business and was a co-founder of the Watkins Coal Co.; and James Mulford Townsend, Jr. (1886–1950), lieutenant, became a businessman in New York and another founder of Watkins Coal Co.

As a matter of fact there is practically no one higher up now except the commissioners. This sounds cocky, but it is the truth. When we started the assistant secretaries of the Commission and the Military Intelligence assumed that they were going to give all the advice on policy, taking facts from us when and as they wanted them. The conferences we had with the President on the boat changed this attitude a little. Then when they got here the assistant secretaries (who know nothing of policy anyway) found that their time was taken in arranging for social functions and that anyway they were *unable* to write the memoranda the Commissioners wanted. As for Military Intelligence their Chief, General Churchill (a very good sort) went to Bliss and said: "Here we are, what can we do for you?" Bliss said: "I don't want you—I am a commissioner of peace now and have forgotten my military point of view entirely." So in the reorganization we eight specialists are to report directly to the Commissioners, all the Military and Political Intelligence reporting to us and getting information for us as we require. This is the way we hoped things would turn out, but we feared for a time that it might be otherwise.[14]

I had a pleasant talk with Gordon Auchincloss who was quite cordial and not discernibly condescending. One of my classmates is ensign on naval commission actions here[15]—(Colonel House is attended by the Navy). And a pupil of two years ago, a captain wounded at Château-Thierry, is aide to Gordon. The hotel is guarded by the military—sentries before the doors—and orderlies in the halls and guard-

14. The final composition of the American Commission included:
   a. Personal aides and assistants for each of the five Commissioners.
   b. A Secretariat, headed by Joseph C. Grew and consisting largely of State Department personnel. Here there were the Division of Current Diplomatic and Political Correspondence with geographical subdivisions corresponding to the sections of the Inquiry, a division on Current Intelligence Summaries headed by Bullitt, and various military intelligence and information divisions.
   c. The Technical Advisors on international law, economics, finance, food, labor, shipping, military and naval affairs.
   d. The Division of Territorial, Economic, and Political Intelligence consisting of the former members of the Inquiry.
   15. Presumably Francis Goodell (b. 1886), Yale '08, who became a writer and consultant in later life.

ing the chief conference rooms. The poor boys have to rise from their seats when we come down the hall.

Monday afternoon late I went out with Clive, the first chance I had had to get out that day. We went to establish financial connections. The boulevards were crowded with people anxious to see Wilson drive home from the Hôtel de Ville. Always *en fête* but rather sadly. I ended up at the Union to bring Clare and Sam over for dinner. To my horror I found that Sam had gone to the hospital that morning with pleurisy.

Clare came in and we had dinner together and then took the metro up to Notre Dame des Champs to the hospital. It was long after visiting hours but they let us in. We found him, in the midst of convalescent wounded, in a temporary shed erected in the main court of the building. He was reading and very cheerful, and said that he was feeling much better already. He said that he had had a pain in his side for weeks, and had talked to the doctor who only decided it was pleurisy Monday morning. He was not really sick enough to go to a hospital, but it was the only place where he could get a really good rest. The doctor thought he would be out in two or three days. Clare does not believe it is pleurisy at all, but says it is a muscular strain on his side which comes from his flat feet which are very bad. The hospital room is very attractive—it is about 40 by 30, with some 60 beds—not crowded. It has a glass roof and is evidently cheerful. There are flowers about, and each soldier has a box of chocolates—they can buy all the cigarettes and tobacco they want. They seem cheerful, and jolly the nurses continually. This is said to be the best American hospital in Paris. It is supported by Mrs. Whitelaw Reid at a cost of a million or so.[16]

Clare and I walked back by the Luxembourg, very fine in the clear moonlight, and the rue Bonaparte. He said the thing that infuriated

16. Whitelaw Reid (1837–1912), journalist, author, and diplomat, elevated the *New York Tribune* to national prominence during his editorship. He ran unsuccessfully for Vice President in 1892 and then served in ambassadorial posts in France and England (1905–12).

him most about the Big Bertha was that one of the shells struck in the middle of the Luxembourg Garden, so that the children couldn't play there at all.[17] He reminded himself, as we crossed the Seine, of a night on the same bridge when he got caught in a raid; shrapnel began to fall and he had to run (as from a thunderstorm) to the arch under the Louvre. He has just been to Rheims and says that the cathedral is far more than a shell. The facade and exterior are battered but handsome; the interior is by no means gone; part of the roof is intact and this can all be easily repaired. Two-thirds of the glass was taken to Paris and is safe. He is filled with admiration of the French and says that only Foch's tactics and German weakness saved Pershing from disaster in the Argonne. You can take this for what it is worth. He came back to the hotel with me and he and Clive and I talked for an hour. The worst of this whole game is that one gets so little sleep. I don't think I have been to bed before midnight since arriving.

Yesterday was spent in seeing people—important and unimportant. Most of the morning in conference with Colonel Buckley—attaché at Rome—going over Italian claims in the Adriatic and Asia Minor. He is so far under official Italian influence that he was not of much help. Believes that Italy should have the London Pact line of 1915, and even Fiume. Says that if the Italians don't get this there will be a revolution, etc. Italian army wonderful—etc., etc. Then a conference to revise one report for the President in slight detail (by no means as a result of our talk with Buckley).

Then at 12:30 a conference with Colonel House on general matters. He looks tired but says that he is taking care of himself. The oftener one sees him the more enthusiastic one becomes. He is very quiet in manner, suave, absolutely simple. I think his ideas are rather further developed than the President's and that he will help him to

17. The Big Berthas, one of Germany's surprise weapons, were 420-mm. mortars which hurled one-ton projectiles. These siege guns were first used in 1914 to wreck the forts at Liège and to batter Antwerp. Actually this was not the weapon used in 1918 to bomb the French capital. The Paris Gun, of which only three were made, was a reconstruction of the navy's 15-inch rifle. A relatively small projectile and a tremendous powder charge gave this weapon a 75-mile range. In the spring of 1918 several hundred rounds were intermittently fired on Paris.

crystallize on a good many points. House has made a fine impression over here, although he has succeeded in staying so far in the background even lately that the French people hardly know him. Unlike White, Bliss, and Pershing he has not been riding in any of the parades of the last few days.

I find that the higher one goes the easier it is to meet people—neither in the case of Wilson or House did I feel any nervousness or timidity. Clive has had a long interview with Venizelos today and says that absolutely he is the easiest man to get on with and the nicest old gentleman he ever met. Clive, by the way, is making a great diplomatic success. Henry White is obviously very fond of him and he got on very well with the President. He is a good deal more than earning his salary.

After lunch yesterday (which was late because of the talk with House) I had to make some notes and later went out to get some air, stretch my legs and see Sam in the hospital. I have to admit that, not knowing that part of Paris—Montparnasse—I strayed quite a bit, a fact which I should have been ashamed to confess seven years ago. But I did not ask my way of anyone—which would have pleased you I know—and ultimately got there. Sam was quite cheerful, said he had had a perfectly comfortable night and looked much rested. He talks of getting up but says he is so comfortable that he dreads going back to the bustle of the Union.

I hurried back to the hotel for a long conference of the specialists (as we are now called) discussing arrangement of offices and allocation of assistants and points of detail. There are now eight regional specialists—delightfully paradoxical term, who form a committee directly under the Commissioners and responsible to them. Kerner is excluded from this inner circle—necessarily, but I am sorry for him. I have him working on jobs for me.[18]

I hurried from the conference to dinner with Bob Taft and Phil-

18. Robert Joseph Kerner (1887–1956), Harvard '14, professor of modern European history at the University of Missouri and later (1928–54) at the University of California, served under Seymour in the Inquiry and at Paris. A Czech, he was an expert on Slavic history. In 1952 he was appointed to UNESCO's Commission for the Scientific and Cultural History of Mankind.

bin.[19] I wanted to see them on general grounds, of course, but I was particularly anxious to get in touch with Bob, who is Hoover's first assistant and can give me Hoover's point of view on food conditions in Austria-Hungary. I also want to establish a point of contact in case I need to get information on economic points from Hoover personally. I wanted to find out what Philbin had to say on Italy—people and politics. I found out briefly that Steve is at the opposite pole from Colonel Buckley—nearer the truth I imagine. He says the Italian officers are impossible—the worst *embusqués*[20] imaginable. He told of instances in which they bluffed sickness so as not to fly—their frank cynicism in confessing it, their failure to lead their men. Caporetto, he says, is generally agreed to be due not to German propaganda or even particularly bad morale on the part of the Italian fighting soldier, but simply to impossibly poor strategic and tactical defense by Cadorna[21]—Diaz is said to be just as bad as Cadorna. A new story, not absolutely vouched for, is that the Italians before their last offensive contracted with the Austrian general (who commanded Jugoslav divisions) to retreat and expose his flank. I got this from a newspaper correspondent who says that he was sent to Trumbić, the Jugoslav leader,[22] to try and find out whether the contract had been definitely arranged. The Italians didn't want to attack unless it had been.

19. Robert A. Taft (1889–1953), Yale '10, lawyer and later U.S. Senator from Ohio (1939–53), was assistant counsel for the U.S. Food Administration (1917–19). He served as a member of the Yale Corporation from 1936 until 1953 and thus participated in Seymour's selection as president.

20. Term used to denote avoidance of front-line action in World War I.

21. The Battle of Caporetto, which commenced on October 24, 1917, was a disaster for Italy and a serious blow for the Allies. Italy had declared war against Austria in mid-1915 and against Germany 15 months later. General Luigi Cadorna, Chief of the Italian Army, opposed an offensive against Austria because of extreme topographical difficulties. Lured on by territorial greed, however, the Italians initiated a series of fruitless attacks. Finally the Austrians struck back and crushed Cadorna's forces, which suffered 305,000 casualties, most of them by surrender. The Italians reeled back for 100 miles to the Piave River. General Armando Diaz replaced Cadorna, later becoming Minister of War in Mussolini's Cabinet and Marshal of Italy in 1924.

22. Ante Trumbić (1864–1938), Yugoslav politician, was co-founder of the Serbo-Croat coalition, the majority party of Croatia before the war, and became president of the Yugoslav Committee in London (1914–18). He then served as the first Minister of Foreign Affairs of Yugoslavia (1918–20). At the Conference, where he was a representative of Yugoslavia, he opposed Bratianu on the question of dividing the Banat.

We talked very late and again I didn't get to bed until after midnight. This morning I had a request for a memorandum from General Bliss and worked most of the morning on it. At 12:20 we had a conference with him. I had assumed that he would be a conventional West Pointer with simply the military point of view and on the Commission simply to represent the military. What Colonel House told me about him indicated that this was all wrong. House says that he is a very quiet man who won't get into the newspapers, that he is modest and unassuming; but that he is very thoughtful and scholarly (he is the son of a college professsor)—broadminded and liberal and very able. House reported that a man who knows Bliss and the other big men here said that "Bliss is the ablest man in Europe bar none." House said that last year when he and Bliss were in Chesterfield House in England with all the magnates, they came to a room where there was a Latin inscription on a mantelpiece. Of the whole crowd, English and American, Bliss and Lord Loreburn[23] were the only ones who knew that it was from Horace and whereabouts in Horace. So I was enormously interested to meet him. He is tall, bald, with his head a bit pointed at the top, with "beetling brows," heavy white moustache. His manner is very simple and direct. Unquestionably he knows what he wants and he looks as though he would put it through. Actually of all the Commissioners (and I have met them all personally) he gives the impression of having greatest force of character. There is a very distinct reminiscence of Bismarck, but a Bismarck without the lines of brutality and the heavy pouches under the eyes.[24]

From this man came the most extraordinary talk you can imagine. Every military person I have talked to has had nothing to say except about strategic frontiers and the necessity of strong armaments and improvement of weapons. From him nothing of the kind. If you can't prevent war, he says, the human race is going to destroy itself. "The next war, if there is one, is going to be just as much worse than this

23. Robert Threshie Reid, 1st Earl Loreburn (1846–1923), scholar, lawyer, and statesman, served as Lord Chancellor from 1905 to 1912.
24. Prince Otto von Bismarck-Schonhausen (1815–98) was the Prussian statesman who united the German people and became first chancellor of the new German Empire.

one as human ingenuity can make it." To prove how bad it would be he read us a letter from Secretary Baker describing a new weapon of war which had been tested and approved in the United States. (Remember to ask me to tell you about it—Bliss said that it was sufficient to destroy completely a city at a distance of 60 miles—when improved, London could destroy Paris or Paris London.) With the new weapons strategic frontiers cease to exist—there are no such things. War would be simple suicide on a grand scale. The only answer was disarmament and an effective League of Nations to prevent war.

Coming from such a man it was very impressive. And as I say he gave the impression of knowing what he was talking about and being minded to put it through. (Compare with what I wrote in a previous letter on Henry White's idea of a League of Nations.) I talked with several of Bliss' staff afterwards and they confirmed absolutely what he said about the new weapon of warfare, one of them having seen the test.

I was delighted with the conference, having fought continually against the idea of strategic frontiers.

Thursday, December 19, 1918

I will just finish this up and send it off. Last night Clive and I had dinner with George Nettleton at a very good cercle—the Cercle Volney, the Paris equivalent of the Century Club—wonderful atmosphere and excellent food—although we had to have bread checks—I haven't got mine yet and must needs borrow. Clare was there, Paul Van Dyke, our friend of the evening before—Colonel Buckley—and Jepson.[25] The latter is very friendly, being, possibly, a little homesick. Clare and I talked over the arrangements we could make if his transference were effected. He and Clive and I left early. I had some

25. Paul Van Dyke, a Princeton professor, was the director of the Princeton Bureau of the American University Union. Harry Benjamin Jepson (1871–1952), Yale '92, was professor of applied music and university organist, who took a leave to direct the Yale Bureau, succeeding Mendell.

work to do and wanted to get to bed as early as I could (I finally made 11:45).

Until yesterday we have had wonderful weather—warm and sunny, the rain coming at night. Yesterday it rained most of the day and left the typical Parisian liquid mud on the streets—(I forgot that I owned rubbers when I went out). It is unseasonably warm. I haven't had the excuse for my fur coat and have worn nothing but my raincoat. Our rooms both in the hotel and in the offices are very well heated and I think that there is no question of our comfort. I am living more luxuriously than I ever did in all my life before.

It looks as if I should not be able to get away for Christmas in England. I have written to Beth[26] and hope to hear from her soon, and at the last minute may go over for a couple of days. If I stay here I shall eat Christmas dinner with Clare and Sam at Foyot—on K's[27] present to Clare—then I can give a birthday dinner to them on your present to me.

A big batch of cables has just come in from Berne and I must get to work. Let me know when my letters arrive. I am certainly waiting anxiously for news from you. Happy New Year—even if this reaches you late.

Friday, December 20, 1918

As usual I try to take advantage of a spare few minutes to get my letter started to you. One finishes a job and expects some free time when another bobs up, and every free second is taken up with chats or interviews with persons who want to put some ideas over. The oppressed nationalities have myriads of agents, each with their own particular propaganda. They evidently think that we are going to swallow everything they say; I don't know much but I can usually discover when they are trying to put some egregious lie across. My attitude,

26. Seymour's sister, Mrs. John Angel, wife of the English sculptor, née Elizabeth Day Seymour.
27. Mrs. Clarence W. Mendell, née Katharine Webb.

however, is one of ignorance and desire for information and I am getting thereby a pretty good idea of what they are after. I am hampered by the difficulty of distinguishing between claims with official backing and those set up by individual enthusiasts, and this difficulty will not be obviated until I get in touch with some of the big men who are not here now.

Clive has had a great advantage in his Balkan and Greek work from his interviews with Venizelos. He says that he is just as nice as he can be—priestly and paternal. I can see how he gets his reputation for great statesmanship. In this way: I think he found out very soon that Clive knew the difference between truth and fiction; realizing that his strongest asset would be *our* belief in his honesty, he determined to lay his cards on the table and speak with absolute frankness, and I think that he did. This policy was almost Bismarckian in cleverness. Any double-dealing of the kind others are trying would have been useless; now he has our sympathy. His policy is one of moderation.[28] What appeals to me is the universal demand that the U.S. take practically all disputed and difficult districts under her protection. Then not merely is it suggested that the U.S. assume responsibility for Constantinople and the Straits, but even Armenia. If they can't get U.S. protection they want British, and there is jealousy in certain quarters of an increase in British protectorates. This is a big problem which we may have to face.

Yesterday morning came a call for a memorandum for General Bliss. It was very interesting, as it was a request for a modification of the line we had drawn on Monday between Jugoslavs and Italians, but leaving questions of a strategic nature out of account. It is extraordinary that the one military man on the Commission should be working in this direction, and it shows the independence of his thought. We had a conference (Clive, Lunt, and I) over maps in our bedroom and after lunch went over to the office and worked it out

28. Seymour considered the Greek leader one of the very influential personalities at the Conference and later reevaluated this initial impression, for he made the following note in 1963: "Venizelos—'Moderation'!?"

with the accompanying statistics and memorandum. We got in Bliss' aide, Colonel Stanley D. Embick, to talk it over. He is an exception to many of the military crowd—very intelligent, pleasant, a man you can do business with easily. He has caught Bliss' point of view, which is to use the men who have the stuff, which is different from the attitude of less eminent officers who assume that if a man has not a uniform he knows nothing practical.

The stress and hurry of these calls for Jugoslav memoranda result from the visit of the King of Italy, with whom the President will have to talk—while our Commissioners are meeting Orlando and Sonnino.[29] They all came yesterday afternoon, the King driving with Poincaré, the Prince with Clemenceau, then the ministers. The King looks small, even sitting, and is not impressive—almost fatuous in his smile. The crowd gave him a good send-off but not nearly as enthusiastic as Wilson's. The Prince is delightful.

Clemenceau really got the biggest noise. Curious to think how unpopular he was as Prime Minister when I was here ten years ago— then he was looked on as merely a tricky politician; now he, with Foch and Pétain, has saved France. The controlling force in the Italian Government now is Foreign Minister Sonnino, who is blunt and less tricky in his methods than the orthodox Italian, but an old-style diplomat, opposed to the League of Nations, hates the Jugoslavs and wants to take in lots of their territory in order to get strategic fron-

29. Vittorio Emanuele Orlando (1860–1952), jurist and politician, served in several lesser Cabinet posts before becoming Premier in 1917 after Caporetto. He led the Italian delegation to the Conference and was a member of the successive Councils of Ten and Four. The weakest of the "Big Four," and also the only one who did not speak English, he left the Conference in anger when the Allies opposed Italian annexation of Fiume. Orlando was overshadowed at Paris by Baron Sidney Sonnino (1847–1922), an older and more experienced statesman who had served one term as Premier and who was Foreign Minister until June 1919. President Wilson grew fond of Orlando, but never accepted Sonnino. King Victor Emanuel III of the House of Savoy (1869–1947) lost his power to the Fascists when Mussolini became Premier in 1922, but remained on the throne until 1946, when he abdicated in favor of his son, Prince Humbert II (b. 1904). Humbert, a boy of 15 at the time of the Conference, spent most of his life in the Army and was not a popular prince. He led the Italian troops that invaded France in 1940. King for only a month, he joined his father in exile when Italy voted to do away with its monarchy and set up a republic.

tiers for Italy—i.e. to play the same game on the Jugoslavs and the German Austrians that Austria played on Italy in 1866.[30] Orlando, the Premier, is supposed to be more liberal; he is willing to shift to whichever side seems to be getting the upper hand. Nitti, Finance Minister, is probably the ablest man in Italy; crooked in politics and playing his own hand, like the other two, he is staying behind and is likely to stage something behind their backs.[31]

Saturday, December 21, 1918

As usual I was interrupted, and for 24 hours. Now I shall hope to have a clear half hour. Yesterday morning I was busy for half the time seeing Jugoslav and Czech representatives, and the rest of the time working on a new memorandum for General Bliss, who is thirsty for information on Italian-Jugoslav relations. Then a difficult half hour with Kerner whom they want to send to Austria, and who is torn with desire and fear that if he goes he will miss the fun here.

This week, of course, all the interest is here; next it may shift, but it is bound to be the center of things permanently after January 1. The general conferences are evidently to be held in Versailles, but all the work, and gossip, and intrigue will go on here.[32] The Americans

30. The reference is to Venetia. Count Camillo Benso di Cavour (1810–61), Premier under King Victor Emanuel II, undertook to unify the separate Italian states, a task which was not completed until 1870, long after his death. By 1866 one of the few remaining states not under the monarchy was Venetia. Italy, backed by France, joined Prussia in the Seven Weeks' War against Austria in order to seize this prize, but was quickly defeated, especially since France's neutrality had been bought by Austria's secret promise to cede Venetia to France regardless of the outcome of the war. France then retroceded Venetia to Italy.

31. Francesco Saverio Nitti (1868–1953), educator, economist, and politician, held numerous Cabinet posts and served the Orlando Cabinet from 1917 to 1919, when he became Premier and Minister of the Interior (1919–20). Exiled by Mussolini in 1924, he returned to Italy in 1945 to help reconstruct the ravages of war and Fascism.

32. This expectation did not prove to be entirely accurate. The general conferences were held at the French Foreign Office on the Quai d'Orsay. The elaborate Hall of Mirrors in Louis XIV's Palace of Versailles, a Paris suburb, was used only to present the draft treaty to the Germans on May 7, 1919, and later to accommodate the signing ceremony on June 28. There was historical importance attached to this site, for here in 1871 William I was proclaimed Emperor of United Germany, the fruition of Bismarck's labors.

are being watched; you know your waiter is probably in the pay of some other government; I have had certain clear indications. But I am going on the principle of leaving all my papers except a very few in plain sight for anyone to read and putting nothing in a letter which would tell them what they don't know already.

Yesterday afternoon Clive and I simply broke away from everything and went for a long walk up the boulevards to the Guaranty Trust Co., to get some money and try and locate Gilbert Stanley.[33] In the latter I failed, getting only his military address. Then we walked down the rue de Richelieu, past the Bibliothèque and through the Palais Royal. The glory of its little old shops has largely departed, and the shops noted for vulgar postcards are now filled with military pictures. We passed a pitiful group in front of "le Comité Ardennais," where a sign (probably dating from 1914) informs one that the return to the Ardennes is closed.[34] They seemed to be hoping to get permission now to get home; their faces were drawn and haggard and they looked the part of refugees. It was a far cry to the brilliant windows of the Magasins du Louvre with their *étrennes* and dresses— except for the number of black dresses displayed and the crudity of the *jouets* it was almost as gay as in the old days. Judging from the feminine dummies in the windows, large busts, thin waists, and large hips (à la 1888) are going to be the style. (This for your private information bureau.)

We walked through the Cour du Louvre, following the path I used to take from the Bibliothèque ten years ago and crossed the Seine by the Pont Neuf. On getting to the Quartier we at once found indications of the raids and the Berthas. Most of the houses struck are now completely razed to the ground, but a few show up much as they must have done soon after being struck. This arrondissement (VIe) is said to have got much the worst of the business. We walked up the rue Dauphine (being in the Latin Quarter we felt that we were at last in Paris), past a little hotel where Clive lived 20 years ago, then up the

33. Gilbert Stanley (b. 1897), Yale '19, lieutenant in the Air Service, was wounded in combat. After the war he became an investment banker.
34. The Ardennes Province is located in northeastern France.

Boul. Miche past no. 18 where I lived 10 years ago. We didn't have time to see whether Mme. Adam is still there.[35] I went up to the rue de l'École de Medicine to find out the name of that restaurant where we met Mrs. Wyeth—and it has been taken over by Duval, so we shall never know.[36] But the delightful little patisserie opposite is still going —do you remember it? Then we went up the rue Racine so that I could show Clive the windows of our old room and the patisserie where we used to get cold chicken. Again I should have liked to look in and see whether Albert is there—probably not; chances are he has been shot. We walked along the Bvd. St. Germain to the rue Bonaparte where I insisted on stopping at the Deux Magots and having "deux demis-brunes," just as I used to a decade ago after fencing. The beer was very good.

We got back at 5:30 and I was immediately called into conference by Mezes who had just received word that the President wanted a memorandum by 9 o'clock this morning. It was not a very difficult thing to prepare, except that it required materials which were as yet not unpacked, and the proper volume was not forthcoming. It was a small volume and withal a small job, but without it impossible. But the President was leaving his house at 9:25 in the morning and was going to have a conference with Sonnino and Orlando at 10 and had to have the memorandum by 9:20. Well, I got Major Martin of the General Staff over; he is a very good sort and full of pep and afraid of neither man nor devil. He knows everyone in Paris and immediately agreed to rout out a high French official and get the volume if in Paris. Then everyone else went to bed and I sat down to wait. At midnight Martin was back, said he and his official had been to everyone except Clemenceau; that the only copy of the volume was in the French Foreign Office and we couldn't get it at any time least of all at 12 o'clock at night.

Well, we talked it over, discussed it with Bowman and finally I

---

35. Seymour lived at Mme. Adam's *pension* during his student days in Paris. He also resided on the Place de l'Odéon in the Latin Quarter where Albert was his concierge during his honeymoon.

36. Mrs. John A. Wyeth was the wife of Dr. John Allen Wyeth, New York surgeon, and the daughter of Dr. Marion Sims, who had been physician to the Empress Eugénie.

routed Kerner out of bed, got an army automobile (there are always three for our use) and hiked over to the Jugoslav headquarters. They were in bed, but Kerner knew them well enough to get them out. It was a delicate matter and had to be presented as one purely personal to Kerner, for if they thought anything lay behind it four cables would have gone off at once to Laibach, Agram, Belgrade, and Fiume.[37] They were very hospitable but didn't have the book. But one of them thought he knew where to get it, and promised to bring it around *n'importe quand.* So we went back to bed. I got up early chafing at the non-arrival of the book; just as I was sitting down to breakfast at 8:15 it arrived—not the one I wanted but good enough to fake a pretty good memorandum and map. I got six assistants and for the next hour we fairly worked. I had the job pretty well divided up, but even so it was exciting at the end. I stood with my eyes on my watch shouting to one draughtsman—"five minutes left" and to a typist—"four minutes now." At 9:19 I left the office on the run with map and memorandum and entered the hotel at 9:20. The President had it in time for his conference, but it was not a very good report. The worst of it is that the missing volume is only one of several which I packed in New York, and which were subsequently unpacked without my knowledge. We are sending a courier to Berne tomorrow to see if he can buy them there or get them bought in Austria.

I had not had much sleep, but found a number of despatches to go over and had to write comments for Colonel House on an Italian memorandum just sent in. That kept me busy till noon when I had lunch with Dulles,[38] just arrived from Berne. He is Lansing's nephew and of a diplomatic family—his grandfather was Minister to Spain.

37. Laibach (Ljubljana) was the capital of Slovenia. Agram (Zagreb) was the capital of Croatia. Belgrade was the capital of Serbia before becoming the capital of the new nation. The port of Fiume, of course, was the focal point of the dispute between Italy and Yugoslavia.

38. Allen Welsh Dulles (b. 1893), Princeton '14, lawyer and government official, remained in the State Department until 1926 when he joined the law firm of Sullivan and Cromwell. Thereafter he periodically took part in international negotiations, principally relating to disarmament. In 1951 he turned once more to full-time government work with the Central Intelligence Agency, which he directed from 1953 until 1961.

But he is, nevertheless, absolutely first-class—just as nice as he can be—young—very willing to work in any capacity, and very well acquainted with politics and persons in Austria. He was Secretary of Legation at Berne and wrote all the despatches on Austria for the State Department.

He has just come on for a day to see me and find out how things were being organized, and is going back tomorrow to close up his place in Berne and come on here permanently. I think that I will have him organize my whole service of information—getting out daily and weekly reports, having newspaper clippings translated and despatches summarized. He will bring on two secretaries from Berne. I have another assistant—a Captain in the M.I.D., who is said to be a Czech expert. I have also arranged for Clare Mendell's transfer, and he is assigned to my office on Monday. So I shall have a good working force of good men. You see the reorganization here has put us Inquiry specialists directly next to the commissioners. I am now running the entire show as far as Austria-Hungary is concerned and have the entire responsibility for seeing that the Commissioners get the right facts as well as the advice on policy.[39]

I don't think that we shall be doing much work for either White or Lansing. The former will do his social work, the latter is interested chiefly in international law. Wilson and Bliss will be the ones that will keep us busy. The mind of the latter is active as a ferret and he is never satisfied until he gets what he is after. He was much pleased, sincerely, I think, with the report on Jugoslav boundaries. This afternoon he came back with another call—nothing else than a report on how Germany will look when we get through stripping her. There is no one person looking after Germany amongst the specialists; we have a sort of committee—Haskins (who has charge of Alsace-Loraine, Belgium, etc.), Lord (Russia, Poland), Young (general economics) and myself. We are going to get out a summary report first, and then

39. Seymour's responsibility for the Czechoslovakian settlement led him to write a strong denunciation of Hitler in 1938. See "Czechoslovak Frontiers," *Yale Review,* 28 (December 1938), 273–91.

some details, if necessary, later. The General is beginning to look on me as his personal property—but he is a fine old soul, has lots of pep, and a good head.

I went out for a brief walk this afternoon to the University Union. Almost the first person I met on the rue de Rivoli was Tom Miller.[40] He was in a great hurry but had his usual bluff cordiality and sent his best remembrances to you. Then at the Union I found Alfred Bellinger, just back from Coblenz. He looked thin and tired; had nearly got his discharge, but now felt that he was over here for some time. He said that Bush and Ken Simpson were coming to town soon and he would send them over.[41] He said that it was rather good fun being in Germany—treated well, etc., but that it was cold and the soldiers were pretty well bored. Sam came in and we had a brief chat. His few days in the hospital seem to have done him good, but he was much disappointed at not being able to go down to Nice. It is closed to the Y.M.C.A.! He really ought to come home to his wife, I think; his constitution simply isn't strong enough for the work. But don't tell that to Mrs. Hemingway. His conscience is too strong—also, I guess he hates to get out of the interest of things.

Tomorrow, Sunday, I am going to have lunch with Hugh Bayne and Mrs. Ward[42] and take things easy if it is possible after the stress of the

40. Thomas Woodnutt Miller (b. 1886), Yale '08 S., was a lieutenant colonel in the Ordnance Department who later had a varied career in public service: congressman from Delaware, commissioner of Nevada state parks, director of U.S. Veterans Employment Service.

41. Alfred Raymond Bellinger (b. 1893), Yale '17, lieutenant in the Air Service, was another destined to be closely associated with Seymour and Yale. He returned to the faculty and became Lampson Professor of Latin. In 1953–54 he served as acting dean of Yale College. Prescott Sheldon Bush (b. 1895), Yale '17, banker and politician, served as a captain in the Field Artillery. Later he became U.S. Senator from Connecticut (1952–62) and also a member of the Yale Corporation (1944–58). Kenneth Farrand Simpson (1895–1941), Yale '17, also an artillery captain, served with the French Army and then became commandant and dean of the American School Detachment, University of Aix-Marseille. After the war he turned to law and Republican politics, being elected to Congress in 1940.

42. Hugh Aiken Bayne (1870–1954), Yale '92, international lawyer, served as a judge advocate, 80th Division and 9th Army Corps, and later was a member of the legal service of the Reparations Commission (1919–28). He married Mrs. Ward, practiced law in Paris until 1928 when he retired, moved to New Haven, and entered the Yale Art School as a student.

last few days. I fear my letters aren't very exciting. I should have gone this afternoon to the reception at the Sorbonne and see Wilson get a degree—but the inside game is more interesting and it takes time.

American Commission to Negotiate Peace
4 Place de la Concorde, Paris

Monday, December 23, 1918

At last I am back to a typewriter, a Remington, and although it clicks in a rather French fashion, has no bell to warn me at the end of the line, and some rather curious tricks, still it will save time writing and make my letters legible for you.

I have had a fine weekend, socially, and a certain rest from business. Fortunately the memoranda I sent in at the end of the week seem to hold the powers that be, for the moment at least. I stayed in bed late Sunday morning, getting my breakfast sent up at 9 o'clock and then turning over and getting to sleep again. I was fighting the regular old "Day cold" which comes from getting tired and knew that the best thing was to get rested.[43] So I did not turn out until half-past eleven, dressed comfortably, and came downstairs at noon. While waiting for Hugh Bayne I ran into O'Brien, who used to be Obie Cunningham's roommate and best friend.[44] He looked worn out and evidently feels Obie's death keenly. Hugh came in and we walked over to Voisin's, where we met Mrs. Ward. She looked very attractive and became more so as she talked. She has a very flattering way with her. She had seen Law when he was in Paris six weeks ago and said, as we guessed, that he was fed up and tired, but that a few days

43. The "Day cold" was a familiar reference to a persistent, debilitating kind of minor ailment frequently suffered by all descendants of Thomas Day of Hartford, Yale 1837, Seymour's great-uncle.

44. Kenneth O'Brien (1895–1954), Yale '17, a captain in the Field Artillery, was to become a justice on the New York Supreme Court. His classmate, Oliver Baty Cunningham (1893–1918), also an artillery captain, was killed in September 1918 near Thiancourt, France.

of Paris had put him back on his feet. She and Hugh thought that he had been sent further east with his battery, but did not know whether or not this meant that he was going to be part of the army of occupation. But Hugh seemed to think that he would be able to pull out when the preliminaries were signed.

We had a delicious lunch, even surpassing the luxurious food that I get at the Crillon—oysters, wonderful eggs, steak, ice, and petits pains, which are real luxuries to me, for at the hotel we get American army bread, which is very good but not crusty like the French. One of these days I shall take my bread card and go out and buy some. I enclose a sheaf of bread card tickets as a curiosity. They are good for the week, theoretically, but actually can be used any time during the month. We don't have to have them at the hotel. To illustrate prices I saw sole advertised the other day at 16 fr. per lb. The restaurants where one used to get good table d'hôtes for 3 fr. now furnish them for about 7. The menus are about the same, so far as I could judge, but they cost rather more than twice as much.

After lunch I came back to the Crillon and walked right into Walter Davis. He had been ordered up from Berne and is probably going to Austria with Coolidge.[45] I am very much disappointed that he is not going to be here; he would probably have come into the office here with me and cooperated with Dulles in organizing my service of information. In this respect he would have been invaluable, but he is sadly needed in Austria, from his experience of the last year on the border, and if he isn't here I shall be glad to have him on the other end of the line of communications. He looks well, decidedly better than last year; his moustache is of the most pronounced British type, a mere bunch of fur on either side of his nose. I didn't get a chance to

45. Archibald Cary Coolidge (1866–1928), Harvard-trained educator and diplomat, served at several American legations in Europe before turning to full-time educational work at Harvard in 1893 where he became professor of history and the pioneer American scholar in the study of Eastern Europe and the Middle East. He joined the Inquiry as head of the Eastern European Division until 1918 when he went overseas to serve the State Department as chief of mission in Vienna and was replaced by Lord.

talk to him at all for I had a date with Vošnjak,[46] who is a Slovene in close touch with the three Jugoslav Commissioners.

My conference with Vošnjak lasted about an hour. He was not disposed to compromise any of the Italian claims; showed himself perfectly willing to go on national lines and not claim anything that was not Jugoslav, but couldn't see why the Italians shouldn't do the same. Of course I agree with him largely in this, but I rather hoped to find a tendency to meet the Italians part way. Of course he is absolutely firm about Dalmatia; I tried to get him to indicate a line of division in Istria, but although I dropped the matter and then would bring it up again casually when he gave me an opening, he would not not admit that Istria could be divided. Last spring at Rome the Jugoslavs had practically settled on a line of division, but you see the extreme claims made by the Italians since the armistice have had the effect of spoiling the conciliatory spirit of the Jugoslavs. Trieste, of course, he thinks should be Jugoslav, but does not hope for anything more than an international free city. As a matter of fact I suppose that the Italians are sure to get it; I asked Vošnjak if he would not be satisfied if its freedom of trade were guaranteed by a League of Nations, but he stuck at the idea of Italian control. So the Adriatic problem becomes more difficult.

On the other hand I saw later in the afternoon a man who brings word that in Bohemia matters are looking up; the Germans of the north, over a million of them, have formed part of the economic life of Bohemia but if they don't want to live under Czech rule we could hardly make them. But it looks now as if they preferred to stay under the Czechs; their economic interests will be better served, they will not have to meet German industrial competition, and will not pay such heavy taxes.

46. Bugumil Vošnjak (1882–1957) had served with the Yugoslav Committee in London during the war and became secretary-general of the Yugoslav Peace Conference Delegation. During the 1920s he was to hold various posts in the Ministry of Foreign Affairs. After the Communists seized Yugoslavia he came to America and became a leader in the Slovene Democratic Party in the United States.

Tuesday, December 24, 1918

I was stopped last night, as I was writing, by a call to a conference with General Bliss to go over the question which we are handling in a memorandum today. I'll go back to Sunday again. After my interview with Vošnjak I had a talk with Harold Stokes who is looking for a job with the Commission.[47] He is only one of many; every soldier is now anxious to get out of the army and into this work. I am really awfully lucky to be in on things and realize it when I see how intrigues are being multiplied to get in.

After disappointing Stokes I went over with Clive to see our new offices. We had steadily refused to move into the ones which had been assigned to us at the beginning because they were so absolutely inadequate; practically all of our work of the past week has been done in our hotel rooms. But now that our crowd is recognized as one of importance we have at last been given the best to be had.

Clive and I were moved down from the inside room on the court to a big gorgeous suite with two windows running from floor to ceiling and each five feet broad, with a little balcony on the rue Royale. We look out across the Place de la Concorde, and by stepping on the balcony, up to the Madeleine. The room is really superb, done in white paneling, with three huge mirrors extending up to the ceiling and white wood carvings over the panels. It was, I imagine, formerly a private banquet room over Maxim's. We have four desks, typewriting table, and two files in it now, and it looks empty. We are planning to have two more desks and a map table. It is heated with a very cheerful coal fire. It has five electric lights in it and there is an electric reading light for each desk. So now we have room for work and a dignified place to receive visitors. I hate to think the price our windows would carry in case of a big parade. I don't think that I can go home until the grand review of the troops.

47. Harold Phelps Stokes (b. 1887), Yale '09 (brother of Anson Phelps Stokes, Yale '96 and Secretary of the University under President Hadley), a lieutenant in the Field Artillery, returned to civilian pursuits as a journalist. Once secretary to Herbert Hoover, he was an editorial writer for the *New York Times* from 1926 until 1937.

Sam came to dinner with me Sunday night. He looks much better but is obviously tired. After dinner he came over to the office and we talked before the fire for an hour or so.

Yesterday I got down to the sordid job of getting my material arranged and my maps unpacked. We have two stenographers—the one French and very good, who takes dictation in both French and English and is very rapid on the machine. The other is an American Red Cross stenographer and is rotten. We shall hope to fire her and get an army stenographer.

The Red Cross reminds me of what Sam says of the Y.M.C.A. He says that it is not popular with the army as a whole, although in spots it has done marvelous work. It got in wrong at the start by selling at higher prices than the Q.M., which it had to do because it bought at higher prices. The smaller organizations, like the Knights of Columbus and the Salvation Army, give chocolate and cigarettes away, which they can afford to do because they work on so small a scale. Some of the Y.M.C.A. men have been stupid. Sam told me of Mr. Houghton of New Haven,[48] who had a thousand dollars' worth of cigarettes and chocolates to sell and was with the first line at Château-Thierry; the army supply broke down and Houghton simply distributed all that he had, giving it away; he could hardly sell it to those men. When he got back to Paris he was told that he was personally responsible for the gifts and would have to pay for them out of his own pocket! He explained the circumstances, but was told to pay up. He said all right, but that he would cable the circumstances to New Haven and ask his church to raise it and the Y. would see what New Haven would think. Then he was told that it was a closed incident. Sam says that the personal characteristics of many of the men who have come over in the Y. have been very unfortunate. Take this only as symptomatic and not as a generalization.

48. The Rev. Roy M. Houghton (1876–1958), Yale '05 Div., was minister of the New Haven (Congregational) Church of the Redeemer from 1906 to 1931. He served as a Y.M.C.A. secretary during the war. In 1931 he moved to the Milford (Conn.) First Congregational Church where he remained until 1945.

Well, to go back to yesterday, I had my military intelligence assistant, Captain Kramarzin, report and set him to work to find out something about the situation before getting to work. He knows little of politics but as an engineer will be good at mapping out certain facts. Then I worked on my memorandum for Bliss, and discussed with Bullitt the methods of getting information to the Commissioners rapidly and easily. It is obvious that the more the reports can be verbal and not written, the less time will be wasted.

In the middle of the afternoon who should walk in but Biglow. I had several dates, but none of them with persons of consequence, and I simply picked up my hat and said that I would not be back again. He is enormous—big as a house and looking very healthy. Also in very good spirits and obviously glad to see a friend. We walked down the quais of the right bank over to the cité, around Notre Dame and back to the Boul. Miche, where we entered the Soufflot, and sat and talked on the red plush seats. Then we came back through the Quartier to the Crillon and had an early dinner; he had to get an eight o'clock train for le Mans. We talked about everything in the world, chiefly his military experiences which were certainly thrilling. It would be nice thing if you could drop a note to Marian and tell her how well he was looking and what a treat it was to be with him for half an afternoon. I told him to lead a selfish life in the future and think less of doing the things he doesn't like to do, and found him fairly receptive. He is going to drop out of all things military; he certainly has done his bit.

Christmas Morning, 1918

My attitude toward life is much altered by the receipt of your cable, which I found at the Union yesterday afternoon. I could not tell when it was sent but judged that as it was dated from New Haven it was some time on the way. I was hoping for one but did not hope that I should get it before a day or so after Christmas, and it makes a lot of difference to the day.

The atmosphere is not particularly Christmasy, for it is typical of
Paris winter, grey, rather raw drizzle. But I have more of the spirit
of Noël than the poor doughboys, who look utterly disconsolate and
homesick. I wanted to say "Merry Christmas" to the orderly outside
my room, but was afraid that he would kill me if I reminded him
of the season. I have been too busy this morning to be homesick; after
lunch I am going to open my hard candy, put my wristwatch on the
table in front of me, marshall my shirts and my neckties, and count
my presents. The reason for my business today is the insatiable curiosity of General Bliss, who when every other Christian is celebrating
the season is anxious for more information. We took in our report
yesterday afternoon and he came back with more questions. I could
have prepared most of my stuff last night, but I had made up my mind
to *faire la bombe*, at least mildly, and postponed the evil hour. So I
have been over in the office here this morning instead of going to
church.

But I got a good Christmas feeling last night. I went over to the
Union late in the afternoon to see if there was any news for me, found
your cable and determined to celebrate as well as possible. Sam was
going with Van Santvoord, who has been wounded and is just out of
the hospital,[49] to hear carols at the American church. This hardly
suited me at the moment, and I tacked on to Clare and Ridgely Hunt,
who is just back from Nice.[50] He is supposed to be there still, but
wanted to be with Clare and Sam over Christmas. They were going
to have a good dinner and go to the Grand Guignol. We had the
good dinner at a restaurant near the Opéra Comique, apéritif, co-
quilles, and Asti Spumante which didn't spume very well but tasted
just right. Also very good cigars from the stock which Mr. Heming-

49. George Van Santvoord (b. 1891), Yale '12, first enlisted in the French Army
in 1916, then transferred to the American Army in 1918, was decorated and spent
nine months in the hospital. Later he became headmaster of the Hotchkiss School and
also served as a member of the Yale Corporation during Seymour's tenure as president.

50. Ridgely Hunt (1887–1933), Yale '14 S., an infantry lieutenant, returned to
the publishing business in New York. In 1930 he was named librarian of the Linonia
and Brothers Library at Yale and soon thereafter lost his life in an automobile accident.

way sent to George Dimock but which he didn't get as he had started for home.[51]

Then we tried to get a taxi, which is difficult in Paris these days; there are so few on account of the scarcity of *essence* that they are very cocky. We tackled three in front of the Opéra Comique, but they all refused to drive us, saying that they wanted their dinner. Five more passed us, *libre* but unwilling to take us in. It must be an amusing pastime thus to pass customers haughtily, but one could hardly expect good financial results. Finally we boarded one by main force and drove up to the Guignol. Arrived there we found that nothing was left but loges, at double the ordinary price (50 fr.). This seemed rather expensive an amusement for an hour, so we decided to come back to a cafe and talk, and went into the Café de l'Univers on the Avenue de l'Opéra.

I was anxious to hear Hunt talk, for he has a picturesque manner of description and saw good fighting both in Flanders and in the Argonne, and rose from the ranks to his lieutenancy. He agrees with Biglow that the English troops of the last year were of poor quality, the colonials and Scotch were fine. The latter got on well with our men. Biglow had described the difficulty of the positions so long as the Germans held Mont Kemmel; he said it was just exactly as though our men were in Orange Street and the Germans on top of East Rock.[52] Hunt described the land around Ypres and Verdun as the most desolate and horrible desert that could be imagined.[53] The shal-

51. George Edward Dimock, Jr. (b. 1891), Yale '12, another infantry lieutenant, returned to a long career as head of the Classics Department at the Pingry School in Elizabeth, N.J. His sister Mary married Professor Samuel B. Hemingway.

52. Mont Kemmel is located south of Ypres in the Flanders section of Belgium, the Allied bastion which held out against three massive German attacks between 1914 and 1918. Ypres was also the scene of a bitter, four-month Anglo-French struggle to gain the 150-foot heights that curved around two sides of the city. This battle caused some 245,000 British casualties. The Orange Street–East Rock analogy referred to New Haven topography.

53. Verdun, the battle that raged in confused fashion for most of 1916, has been considered the greatest single battle in the history of the world. It cost the French 500,000 casualties and the Germans 400,000. Both sides expended some 40 million artillery shells. General Falkenhayn felt that the capture of this stronghold, located on the Meuse River some 120 miles east of Paris, would cause the collapse of the alliance.

low graves of 1916 are being washed out—feet sticking out of the ground, helmets with skulls in them, etc. He also told of the tricky mines the Germans left behind them, helmets with grenades attached, etc.

We had to get out of the cafe at 9:30, that being the closing hour even on Christmas eve, and walked over the river to Clare's room, just off the rue des Saints-Pères. It is in a nice clean house, with electric light; it cheered me up, because you and Katharine Mendell would be quite happy, I should think, in such a place, although it is simple in the extreme. It costs him about 125 francs a month for bed and breakfast (that seems queer, I must ask again). We looked at his *affiches*[54] which are wonderful; I shall take the first chance, probably tomorrow, to go over and buy a set.

At 11 Jepson and Sam came in and we all went over to Saint Sulpice. We found the church crowded and were rather pessimistic about seats, but Hunt's uniform attracted the attention of a beadle who led us around behind the high altar to the apse, where we were placed in stalls, which I suppose were the seats of the old monastic choir before its dissolution. We could look down the nave and see the great crowd and were close to the little organ and orchestra and the choir.

We had to wait an hour for the midnight mass, but it seemed short watching the people of all sorts and conditions, many poilus of the roughest sort. The pictures we have of the rough ones are typical; they are round-shouldered, squat, mustachioed, unshaven, and very dirty, typical Paris cabbies or *colporteurs* in dingy uniform; but they certainly did the fighting. They munch a piece of bread whenever

---

General Pétain was called upon to save Verdun, despite the fact that by 1916 German bombardment and Allied redeployment of troops and supplies had greatly reduced the military value of the city. By October the Germans had advanced two to four miles through the hills of Côtes-de-Meuse and over the plains west of Verdun. They also over-ran several of the forts that once seemed to make Verdun impregnable. The French then counterattacked and by December had pushed the enemy back two miles to a point where the front remained stabilized until late in 1918.

54. War posters which made excellent souvenirs; now preserved in the Yale Library.

possible; several had bread with them last night. Then there were officer types, some of them very handsome; it may be imagination, but I think the officer face is finer than ten years ago. All faces are rather expressionless; it is not a picture of active suffering or of obvious weariness, although the result proceeds from both, but a certain fine and rather intelligent stolidity. Very different from the old Paris face.

Exactly at 12 the small organ and orchestra began the prelude to a carol which was sung by the choir as the priests came in; they celebrated mass in all the small chapels and before the high altar. When the choir had finished the carol the big organ at the other end, played by Widor,[55] took it up; he often improvised on the prevailing motif of the carol which had just preceded. We could see the baritone soloist plainly and he was the most impressive part of the whole thing, tall handsome, rather haggard, with a superb voice which rolled way over the arches—and in a poilu's uniform! Each carol had a chorus and the leader turned to all of us sitting in the stalls and asked us to sing, and to my surprise everyone not merely sang but with all their lungs; it was such a nice, homely, worshippy touch, which I had not expected in a Roman Catholic mass. A very large proportion of the congregation took mass, at least three times as many as before the war and probably ten times as many men. I am glad to have been at the first *messe de minuit* after the war.[56] Some of the poilus coming back to their places after communion remained on their knees for 15 minutes. Many American doughboys were there.

Now I must stop and get my Christmas dinner. We hope to go out to Foyot tonight. The sun has come out and the day is cheerful after all. Naturally my mind is continually with you and your Christmas.

55. Charles Marie Widor (1844–1937), composer and organist, was a famed performer in churches in both Lyon and Paris and taught at the Paris Conservatory (1891–1905).
56. Seymour was a member of the Church of Christ in Yale University (Congregational).

American Commission to Negotiate Peace
4 Place de la Concorde, Paris

Friday, December 27, 1918

I am writing on this thick stuff in order to show you our correspondence paper; pretty sporty we consider it. Now when our official
calling cards are issued, we shall be nicely equipped. I have had to
answer letters from many persons today who saw my name in the papers as one of the "President's suite"; it was evidently published all
over Europe, for I had a note from a Dutch girl whose family I knew
in the summer of 1902 in Baden, who wrote to know "if the distinguished professor" was one and the same as the "young student"! I
enclose General Bliss' calling card to amuse Charles (if it does). I
am sorry not to have Pershing's. Bliss and the other Commissioners
pay their respects and return calls by sending their cards around by a
captain of the "ceremonial office." I also enclose tickets of invitation
to the presidential ceremony at the Sorbonne.

The great excitement of the moment is, as I have just cabled you,
that the chances of getting a passport seem pretty good. It is not certain, but I think that we ought to know definitely in a week or so. The
only hitch is that a good many want to have their wives over; if there
were only one or two I think there would be no difficulty. I have
cabled you so that you would be prepared and be thinking seriously
what you wanted to do. Of course your passage would not be very
comfortable. On the other hand it would unquestionably be something
for both of us to look back on all our lives to be here together now.
I say nothing about my personal happiness.

I wanted you here particularly Christmas afternoon when Clive
and I went for a walk. I have never seen the Place de la Concorde so
beautiful; it was glistening with the sun on the wet pavement with a
rosy haze over everything, the pennants streaming from the great
flagstaffs they have erected around the Place, and thousands of people
looking at the big guns and tanks (German captured ones). They let
the children play soldier with the 75's and trench mortars and you

can guess what fun they have. Some time ago in a celebration they began to take the smaller guns, wheel them off; they are scattered all over Paris; many are in backyards, where they are being left. They say that Clemenceau was interpellated in the Chamber as to what protection he was providing for the captured guns, and said "Oh, let the children play, we have plenty more."

We walked down by the quais; the river which has been low is now a torrent and rising rapidly so that if you come over you may run into another flood. We dissipated by looking in shop windows and watching the crowd and taking an aperitif and I cut out the dinner at Foyot's. It would have meant little for it had developed into a big affair and would have cost 60 francs. I preferred to wait until I could have one with Clare and Sam alone. Also we had a conference of the Inquiry in the evening (the Inquiry is now the "Section of Military, Political, and Economic Intelligence"), which was largely social and I wanted to pick up the gossip which flies around. Now that we occupy a real position there is no better place to piece together all the inside happenings than at such a gathering of six or eight. Ken Simpson who is a Field Artillery captain and Neil Mallon who is a major came in to see me a couple of days ago and I think that I can use them to take charge of all the statistical and map work.[57] They are on leave, but I shall hope to get them in ten days' time. As they are former pupils and well grounded in political history as well as in map work they ought to be valuable.

I learned that our elevation to our present position of importance was due to a *coup de force* on the part of Wilson. Lansing was determined that we should be pushed off to the side and had made all arrangements to have control put in the hands of his own men; Austria, for example, was to have been in the hands of Dulles, who is now to be my assistant. In this connection remind me to tell you interesting things about Wilson's inaccessibility to big men and the

57. Seymour was disappointed in his hope to obtain the assistance of Simpson and Henry Neil Mallon (b. 1895), Yale '17, who became a Texas industrialist after the war.

work done by House during the past two years. Hoover has come to the Crillon; I met him for a moment yesterday in the hall and sat at the table next to his at dinner.

This is a comparatively slack season and gives us time to get going, for the President is in England and House has been away, at the front I think. (By the way, I am going to spend two days at the front next week if nothing intervenes.) Bliss however is still active and spoils my chance to get to England just now by demanding daily memoranda on the political events in Austria-Hungary. As Dulles has not returned from Berne I have to go through the mass of cable information that comes in daily. Fortunately we are now well supplied with stenographers, and have got a good Red Cross one instead of the loss which we had.

I do not think that things will be very lively until the President returns from Italy, and that may not be before two weeks. We are rather disgusted that things are moving so slowly and that no preparations are being made for the opening of the preliminary conferences. I heard a sharp remark from a poilu in the métro yesterday; "Le président Wilson fait la bombe avec beaucoup de charme, mais sa permission va expirer sans que la paix soit signée."

I had a long letter from Law yesterday, the gist of which I cabled to you today. Tell me when you receive my cable; I am anxious to know how long it takes. This afternoon I went over to the Union in the hope of finding a letter from you, as some of the men at the hotel have had them, mailed on December 7. There was nothing there; Clare had had some but not Sam; probably there is one from you in the country, but it seems a matter of luck when they get distributed. Then I got Sam to go across the river with me to buy *affiches*. It was a delightful shop, with hundreds of them. I am ashamed to tell you how many I bought, and how much they cost me; but I thought we should be really glad to have them in the future, and I thought Charles might like one for his room. I got the stunning one of Cardinal Mercier,[58] the *On les aura*, and the discourse of Poincaré on Alsace. There

---

58. Désiré Mercier (1851–1926) was the noted religious educator and leader of the Neo-Thomist movement at the Institut Supérieur de Philosophie at Louvain, Belgium.

was Von Bissing's proclamation of the execution of Edith Cavell for 30 francs, but I do not think it was genuine; I would have paid 50 or 100 for a real one.[59] The decree of mobilization in 1914 cost 125 francs and I couldn't go it.

Sam has written to Don[60] to send helmets to the children if he can get them, and Clive has asked Hugh Bayne to try and get them also; I shall hope to pick up some relics at the front next week. They are terribly expensive here. Because of my cold, I have avoided all the diplomatic interviews that I could these last few days; that is why I have so little of interest to report. Give my very best love to your father and mother. As you doubtless guess these letters are for them too. Kiss the children for me. Don't let them bother your nerves and don't worry about their education—mental or moral.

Sunday, December 29, 1918

I have just come back from the Union with your first three letters and the result is that my spirits are very high; you have no idea of the effect of receiving them. I find it difficult to take time from rereading them in order to write this. If you could see me you would think your time really well invested.

We are settling down to real working conditions now and the re-

---

He became a cardinal in 1907. When Belgium was occupied in 1914 and Louvain burned, he advocated a policy of peaceful civilian opposition, arguing that the army alone had the right of open resistance. In spite of German pressure he continued through sermons and pastorals to protest the illegality of the occupation and to proclaim the inevitable final victory of justice. His activities clearly established him as the spiritual leader of the Belgians during these difficult times.

59. Edith Louisa Cavell (1865–1915) was a British nurse in Brussels. At the outbreak of war, her medical institute became a Red Cross hospital where wounded soldiers of both sides were given care. Miss Cavell and others aided some 200 English, French, and Belgian soldiers, stranded behind the German lines, to escape. In August 1915, she and a Belgian patriot, Philippe Baucq, were arrested, court-martialed, and executed by order of the military governor of Belgium, Freiherr Moitzu Von Bissing (1844–1917).

60. Donald Hart Hemingway (1892–1941), Yale '14, youngest brother of Samuel B. Hemingway, served as an infantry lieutenant and was assigned to the army of occupation. When he returned to New Haven he entered banking and became vice-president and director of the Second National Bank, serving with his second brother Louis (b. 1886), Yale '08, who became president and chairman of the Board.

sult is that our lives are going to be rather humdrum. At first we
courted interviews in order to pick up information; now we avoid
them so far as possible, in order to have time to get through our regular routine. The Commissioners have asked us to present daily
memoranda on the conditions in each of our areas, with recommendations of policy. This means going through the mass of cables that
comes in, picking out the salient points, and making up one's mind
as to the proper action, if any.[61] It is my work at Washington over
again, with the knowledge that here the recommendation is likely to
have some result.

As always, Bliss is the one who is most serious in his search for
information and the one most ready to discuss until he gets the main
points. His mind works slowly and when he has made it up I should
say that he was not likely to change it. He has ingrained in him a firm
belief in principle and honesty; he will, I think, fight to the end
against any compromise, for the sake of expediency, with what he
thinks is right.[62]

A certain tendency to look on our point of view as overidealistic,
which is obvious among the old-style diplomats here, is having the
result of turning our Commissioners to more liberal views; even
Lansing is losing much of his Bourbonism.[63] I had a long talk with Bullitt yesterday and found him jubilant because of the growing determination to establish a real League of Nations. Bullitt is likely to be
the most useful man at the Conference; he acts as the personal intermediary between us and the Commissioners, making all the dates

61. One of the organizational deficiencies of the American delegation was the lack
of systematic circularization of information. The American specialists worked in something of a vacuum, regarding it poor form to inquire what colleagues in other fields were
doing. Only the exchange of gossip at luncheons or other casual meetings kept them
vaguely informed. See Bailey, *Woodrow Wilson and the Lost Peace*, p. 135.

62. General Bliss himself wrote on December 18, 1918: "I am disquieted to see
how crazy and vague our ideas are. We are going to be up against the wiliest politicians in Europe. There will be nothing hazy or vague about their ideas." Bailey, *Woodrow Wilson*, p. 134.

63. Lansing, the lawyer and political realist, was perhaps not fully understood by
Seymour. At almost this same moment, Lansing was writing that Wilson's attachment
to self-determination "is simply loaded with dynamite. It will raise hopes which can
never be realized . . . What a calamity that the phrase was ever uttered! What misery it
will cause!" Bailey, *Woodrow Wilson*, p. 18.

for our interviews. If I have a point I want to get over, he calls up the Commissioner's secretary and fixes the hour. He finds out what each Commissioner's point of view is each day and tells me, and I know what recommendations are absolutely out of the question, or when they are weakening on a certain point and ought to have a little more hammering. The Commissioners are very nice and very anxious to learn, for of course they now have no knowledge whatever of details. When Dulles comes he will take off my shoulders the work of going through the cables and make a digest of them; until then I shall be up to my neck in routine.

I have decided however to get exercise regularly by taking an hour's walk after lunch each day. Yesterday Clive and I walked up to Montmartre. As usual it was misty and wet under foot, but not raining; it was as warm as in May. I have blessed you continually for making me get that light raincoat; it has been practically my only outside garment and without it I should have been miserable; my green coat is too heavy and not waterproof, and my fur coat would have been impossible. Even the French admit that there has been a lot of rain; but of real raw cold there has scarcely been a trace. Yesterday we perspired. We walked up past the Gare St. Lazare to the Boulevard Clichy and then up those winding streets and interminable steps to Sacré-Coeur. I had forgotten how ugly the church is when you come to it; it is so ethereal from the distance. The view we didn't like particularly, chiefly because there wasn't any, Paris being swathed in mist. But it was good to stretch one's legs and feel physically tired, and also to get away from crowded metropolitan Paris.

We walked down to the Bvd. Clichy, took a métro to Pigalle, a Nord-Sud to St. Lazare, and another Nord-Sud to Concorde—quite a trip. I have never been so crowded in my life. We were struck by the invariable French politeness even in the jam; as we came to a station a passenger, evidently anxious to get off and fearful that he could not because of the crowd, would say "descendez?" in order not to crowd by us if we were going to get out. An American would just have pushed.

I had dinner with a group who were saying good-bye to a Major

Dexter, who is in charge of the Red Cross expedition to Montenegro.[64] I was anxious to entrust him with getting information on several questions connected with the Adriatic problems. He looked like
Lloyd George and seemed a good man. He spoke highly of the work
of the Knights of Columbus, said the Salvation Army had done spotty
work; that perhaps unjustly, but nonetheless actually, the doughboys didn't like it and were persuaded that it was a money-making
institution. He had just come from an interview with the King of
Montenegro, whom I saw the other day at Meurice's; a large fat old
man. Dexter had been gassed two weeks ago; an old German ammunition dump had caught fire and the shells were flying around. He
has a nasty cough as a result. They say that it is going to be almost
impossible to plough the fields where the fighting was thick, there are
so many unexploded grenades.

This morning I stayed in bed until 11 in the hope of killing my
cold. I read Wells' *Peter and Joan,* which seemed uninspiring but re-
laxing. There is something of an unconscious strain in knowing that
at any moment you may be called on for a piece of information and
in wondering whether you can get it. After lunch I went around and
picked up Sam and we walked along the quais watching the river with
the crowd which seemed pleasurably excited by the current, although
if it floods it will cut off bread. We walked down past St. Gervais,
which was hit by the Bertha and on to Notre Dame for vespers.

It was the first time I had been in and I had forgotten how lovely
it was, with the high nave and stained glass at the end of the apse. The
cardinal archbishop was sitting on his throne in his robes of state,
and as we came in and all the time we were there a beautiful boy's
voice was singing "Adeste Fideles." They have taken out the glass of
the big rose windows in the transepts but left that in the west rose
window. In front the sandbags have been taken off all the portals but

64. Edwin Grant Dexter (1868–1938), trained at Brown and Columbia, went into
the educational field in Puerto Rico, serving as chancellor of the university from 1907
to 1912. During the war he served with the Red Cross. After his mission to Montenegro
he later headed Red Cross activities in South Russia.

one, which is still blocked right up, covering all the sculpture. They are taking the sandbags from the Madeleine now. The church was full of persons at vespers and before the chapels burning candles; one chapel is dedicated to fallen soldiers, wreathed in flags and brilliant with candles. People are coming in with straw for the mangers.

Sam had to usher at the American church and took the métro; I walked down the rue St. Honoré to the office here. Now I must write to Walter Davis' mother, telling her that he is going to a very safe and interesting place; the latter is true but not the former. Forgive the *banalité* of the epistles I am sending; some interesting things are happening underground but I don't want to put them on paper; they are in any event quite technical. I enclose Beneš' card; he will be one of the cleverest men at the conference.[65]

65. Seymour later confirmed this impression of Edouard Beneš (1884–1948), Foreign Minister of Czechoslovakia. He presented the Conference with the independence of his nation as a *fait accompli*. See Seymour, "Czechoslovak Frontiers."

WAITING FOR THE CONFERENCE
TO BEGIN

January 1–17, 1919

DURING EARLY JANUARY 1919 Seymour found that the tempo of his own individual work increased rapidly, although he still fretted over the delay in the opening of the Conference. His immediate work was connected with one of the many major tasks of the Conference, namely, serving as "the executor of the Hapsburg estate," in his own words. The collapse of the dynasty was now a fact, not a theory, and while the statesmen in Paris discussed and debated new forms of political organization for the naturally interdependent area—a group of autonomous states within a federation or completely separate nations—and while they labored over texts and maps to draw boundary lines so as to accord with various principles, the Germans, the Slavs, the Magyars, and others who made up the former polyglot empire were striving to settle their own destinies. They sent representatives to Paris; they established their own committees and governments; and in at least five different areas they fought one another.

Seymour and his growing staff were so busy laying out the lines of their reports, dialectic as well as topographical, that they were actually unaware of the arrival of the British Commissioners or of the real beginning of the Conference on January 12, when the representatives of the major nations met and decided on the organization of the Conference. It was decided that plenary sessions were impossible if any progress was to be made and that a Council of Ten—two representatives each from the United States, Great Britain, France, Italy, and Japan—would serve as the executive committee of the Conference and the official source of authority. The lesser powers and all the other delegates would be engaged in ad hoc committee work; eventually 58 different commissions—territorial and topical—were established. The Council of Ten began to meet on January 13 at the French Foreign Office; in many respects it was a continuation of the Supreme War Council which had brought the war to a successful conclusion.

The plan of procedure was made public on January 15, and the formal, ceremonial opening of the Conference took place at the Quai d'Orsay on January 18 at 3:15 P.M., with President Poincaré presiding.

Other symbolic events provided a backdrop for these organizational developments. The statesmen in Paris finally took cognizance of Europe's sufferings by appointing Herbert Hoover as the head of the Council of Relief and by establishing the Supreme Council of Supply and Relief on January 12. On the same day the Big Ten also recognized the independence of both Poland and Czechoslovakia. Two days earlier an attempt was made to assassinate Czech Prime Minister Kramář; four days later the two German Communist leaders, Karl Liebknecht and Rosa Luxemburg, were murdered. Back in the United States the colorful, controversial Teddy Roosevelt—who once espoused the idea of a league but who had turned against Wilson for partisan reasons—died on January 7, while the Senate, having nothing concrete to debate, continued to insist on a quick, severe peace. These events only strengthened Wilson's determination to make the League the first item on the agenda.

❧

American Commission to Negotiate Peace
4 Place de la Concorde, Paris

Wednesday, January 1, 1919

Another holiday and thus an opportunity to catch up on my letter writing, although goodness knows I ought to be working hard in preparation for the calls that are likely to come in soon. Fortunately for our peace the President, who arrived again last night, is off to Italy today and I think that General Bliss is taking a holiday, so I feel fairly secure for the moment.

I had a great time Sunday night after writing you. The Chamber

of Deputies has been debating the budget for four days and the Socialists have been heckling Clemenceau, trying to get from him some expression of his views on the international settlement. He had kept
absolute silence and refused to rise from his seat. Sunday night was
to be the last of the debate and people had about given up hope of getting anything out of him. But we thought that we should like to go
over and see the big men and Clive, Frary,[1] and I set out across the
river at 9:30. It is not easy to get in without a special card, but when
we explained that we were attached to the American Commission
and showed our cards attesting the same, we were put in the charge
of a gorgeous individual who led us up and around and put us in a
loge marked as reserved for generals! We were close to the floor of
the Chamber, which as you know is small as compared to our own
House, from where we could see the faces of the deputies plainly
and hear perfectly.

Deschanel was presiding, Clemenceau sat in the front row in the
center with Pichon on his left, Deschamps and Klotz on his right.[2] On
the extreme left the Socialists, with Albert Thomas and the pro-
Bolshevik, Longuet, prominent.[3] Renaudel, who stands politically
between Thomas and Longuet, was at the tribune speaking when
we came in; Briand entered and talked with the Socialists and several

---

1. Donald P. Frary (1893–1919), Yale '14, was a member of the Inquiry who
served in the Reference and Archives Section. Previously he had collaborated with Seymour in writing *How The World Votes*. He was to die soon in Paris (see p. 200).

2. Paul Eugène Louis Deschanel (1856–1922), lawyer, orator, and long-term
member and officer of the Chamber, became President of the Republic in 1920 when he
ran against Clemenceau. His victory reflected French opinion that the Treaty of Versailles had been too lenient. He served only seven months before illness forced him out
of office. Auguste Hippolyte Deschamps (1863–1935), jurist and educator, had been a
lecturer at the University of Lille and later became professor of law at the University of
Paris. Louis Lucien Klotz (1868–1930), barrister and politician, held two Cabinet
posts prior to becoming Minister of Finance in 1917. He was the fourth French Peace
Commissioner.

3. Thomas (1878–1932) was a Socialist member of the Chamber from 1910 until
1921, after which he became director of the International Labor Office of the League of
Nations. Jean Longuet (1876–1938), grandson of Karl Marx and deputy from the
Seine District, was leader of the minority during the war and a member of the execu-
tive committee of the Labor and Socialist International. Later he founded a newspaper,
Le Populaire.

other big lights; Millerand was the only big man we missed.[4] Clemenceau listened with absolute unconcern to Renaudel's denunciation of the silence of the government, acting as though he didn't hear. This infuriated the Socialists, who made more and more noise; the president continually rang his bell and called for order.

Finally Thomas rose and in an impassioned appeal begged Clemenceau to take the Chamber into his confidence. To our delight Clemenceau got up and speaking for about three-quarters of an hour sketched in a very general way some of his ideas and demanded that the Chamber give him its confidence and allow him to conduct the peace negotiations in his own way. He spoke of his talk with Wilson and admitted that he was not in agreement with him on all points. He will not admit that the old diplomatic system of alliances has failed absolutely; said that France, England, Italy, and America could keep the peace. He spoke of the "noble candeur" of Wilson. (*"Candeur"* means, as you know, naïveté; this aroused storms from the Socialists; I believe that in the official journal the word will be changed to *"grandeur."*)

His speech was greeted with general enthusiasm and the Socialists could raise only some 90 votes against 390. Nevertheless I do not believe that Clemenceau really represents France; I think that if we support fully the complete acquisition of Alsace-Lorraine and full reparation for all damage done by Germany, then the French will give up extreme claims both on the left bank of the Rhine and in the Near East and will agree to a real League of Nations. I have a hunch that Wilson has abandoned any support for the German view of the

4. Pierre Renaudel (1871–1935) was secretary-general of the French Socialist Party from 1909 until 1927. His opposition to Léon Blum led to his withdrawal from party leadership and eventually, in 1933, to his expulsion from the party. He then formed a small neo-Socialist group. Alexandre Millerand (1859–1943), political leader, deputy, and minister since 1885, started his career as a Socialist. He served as Minister of War (1913–15) and became leader of the right wing in the split of the coalition which governed under Clemenceau, the *Bloc National*. The other wing, the *Cartel des Gauches*, was led by Herriot. Millerand served a brief premiership in 1920 and then succeeded Deschanel as President, remaining in office until 1924, when Herriot refused to form a government for him. Millerand later became leader of the right wing in the Senate.

freedom of the seas and that we are really fairly close to a good understanding with Great Britain; this, however, is only a guess, for I
have not seen anyone who has been in England this past week. A great
deal depends on Wilson's nerve. Personally I hope that a big outcry
will be started at home against a greater navy and mercantile marine
and against anything that will tend to separate us from Great Britain.
With French aspirations we have no quarrel whatever, except that in
Syria and on the left bank of the Rhine their claims have lately
passed the limits of international safety and, I think, what the mass of
the nation really wants.[5]

We got back to the hotel well after 12, but very well satisfied that
we had by luck fallen into the most interesting and historic session
since the armistice. Monday morning Dulles turned up from Berne
with an assistant, and I spent the morning talking over organization
with him and getting him established in the office here. He is taking
over the intelligence work at once and thus I am left free to plan out
the kind of memoranda which will be wanted during the next weeks.
This planning results partly from guesswork, we judging what issue
is likely to be of the first importance, and partly from our own de-
sires, for we can call the attention of the Commissioners to any one
point we think they ought to hear discussed.

I want Mendell badly to help me on the organization of the material for the memoranda. He came in at the end of the morning and
said that the order for his transfer had come into the office, but that
his colonel was unwilling to have his organization broken up and
was holding up the transfer. Later in the day I learned that the order

---

5. The vote of confidence Clemenceau received was the greatest of his tempestuous
career. The official record of the address was altered, as Seymour predicted, but he erred
in his estimate of decreasing French bitterness. Clemenceau and Wilson did reach compromise solutions on the questions of the left bank and the Near East: a demilitarized
zone with temporary French bridgeheads and the mandate system, respectively. But
Clemenceau was accused of treachery because he failed to break up Germany, and lost
his support. American failure to implement a security treaty with France or to join
the League did not help Clemenceau. Wilson's realism, however, persuaded Seymour
that the President was fully aware of the nature of international politics. See "Policy
and Personality at the Paris Peace Conference."

for the transfer had gone to General Harts, commander of the S.O.S. [Services of Supply] in Paris, and thence to General Harbord, who is commander of the S.O.S. for the entire A.E.F.[6] So Clare's name is moving in high circles. I immediately dictated a memorandum for the Commissioners Plenipotentiary, insisting on the transfer and emphasizing the fact that Clare is absolutely essential to the efficiency of the Commission; if Harbord disapproves the transfer, it will, I hope, be effected over his head by the all-supreme Commissioners. Speaking of the S.O.S., in which a large part of the A.E.F. is engaged, there is a popular song going the rounds here now, "Mother take down the Service Flag, Your boy's in the S.O.S." Nothing counts for prestige here except actual service in the line, preferably in an infantry or machine-gun unit.

I had dinner with Clare Monday night at a pleasant brasserie: five francs for soup, "rumstek," and a demi-bière; very good but at least twice what it would have been ten years ago. We went over to the Union and sat around for an hour or so talking with the boys on leave; they can spend only 24 hours in Paris but manage to extend their stay by various subterfuges. Their leave is generally for seven days, but this means seven days at the place where they go, and the time spent en route does not count. Yesterday who should turn up but Jim Thornton on his way back from leave at Nice.[7] He came in very brown and having had a fine time. I could not dine with him as I had an important date for dinner, but I hope that he is going to be able to stay over today and that we can stage a party tonight. Now I must stop to do a little business. I have not had time to say lots of things I want to, but I will hope to resume later.

6. Brigadier General William Wright Harts (1866–1961) was a distinguished engineering officer who built the Lincoln and Arlington memorials. During the war he was the American commanding officer in the District of Paris, 1918–19, and also Wilson's military aide while the President was in Europe. Major General James Aithrie Harbord (1866–1947), a brilliant military organizer, served as Pershing's Chief of Staff and then got a combat command. Problems in the communications zone forced Pershing to recall Harbord, who quickly restored the effectiveness of the supply services.
7. See p. 47, n. 13.

Friday, January 3, 1919

Forgive my writing by hand, but I should have to go over to my office to use the machine and I am so comfortably fixed in our room here that I find it too difficult to resist the temptation to stay put. I found your letter of December 10th—received here on New Year's Day—and it raised my morale greatly.

My birthday passed off smoothly with a bit of celebration in the evening. I wrote letters in the morning, as our stenographers did not turn up, and did a little work. Jim Thornton came to lunch; he should have left Paris but got his leave extended on the ground that a "division chief of the Commission" wanted to see him. He is quite unchanged by military experience—retains his old manner and hesitating speech. His guns were like Law's—almost invariably well back of the line and his job rather trying and boring. He said that they suffered no hardships and few casualties.

At 3 in the afternoon of New Year's we had a conference of the division chiefs to hear orders for very important memoranda which each of us is to send on soon. They are the most comprehensive of any we have turned in, and according to Mezes possibly the most important single piece of work which we shall be called upon to do during the whole conference. Upon them the President is going to base the specific proposals he will make during the first sessions of the informal conference which will decide the peace treaty but precede the formal conference. My mind is fairly well made up as to the recommendations I want to make for my area and I shall not have to work very hard. There are two or three problems which I have not yet made up my mind about. The discussion on the general form of our recommendations lasted until nearly 5.[8]

I should have gone back and worked but I was not going to have my fun spoiled, so I went over to the Union and met Jim. We stopped

8. Later Seymour was to comment on the importance of this meeting as producing the first coordinated instructions the Inquiry received.

and talked to Pop Jefferson and Harold Vreeland[9] and then walked up to the Grand Boulevard, stopped at Pousset's and sat on the *terrasse* drinking beer and watching the thick crowd. You know how it is up there on New Year's Day. I was glad to have Jim explain to me the French insignia so that now I can distinguish an *aspirant* from a major. We had dinner in a restaurant near the Comique, drinking Asti Spumante. Then we went up to the Folies Bergères. The show was much the same as it used to be—rather poor—more moral if anything than formerly; some very pretty costumes, quite moderate *nudités*. At last half of it was in English, and three-fourths of the audience was English, Australian, and American. There was wild applause when the American colors appeared on the stage, but I think it came from our doughboys and officers.

It is a myth that our men love the French and vice versa. I think the sooner we got our troops home the better for our national relations. Our men have been affected by the dirtiness of the poorer French country houses and are sore at the way they have been overcharged (largely their own fault for they wouldn't learn the money). The French are sore at the raising of prices by Americans. Then there are lots of difficulties that have come from misunderstanding. I have heard lots of men discuss the reasons but none of them differed on the fact that we and the French ("Frogs" the doughboys call them) do not get on. Where our men come in contact with the English they get on even less; on the other hand we get on very well with the Scotch and the Australians.

Jim and I walked around during the intermission watching the painted ladies and the fighting mob at the bar. There seemed to me a

9. Edward Francis Jefferson (1879–1952), Yale '09, served for two years in the Y.M.C.A. in France, then resumed a lifelong career of teaching history at the Hotchkiss School. Herbert Harold Vreeland, Jr. (b. 1891), Yale '12 S., major in the Field Artillery, was assigned to command the School's Detachment at the University of Bordeaux. A New Haven resident, he combined a varied career of teaching, headmastering, and military service, which he re-entered in 1941 and rose to the rank of brigadier general.

terribly strained effort to have a good time, with very few succeeding. I should have liked it if we could have gone to a café to talk after the show, but everything closes at 9:30.

Yesterday was filled mostly with conferences with other division chiefs to decide where the lines that divide our separate areas should run. After lunch Clive and I took an hour's walk. It was the first really bright day that we have had for nearly two weeks and was really Paris at its best. All the children were out in the parks sailing their boats and kicking their footballs. We stopped as always to look at the guns on the Place de la Concorde and the German tank; then lingered on the bridge to watch the barges shoot down on the stream (which is very swift but not flooded); then we walked down the Bvd. St. Germain to the Ministère de la Guerre. Big Bertha struck in the street.

Saturday, January 4, 1919

No, it wasn't Big Bertha that struck in the street, but a bomb from an aeroplane; Big Bertha struck just around the corner. This bomb hit just off the curb, and it must have been some explosion for the walls of the Ministry of War are simply peppered; some of the holes are about four inches deep and look as if they had been made with a drill; one of them cut clean through the iron rail protecting the window. The marks are so clear on the whole side of the wall that it is possible to calculate almost exactly where the bomb must have hit. Inside the court of the Ministry they dropped a big incendiary bomb which burned up everything in the way of temporary building and equipment in the court. We wanted to get in but were stopped by the guard; but when we showed our passes signifying that we were members of the Commission he bowed, let us through, and told us all about the explosion.

I got a *Matin*[10] yesterday which shows the location of all the places where the Bertha hit; I must try to get one showing the hits of the

10. *Le Matin* was a daily newspaper. Founded in 1882, it ceased publication in 1944.

aeroplanes. They were much the worst and really caused a great deal of damage. One of them hit in the Place Vendôme and others fell around the stations and War Ministry and Credit Lyonnais, indicating that the bombers had definite marks for which they were aiming.

I was too sleepy to finish this letter last night and was glad I waited, for exciting news has come in. John Storck, Bowman's secretary, has just been around to say that the Commissioners have approved a plan whereby the wives of those attached to the Commission are all to be brought over and be given accommodations here. It is possible that transport will be provided and you all come over as we did. But even if that isn't arranged and it seems improbable to me, you will get passports and you will probably be allowed to live at the Crillon paying something like three or four dollars a day. As I say, it seems too wholly perfect to materialize. There is no indication when all this would come off, but the feeling seems to be that it would be pretty soon. It is possible that the boat sent over to take the President back would bring you over.[11]

Well, I'll forget my excitement and get back to telling you what I have been doing. Thursday evening I dined with Mr. and Mrs. Gibbons. He is a journalist, author of *The New Map of Europe* which is an excellent book I have used in my course, has been everywhere and knows everybody.[12] She is adventurous like him, clever, also knows everybody and then some, not good looking but quite a talker. He had more information than anyone I have met in Paris on any topic one introduced. Their speciality is Turkey, and Westermann was of the party. He is a warm admirer of the French but has preserved his American point of view, is liberal and idealistic and hopes Wilson's program is put through. He says that we don't realize its appeal to the peoples of Europe.

Yesterday I spent in working over boundary lines—very interest-

11. Five days after this was written, the wives were notified that they could go to Paris at their own expense. Subsistence and quarters at the Crillon would cost $100 per month. Mrs. Seymour sailed on February 15 aboard the S.S. *Espagne*.

12. Herbert Adams Gibbons (1880–1934), educated at the University of Pennsylvania and Princeton, was a widely traveled author, journalist, and lecturer. For ten years he was a correspondent for the *New York Herald*.

ing but slow work; I need two or three assistants on these lines badly and hope that Clare at least will appear soon. Robert George (Yale history instructor) has been attached to the Commission as Haskin's assistant and I copped him yesterday, but that will be only temporary.[13] Dulles is working out very well; I leave him to himself, as he knows all about political intelligence and I know little. I like his point of view and the advice he gives out. I had a long interview with Bowman and Mezes to discuss my recommendations. I have the final say but Mezes is in a position to block anything I say which he thinks is impolitic. Fortunately, he came around almost completely to my point on nearly everything.

In the early afternoon I went over to the Union and saw Bellinger, Bush, and Jim Gould.[14] I was to have met them this afternoon and gone for a walk but I have not had time. Today I have been working on my lines again. Had lunch with Neeser,[15] Mendell, and Clive at the Cercle Interallié, which is in the Rothschild house with enormous lawns and wonderful vistas. It is just around the corner next to the British Embassy. I shall hope to have more time to tell of this and of my very interesting interview this afternoon with Leeper of the British Foreign office,[16] but I must stop now to get ready for dinner with the Franco-American Society.

Tuesday, January 7, 1919

These are such busy days that there is little time to collect thoughts unconnected with boundary lines, far less to write them. I was to have

13. Robert George, Amherst '11, served on the Yale faculty from 1916 until 1922.

14. James Gould (1894–1950), Yale '18, served as captain in the Field Artillery. A banker and businessman in later life, he also served as treasurer of Andover (1931–50).

15. Robert Wilder Neeser (1884–1940), Yale '06, served as an infantry lieutenant assigned to the American Embassy in Paris, 1917–18. By avocation a naval historian, he remained in Paris with the National City Bank until September 30, 1940, when he was reported missing and later presumed dead.

16. Alexander Wigram Allen Leeper (1887–1935), career officer, served in the British delegation to the conference and later became first secretary in the Foreign Office. At Paris his responsibilities paralleled those of Seymour.

been at the front over the past weekend, but the urgency of the present call is such that it had to be given up; and I have been working like a coon every minute of the day—yesterday and today at least. I am hampered by the fact that my assistants have not yet received their orders to report although they are all ready to appear when they do. But fortunately my materials are in good shape, owing to many months' work in America, and I do not worry about the figuring and computation which is keeping some of the other division chiefs on the jump.

What I am asked to do is to present to the President by next Monday the best boundaries I can for all the states involved in my area. This is the same sort of problem that was put up to us last September; unfortunately they want the lines in greater detail and so much water has gone under the bridge since then and I have seen so many men and heard so many opinions that the September lines serve only as a general basis. Most of the day is taken up with the other chiefs whose areas abut on mine and with whom I have to come to an understanding. Some of the conferences are hot. It depends on how much the individual man lays stress upon strategic frontiers or upon national distribution. When we have settled the main lines upon which we should like to divide, and often we spend three or four hours upon half an inch of large-scale map, we refer the line to a physiographic expert who then proceeds to tell us how little we know about geography and how the line we have drawn is impossible from every point of view.

So we go to work again with him and slowly and laboriously construct a new line as near as we can make it to our first one. Our physiographic expert is Major Johnson, who is really a delightful fellow; he tries his best to subordinate his army point of view and the help he gives is invaluable.[17] In the end the decision of the line comes to me

17. Douglas Wilson Johnson (1878–1944), geologist and topographer, studied at Denison and New Mexico, then took his doctor's degree at Columbia. After a tour of teaching at Massachusetts Institute of Technology and Harvard, he joined the Columbia faculty where he remained until his death. He was appointed Chevalier of the Legion of Honor and named as medalist of various European learned societies. At Paris he served as chief of the Division of Boundary Geography on the American Commission, having previously been in the M.I.D. (C.S.)

and I am responsible for the one finally recommended. It may be changed radically in conference, of course, when the alterations will come back to us for comment. When the Commissioners finally decide on a line it will be in moderate detail; the exact delimitations of the line will be done, perhaps months later, by a special boundary commission which will survey the line on the spot. Let's hope that I am not on one of those commissions. There is little chance of it.

We are using meals for seeing the men from the other commissions whenever we ought to. The British have been very friendly in coming around to call on us in our office, and today Clive and I had two of them to lunch. One of them, Nicolson, is a son of Sir Arthur Nicolson, who has been one of the greatest of British diplomats of the last 20 years or more; he was responsible for the results of the Conference of Algeciras and for the Anglo-Russian reconciliation of 1907.[18] Tomorrow we are to have an interview with Také Jonescu, who is the greatest of Rumanian statesmen, although he has refused to join the present Ministry.[19]

I wish that I could get the opinions on southeastern Europe of other men who are not available now. Seton-Watson and H. W. Steed, the two authorities on Austria-Hungary, are in town now and I hope to see them soon.[20] The British representatives are arriving

18. Sir Arthur Nicolson, Lord Carnock (1849–1928), served in diplomatic posts of importance all over the world, completing his overseas assignments as ambassador to Russia from 1905 until 1910, when he became Permanent Under-Secretary for Foreign Affairs. Seymour became closely acquainted and very friendly with his son Harold, who just at this time described Seymour in his diary as "young, dark, might be a major in the Sappers." *Peacemaking, 1919,* p. 233. The two younger men later discussed writing a joint study of the Conference, but it did not materialize.

19. Jonescu (or Ionescu) (1858–1922) served in numerous Cabinets as Minister of Public Instruction and Finance prior to 1908, when he founded the Conservative-Democratic Party. He represented Rumania at the Peace Conference at Bucharest in 1913 but, after having favored intervention on the side of the Allies during the war, not at the Paris Conference. He attended in a private capacity and publicly split with Bratianu on the Banat question. In 1920 he became Foreign Minister, labored for a Danubian federation, and was one of the chief architects of the Little Entente (Czechoslovakia, Rumania, and Yugoslavia) in 1921.

20. Robert William Seton-Watson (1879–1951), British historian, was editor of *The New Europe* (1916–20), and then co-editor of *The Slavonic and East European Review.* Henry Wickham Steed (1871–1956), British journalist, was an overseas correspondent for *The Times* of London from 1896 until 1914, when he became foreign editor. Five years later he became editor.

gradually. Lord Robert Cecil, "Bobby Cecil" as Nicolson calls him, arrived last night.[21] Nicolson says that he will be the next British Foreign Minister, and ultimately certainly Prime Minister. I suppose that Lloyd George and Balfour[22] will arrive very soon. If the President gets back from Italy on Thursday some sort of informal conversations may start at once. I don't know whether or not the Italians are planning to get here by Monday. Of course the Commissioners for France, England, and Italy are not chosen, or at least announced yet.[23] I have been working so hard on boundary lines for the past few days that I have had no leisure to pick up gossip.

Saturday night I went with the Franco-American Club to dinner. This group has dinners every Saturday at the Cercle Volney, which is the very high-toned (though less elaborate and sporty club than where I lunched with Neeser) club and where George Nettleton took us to dinner our first week here. It was very pleasant. I sat next to Eduard Dolléans, the economic historian whose work I knew, who is sort of a chairman of the reception committee.[24] (I suppose he put me next to himself because I referred in my acceptance to his work.) He has given up his historical work on the Internationale to study international currents of today and is interested in promoting

21. Edgar Algernon Robert Cecil, 1st Viscount Cecil of Chelwood (1864–1958), statesman, parliamentarian, educator, and author, was Minister of the Blockade, 1916–18, when he became Parliamentary Under-Secretary for Foreign Affairs. Very influential in drafting the League of Nations Covenant, he won the Nobel Peace Prize in 1937.

22. Arthur James Balfour, 1st Earl of Balfour (1848–1930), statesman, philosopher, and author, was a leader of the Conservative Party and served as Prime Minister from 1902 until 1905. In the wartime coalition government he served as First Lord of the Admiralty and then as Foreign Secretary, 1916 to 1919. His famed declaration in favor of a Jewish national home in Palestine, 1917, became one of the foundation documents of modern Israel. Later he was chief of the British Delegation to the Washington Naval Conference in 1921.

23. Eventually the five British Commissioners were named: Lloyd George, Balfour, Andrew Bonar Law (the Lord Privy Seal), Viscount Milner (Colonial Secretary), and George Nicoll Barnes (Minister Without Portfolio). The five French Commissioners were Clemenceau, Pichon, Klotz, Tardieu, and Ambassador Jules Cambon. The five Italian Commissioners were: Orlando and Marquis G. F. Salvago Reggi (who did not sign the Treaty); Sonnino, Ambassador Marquis Imperiali, and Deputy Crespi.

24. Dolléans (1877–1964), economist, educator, and author, taught at the schools of law at Dijon and Paris. He later joined the staff of La Nouvelle Revue Française.

friendly relations between the intellectuals of different countries as a basis for the League of Nations. We had interesting stories from the three officers who sat at the same table with us, some of them horrible in showing the callousing effect of warfare; others rather sublime.

After dinner we sat and drank coffee at small tables (it was quite a large dinner, possibly 30 or 40) and I talked with Besnard who is in the French Foreign Office.[25] I found him very sympathetic in his ideas and policies and if he represents French foreign policy fairly, some of our difficulties are less than I feared. Then Risdel or Ruysdael played the piano; everyone seemed to know him and regard him as a celebrity. He certainly played well; much Chopin, of which I knew several because of Ruth's playing.[26] Tell her how much I enjoyed it. I was glad to hear him, for he had a light and beautiful touch for the delicate parts, and I was glad to rest from about an hour of solid conversation in French with Besnard. If I were compelled to talk French all the time I should pick it up again fairly soon; but as it is, I am terribly rusty. I enjoyed the dinner immensely and Dolléans made me promise to come often; I liked the French there but not the Americans who were not attached to the mission.[27]

Sunday I had to work in the morning, which was rather short, to be sure: we did not get up till 9, and hardly got dressed by 10. Then Lieutenant Waters came in to take me out to lunch. I had regarded him as rather a poor boy when I knew him before, but he took me to an elegant place and bought delicious wine. His battalion was brigaded with the French and saw some good hard fighting under Gouraud.[28] The impression that I get from talking to the men here is

25. René Besnard (b. 1879), lawyer and politician, had a long career of public service, including terms as both a deputy and a senator, a portfolio in several Cabinets, and the ambassadorship to Italy.

26. The wife of Louis L. Hemingway, Seymour's classmate.

27. Seymour's experiences obviously strengthened pro-French sentiments created by his familiarity with French history. See his review of Clemenceau's *Grandeur and Misery of Victory* in "The Soul of France," *Saturday Review of Literature,* 6 (April 19, 1930), 939–40.

28. William Otis Waters, Jr., Yale '13, 2nd lieutenant, Infantry, served with the 4th French Army on the Champagne front under the command of General Henri Gouraud (1867–1946), wounded veteran of the disastrous Dardenelles expedition and commander of the French Forces in the East, 1918.

that the British and the French were completely played out last July. I get it from all sources. It must have been an anxious moment when the battle of July 15 started.[29] They say that the individual cannon shots could be heard here in Paris, and the glare of the exploding shells seen.

Thursday, January 9, 1919

I have just come back from a very interesting interview with Také Jonescu. He was responsible for the policy of Rumania during the Balkan wars when she intervened against Bulgaria and did much to bring Rumania into the big war on the side of the Entente. He has refused to go into the Rumanian Ministry as constituted at present, but can speak for Rumania as a whole far better than any other man. He does not rank with Venizelos as a statesman but is equal to Pašić.[30] Probably he has done more to influence history in the Balkans than anyone besides these two. Clive and I went over to the Meurice and up to his room. He is a delightfully mannered man of about 50 or so, not unlike Horatio Parker when he talks;[31] he speaks English very well and like all other big bugs in the little powers treated us with extreme courtesy. He talked for about an hour and a half, outlining Rumania's position and aspirations. I think that he spoke frankly; he claimed that he had never told a lie and that once in the Chamber he had challenged anyone to accuse him of ever having spoken even a half-truth.

He is comparatively moderate, far more so than the responsible ministers of Rumania who expect the earth; but even so I do not see

---

29. General Ludendorff's final "peace" offensive.

30. Nikola Pašić or Pashitch (1846–1926), Serbian and then Yugoslav statesman, virtually controlled his country from 1903 until his death and was Premier on several occasions. His pro-Russian, anti-Austrian policy was influential in leading to war in 1914. Four years later he helped bring about the union of Serbia, Croatia, and Slovenia. He was known as the "Old Fox of the Balkans."

31. Horatio William Parker (1863–1919) organist, teacher, composer of religious and secular music, was Battell Professor of Music at Yale and also dean of the School of Music (1904–19).

how I could possibly recommend the frontiers he thinks merely adequate. Possibly Rumania will get more than I should like when it comes to the dickering around the conference table. His attitude is very friendly toward the Serbs; the Bulgars, he says, have behaved very badly; of the 28,000 Rumanian prisoners taken by the Bulgarians only 10,000 survived captivity; Rumanian officers were flogged in Bulgarian streets. He says that they hate the Bulgars worse than they do the Magyars. So they must be friends with Serbia and he does not want to hog the whole Banat, but will give them the southwestern portion. He wants the mouth of the Maros for Rumania and all of Bessarabia. The latter seems sensible but not the former.[32] We asked him to lunch with us next week and I shall hope to get him talking a little more on the secret history of the Balkans. The Bulgars are liars, he says; fifteen days before Bulgaria went to war in 1915, he had a letter from Malinoff promising that they would never fight with Germany.[33] He says that they were all filled with the belief that Germany was bound to win the war.

Since I last wrote I have done nothing except discuss boundary lines. Yesterday I spent practically the whole day with Major Johnson over a large-scale detailed map comparing topographical data. It

32. The Banat, a district not much larger than New England but very rich in cereals and, to a lesser degree, metals, consisted of several frontier provinces of Hungary and Serbia. It was situated at the present junction of Rumania, Hungary, and Yugoslavia, between the Danube, Theiss (Tisza), and Mures (Muresul) rivers. It contained a mixed population of Magyars, Rumanians, and Serbs (as well as sizable clusters of Germans) and was claimed by all three nations. Its disposition was left unsettled by the Peace Conference, where Bratianu claimed the entire territory for Rumania while Pašić and Jonescu agreed on a division with Yugoslavia. In 1920 it was partitioned evenly between Yugoslavia and Rumania. The Maros (Hungarian extension of the Mures) empties into the Tisza north of the Banat, near the Hungarian city of Szeged. Bessarabia, basically a Rumanian region, is the fertile area situated at the northeastern end of the Black Sea and surrounded by the Danube, Prut, and Dnestr rivers. A gateway to the Balkans it was long a target for conquest beginning with the invasion of the Goths. Taken by Russia in 1878, it was re-annexed by Rumania in 1918 and held until 1940, when it was ceded to Russia by the Vienna awards. Then Rumania reoccupied it during World War II but formally retroceded it to the Soviet Union in 1947.

33. Alexandre Malinoff (1867–1938), Bulgarian politician, was longtime leader of the Democratic Party and three times Prime Minister.

resolved itself generally into a contest between us, he wanting to push
the line a little further to make it better topographically or give a
better strategic line, while I would protest that he was taking in so
many hundreds or thousands of aliens. We are aiming to reduce the
importance of strategic factors in our discussions, but we have to consider the effect of boundaries upon economic relations and cannot follow race by itself. Johnson has had very wide experience and opportunities for study, having been with the general staffs of all the Allies
and flown over practically all the old frontiers in an aeroplane. He
knows the political situation well and is a great help.

He gave in 20 minutes about the best statement of the strategical
weakness of Italy in the Adriatic I ever heard: no harbors as opposed
to the myriad of safe harbors on the other side, which permitted the
Austrian fleet to go down the whole Dalmatian coast behind the islands; sandy bottom off Italy good for hostile submarines which can
"go quietly to sleep" while waiting to attack as opposed to the rocky
shore bottom on the Eastern coast; the Italians forced to fight in the
early morning (when attacks were generally made) with the sun in
their eyes; low land as opposed to high on the Dalmatian side so that
for Italians visibility was always bad.

This morning we had a long conference over the Tyrol boundary,
which is largely a strategic question, with Johnson and Generals
Kernan and Marlborough Churchill (a very good name, isn't it, he
looks it too). It was humorous to note that General Kernan, a professional soldier, was interested in everything except military questions.[34] He wanted to talk about eugenica, or the right of minorities,
or anything philosophical. Mezes is often present at these conferences
and likes to monopolize the answers to any questions that are put by
persons of high rank (particularly when Commissioners are in question); it is vexing to the specialist concerned, for Mezes is generally
half wrong. He is a good-natured old duck; he has a great admiration
for Clive but thinks very little of me, accepting me as a necessity and

34. Major General Francis J. Kernan served the Commission as chief military technical adviser.

treating me with kindly tolerance. Bowman came in last night just as we were getting ready for bed and told us gossip for an hour; chiefly about the incompetence of the regular State Department people and the fights he had with them. I got into a scrap with the "Liaison Office" yesterday over a question of etiquette because I got tired of waiting to have them get something for me and finally sent one of my men and had it done myself. The red tape and the confusions of bureaucracy, whether military or civil, are unbelievable.

It is pleasant having Bob George about to eat meals with and tomorrow Clare will turn up, he having finally received his orders. The great source of enjoyment for all of us is Clive's assistant—Lybyer, who is a typical college professor not able to speak without delivering a lecture, and is, as Westermann dubs him, the "Apostle of the Obvious."[35] Westermann is the typical Middle Westerner of the best sort, very breezy but well mannered, mentally vigorous and afraid of nothing and no one. He gets on very well with the men we meet here, largely because he is the sort of American they rather expect to meet. Lunt I see a good deal of in connection with my work, for he has charge of Italy; I find him quietly dogmatic in manner, although he is interesting. Haskins I have seen very little of, during these latter days, as our work keeps us apart. These are days of stress and, unless one works with a man, one doesn't see him; today was literally the first time I had left the arcades of the Crillon since Sunday, four days ago.

Clive and I took a half hour off, before going to see Jonescu, to watch the Seine, which is still rising rapidly and is more of a flood than I have ever seen it, though you might think little of it. No more boats can get up under the bridges, and the trees below the quais are standing in some feet of water. The river is lined with crowds discussing the excitement, which must be rather tame after the air raids of the last year. We walked up to the Grand Palais and down the

35. Albert Howe Lybyer (1876–1949), educated at Princeton and Harvard, taught mathematics at Roberts College in Constantinople for 17 years prior to the war and history at the University of Illinois thereafter. He was an assistant in the Balkan Division of the American Commission and active in fostering the Crane-King Commission of Study in the Middle East. (C.S.).

Champs Elysées. After next Monday I hope to get out and see some people and take in a show maybe. But that is the day when the informal conferences start and I don't suppose that I can get off to England. It is a great disappointment.

I have no idea whether or not this letter will get to you before you sail. But I will continue to write to you until I have a cable announcing that you are leaving on a certain date. I hope that date will be set soon, for as I wrote I think that the sooner you get over here the more interesting it will be for you.

I must cut and run.

Sunday, January 12, 1919

Your letter No. 11 of December 23 has come and is naturally very welcome. It is the latest letter to be received by any of the people here so I am in a very prominent position and much envied. Some have heard nothing since the 14th.

My present hunch is that we shall finish here about June. I hope that you are going to decide to come over here, see the excitement with me, and go back to normal existence early in the summer. Of course the work here may end before June, in which case we can do as we want.

At present, judging from the slowness of getting started, it does not look as if the conference would ever be over. I believe that they are going to begin informal conferences at the Foreign Office tomorrow, but it will be some time before all the delegates gather. Yesterday I had rather a notable lunch at the British headquarters, invited by Nicolson, who despite the fact that he is only my age exercises a good deal of influence. He asked me to lunch with General Sackville-West, who is the British representative on the Allied War Council; a delightful man, handsome with small gray moustache à l'anglaise, gray hair, simple and casual in manner and very amiable.[36] He was evidently disposed to be very friendly albeit rather bored.

36. Maj. Gen. Sir Charles J. Sackville-West.

I got him talking on the question of strategic frontiers in connection with the boundaries we are working on and he spoke very freely. He is in close accord with General Bliss, whom he says he knows very well, and tends to minimize the importance of strategic frontiers; the war, he says, has changed everyone's notion as to what a strategic frontier is, and no one can agree now as to what is desirable. Fortunately I have picked up enough of the lingo from Johnson to be able to question him as to the relation of frontiers to bases of mobilization and as to necessity of putting frontiers at a certain distance from important cities. He feels, as does Bliss, that the development of new military weapons is going to keep everything in flux.

He says that nothing has been decided as to the constitution and organization of the conference. I judge that the British would like to have the presidency rotate; the presiding officer is going to have a good deal of power in his hands. Cecil and Eustace Percy were in the same room, but none of the other big British guns had arrived.[37] These two latter are the ones who are going to push the League of Nations and I think that they will want something broader than our Senate would approve. I take it that the President will have to stay over longer than was at first expected, possibly only getting back in time for March 3; but I have heard no reasonable dope on this subject. Leeper, who holds a position in the British Foreign Office similar to mine, was the fourth at the lunch. We discussed the various points in question very frankly and are in general very well agreed.

I think that we younger men can do a great deal toward stimulating good feeling by playing around together. Carpenter who has been assigned to Clive as an assistant is a very useful man, for he is an Oxford man, and Nicolson and Leeper are among his best friends.[38] I

37. Seymour was apparently unaware that Lloyd George had arrived on the previous day. Lord Eustace Percy of Newcastle (1887–1958), politician, diplomat, and educator, was private secretary to Balfour, later served as Minister of Health, 1923–24, and as president of the Board of Education, 1924–29.

38. Rhys Carpenter (b. 1889), a scholarly member of the Commission, taught classical archaeology at Bryn Mawr, later becoming the director of the American School at Athens.

find that my being a Cambridge man has been of great help. Nicolson told me interesting stuff about Sir Edward Grey, to whom his father long acted as confidential adviser.[39] Sir Arthur Nicolson really ran British policy for a long time previous to the war.

We are supposed to have our report ready for the President tomorrow and I have been working hard, and shall have to spend most of today (Sunday) on polishing mine up. Fortunately Mendell reported Friday morning and has been a great help. He has caught on very quickly to what had to be done and has handled a mass of detail which would have bothered me for many hours when I wanted to be working out the broad lines of the report. In addition, things have been critical in Hungary and I have had to spend time with Dulles discussing recommendations of policy.[40] The latter, however, takes all the detailed labor of going over the cables from my shoulders. The conferences whether with men of other nations or with our own men

39. Edward Grey, 1st Viscount of Fallodon (1862–1933), longtime member of Parliament, served in the Foreign Office from 1892 to 1895 and was Foreign Minister from 1905 to 1916. Instrumental in the formation of the Triple Alliance in 1907, he worked long but fruitlessly to avert the outbreak of war in 1914. When Prime Minister Herbert Asquith's government gave way to Lloyd George in December 1916, Grey resigned. After the war he served as temporary ambassador to the United States, actively supported the League of Nations, and in 1928 became chancellor of Oxford. Of him Seymour later wrote, "whether or not he was a great diplomat, he is assuredly a great Englishman."

40. Crisis became endemic in Hungary, whose declaration of independence from Austria had symbolized the disintegration of the Austro-Hungarian Empire. Military defeat and the application of Wilson's principles of autonomous development and readjustment of frontiers on the basis of nationality threatened Hungary with the loss of much of its territory occupied by non-Magyars. A Socialist upheaval in late October 1918 led to the establishment of a republic and brought to power as Prime Minister Count Michael Károlyi, a liberal and a pacifist. On January 11 Károlyi ascended to the presidency and commenced a land distribution program. Unable to prevent an Allied decision to give Rumania the province of Transylvania, the extreme eastern portion of Hungary since 1868, he resigned on March 21. Communist revolutionaries established a new government. The Foreign Minister was Béla Kun, a Leninist who soon took over as dictator. War was declared on Czechoslovakia in order to reconquer Slovakia; then Rumanian troops invaded from the east to forestall a similar operation in Transylvania. These military ventures proved too much for the new government. A counterrevolution established a provisional government at Szeged, led by Admiral Nicholas Horthy; in August Kun fled to Vienna as the Rumanians occupied Budapest. Eventually, in June 1920, Hungary had to sign the Treaty of Trianon, which reduced its population by half and its territory by two-thirds. The partitioning of predominantly Slavic areas in the process of creating Poland, Yugoslavia, and Czechoslovakia accounted for most of these losses, but in addition some three million Magyars were left outside the new Hungary.

take a good deal of time and cause nervous wear. Combined with that, we get too much to eat at the Crillon and too little exercise. I am getting fat as a seal. Actually I don't know what to do, my trousers and waistcoat are getting so tight.

Yesterday afternoon I decided that I should have to get some air between conferences, so Clare and I visited his former offices at the Intelligence Service. We then moved down the river watching the floods. The river had dropped two feet or so since I had seen it. It had been up to the waist of the Zouave on the Pont d'Alma but had dropped nearly to his knee; in 1910 you will remember it was up to his neck. Most of the cellars about Alma are flooded and furnaces and electric lights are out. We passed firemen who were pumping the water out of the sewers. The trams on the left bank, which had stopped running, are going to begin again. The trees along the river, however, are still standing in water. We walked back on the rue la Boëtie and I was glad to find that the gorgeousness of the shops is not spoiled by the war—pictures for 25,000 francs and wonderful tapestries and furniture.

Last night I went over to the University Union, not having been there for a week. It was a relief to get away from the foreign and diplomatic back into the purely Yale atmosphere. We talked until nearly midnight on football and its future and what the college would be like.

Wednesday, January 15, 1919[41]

My ambition is to get a letter off every other day and I have kept up to it pretty well, but it seems as if there was not a second yesterday in which I could slip one in, and here it is, the evening of Wednesday, and apparently time for only a scrappy letter. It ought to be appreciated, for I should be going to a reception given by Mrs. Wilson but I am staying home to write.

41. In hopes that his wife was by this time en route to join him in Paris, the author addressed all subsequent letters to Mrs. Seymour's parents, Mr. and Mrs. Thomas H. Watkins.

It isn't that I am accomplishing so much, but as the time for formal opening of the Conference approaches more and more people come to Paris and there are more and more talks. Last night I had a rare treat of a dinner *en famille* with H. P. Davison at his apartment.[42] He and his family have just come over on the *Baltic*. Trubee came up to see me and said his mother wanted me to dine with the family. I call it a treat because they made me feel so much at home; Trubee and his sister were there with an English girl friend; also Foster Rockwell, who is a Red Cross Major,[43] and Jim Gould, who is an artillery officer. Mrs. Davison is a nice homey, simple person, very attractive; they had real American chocolate cake (which I scorn in America but which tasted good here) and mince pie, all made by Mary Elizabeth for the Red Cross.[44] Mr. Davison told us of his interviews with all the kings of Europe and the various prime ministers. After dinner we talked international politics for two hours.

Then we Yale men sat around after the others had gone to bed, and it was finally half past two before Rockwell, Gould, and I left the apartment. Going out it was so late that the concierge was fast asleep and it took us 20 minutes to get the door unlocked. At the Crillon, I had an awful time with the French elevator, going up; I am always scared stiff when they start one off alone, and kept figuring what I should do if it didn't stop. Then if you please it *didn't* stop when it should; I saw myself being crushed against the roof, and hastily pushed all the buttons in sight; the result was a sudden stop between

42. Henry Pomeroy Davison (1867–1922), banker and member of J. P. Morgan and Co., was chairman of the War Council of the American Red Cross (1917–19) and later chairman of the Governing Board of the World League of Red Crosses. His son, Frederick Trubee (b. 1896), Yale '18, served in the Navy as a pioneer in the flying corps in World War I and later became a lawyer in New York City. He was appointed Assistant Secretary of War in 1926, a post he filled until 1933. He then became president of the American Museum of Natural History and served continually in that capacity until 1953, save for military service in World War II as Assistant Chief of the Air Staff. He was also a member of the Yale Corporation (1931–56).

43. Foster Rockwell (1880–1942), Yale '06, served the Red Cross for four years, later turned to orange ranching in Arizona and banking in New York.

44. Mary Elizabeth was the commercial producer of a special brand of bread and pastry.

floors. I pushed another button and dropped 20 feet; then on trying another I soared way over my floor and within two feet of the roof. Finally I got expert and with trembling knees emerged onto terra firma.

I was interested to see the way the young Red Cross majors drifted in for ten minutes' talk with Mr. Davison, who treats them all as if they were in the family. He said that the influenza had killed five times as many men in our army (including the army in America) as all other causes.

Monday night, Dulles took Clare and me out to dinner at La Rue's which is excellent cooking and where one sees handsome and wonderfully dressed women—not so handsome or so wonderful as ten years ago (is it the effects of the war or of my increasing age?), but they do very well. We have had some hard problems put up to us by the Commission and spent the evening trying to thrash them out. The situation in Hungary is bad, very bad, and I shouldn't be surprised by civil war or Bolshevism at any moment. Vienna is hard put to it, but is still apparently gay; food is scarce, but prices are cheaper than in Paris. They run a theater or so and an opera on Sunday night. The Czechs and the Slovenes are apparently pretty well off for food, but won't send any to the other places. On the whole, Austria is better off than Poland, I think, where politics are in a state of chaos.

Yesterday I met Mr. Balfour. Nicolson telephoned me to meet him at the Crillon and to fix up a room where he could wait while Balfour and Lloyd George had a conference with the President. I went over to the British offices, having learned that the conference was at the Hotel Murat, where the President lives, and not at the Crillon; I had to explain, and met Balfour in the process. He is as handsome as ten years ago and has rather gained in charm—a very clever man; I am not sure how good his judgment is.

Today we had Také Jonescu to lunch. He was very genial and told us stories of the Balkans just before the big war, when he, as Prime Minister, was one of the most important figures in the whole kettle of fish. He read us part of his correspondence with the king of Rumania to illustrate some of his points. Bratianu, the present Premier of Rumania, arrives today and it is possible that they may combine, but not likely.

We have been working hard to get Italians and Jugoslavs to be a little more moderate and persuade them to try and come to a compromise. It looks as though Orlando were getting ready to give up claims to Dalmatia; that will help a lot. Now we must see if the Jugoslavs won't give up something and gradually get them to agree. I spent most of yesterday afternoon with a very liberal Italian friend of Bissolati—the Socialist who has resigned from the government —who wants to meet the Jugoslavs half way.[45]

Informal conversations have been going on all week; our reports, however, are finished, and for a day or so we are cleaning up odds and ends before the next call comes in. I believe a formal conference of the delegates is to be held on Saturday.

Sunday afternoon we went across the river to the Invalides, where the great court is filled with captured guns, Zeppelin engines, and two German battle planes—on the ground where it is easy to study them carefully. We went on to the church to see Napoleon's tomb. It is still covered with sandbags but they are beginning to uncover. We walked around by the Champs de Mars and the Eiffel tower; evidently the raiding aeroplanes aimed at this frequently; on every corner house there is still apt to be painted "abri—40 persons," showing where one could take shelter. We crossed over the bridge and walked down "l'Avénue du President Wilson" and up the Ave. Marceau to see where one of the Big Berthas had struck. The marks on the houses are still visible, but it had done little real damage. Most of the shells fell in open places.

45. Leonida Bissolati-Bergamaschi (1857–1920), writer, lecturer, and unionist, was one of the party's founders and editor of its journal, *Avanti!* He fell out with the party in 1912 when he supported war against Turkey, then joined Orlando's Cabinet as Minister for War Aid and Pensions. He opposed the annexation of Dalmatia but felt Fiume was essentially Italian in population.

Friday, January 17, 1919

I have just been having dinner with Seignobos, who is the most prominent modern historian of France and who knows French politics, I suppose, about as thoroughly as anyone.[46] He has been father confessor to a lot of the Radical statesmen for the last 20 years. His French is very difficult, he swallows half of it in his beard, and while he is eating he is talking; all goes on simultaneously; the result is absolutely incomprehensible. But he is very clever, rather cynical, a bitter opponent of tradition, conservatism, etc., and spares no one the lash of his sarcasm when he gets started. He thinks well of the British. Says they are unbelievably stupid, but loyal and do a good job in the end. He believes in the League of Nations, but doesn't think that its mechanism is important; it is the international spirit which counts. (In this I suspect he is close to Wilson.) His admiration of the politicians of today is minimal.

The talk is all of the opening of the Conference tomorrow naturally. The press correspondents have been bitter over the announcement that the debates of the Conference are to be in secret. Personally I never believed it possible to have open debates when dealing with delicate questions, and most of the questions are delicate. They have thrown a sop to the press by announcing that certain of them will be admitted to all full meetings of the Conference, but that when considering certain subjects it will meet *in camera*. If the daily communiqués tell what they are discussing and what decisions they are arriving at, I think that that fulfills Wilson's demand of "open covenants openly arrived at." If they publish everything there would be another war before the Conference ended.

We are still bothering over the Jugoslav question which quivers in nervous delicacy. If Orlando cannot hold his leadership in Italy, and it seems doubtful, and a more moderate crowd comes in, the situation will be helped. But I think the diplomats have made a mistake in not recognizing the Jugoslavs and in allowing Montenegro a sep-

---

46. Charles Seignobos (1854–1942) was a professor at the University of Dijon and later a lecturer at the Sorbonne.

arate delegate. I can't make our Commissioners understand that this is playing into Italian policy, which aims at splitting Serbia, Montenegro, and the Jugoslavs so that Italy can control the eastern shore of the Adriatic. I want them to occupy Dalmatia and Fiume, and possibly Montenegro with American, French, and British troops, but I am afraid they won't do it.

In one respect the situation is promising, in that the Italian pressure is compelling the Slavs to look around for friends and may help to a reconciliation with Hungary and Bulgaria; both of these countries are going to come out of the Conference very much weakened (the former most) and are not to be feared. If we can patch up a working confederation—economic and even loosely political, between all of the Danubian states it is going to be a good thing for the peace of the world.[47]

Both Jugoslavs and Czechs are getting very uppish and are sending troops into all sorts of places that don't and can't belong to them. They have simply got to understand that it makes no difference what they hold; the Conference is going to decide on the merits of the case (at least it will if the Commissioners get their way). I should like to see an Allied Commission go into Vienna and take complete charge of the economic situation—import the necessary raw materials, compel each state to trade with the other, and control food. It's the only escape, perhaps, from Bolshevism.

I talked with a man today just back from Austria; he said the most important leader of the Slovenes[48] is a bandit captain who has turned

47. The weakness of the successor states, so apparent from the outset, suggested to many the need for a Danubian confederation in order to provide viability to the least sufficient, notably Hungary, but this plan was constantly blocked by national jealousies.

48. Scholars are not entirely agreed, but believe the Indo-European Slavs originated from the area of present Poland and the Soviet Union that lies southeast of the Vistula River and northeast of the Carpathian Mountains. They expanded in all directions and by the sixth century were divided into three main branches: western (Poles, Czechs, Slovaks, and Moravians); southern (Bulgarians, Serbs, Croats, and Slovenes) and eastern (Russians, Byelo or White Russians, and Ukranians). The term "Jugoslav," as used by Seymour, connotes primarily the Serbs, Croats and Slovenes, of which the latter two fought on the side of the Austrians against Italy. The Kingdom of the Serbs, Croats, and Slovenes initially included the Montenegrins, but the political situation remained unsettled for some years.

diplomat; he used to be Austrian consul at St. Louis. When asked if he wouldn't use his influence to prevent another war or avoid civil war, he said no, he rather preferred war—he had made a lot of money fighting the last few months!

I had a good walk yesterday in the sun to Montmartre with Clare and Sam. Today it is rainy again, but always warm, thank goodness.

———

THE CONFERENCE COMMENCES

January 20–30, 1919

AT THE FIRST PLENARY SESSION of the Conference on January 18 the politically astute Colonel House had tried to avoid opening speeches. He warned Wilson that they could be used to introduce major problems to the embarrassment of Allied relations, but his warning went for naught. The President himself made a temperate but firm address demanding a League of Nations. Lloyd George, as a means of introducing the reparations question, emphasized the devastation of France. Clemenceau stressed the responsibility of the big powers for the work of the Conference, thus justifying the decision already made to create the Council of Ten and also giving an early indication that even this group might be too large. And Orlando made an open bid for French support of Italian claims.

Thus initiated, the flow of major questions poured forth in an ever-increasing stream during the ensuing days: Turkey, Russia, Shantung, colonies, socialism, and Austria-Hungary. Strangely enough, little was said about Germany. The former Austrian Empire particularly concerned Seymour, and his work in the main began to concentrate on two of the emerging new nations, Czechoslovakia and Yugoslavia. Simultaneously Italian ambitions became a cross-current of confusion and disruption, especially with regard to Yugoslavia, and so remained for the duration of his stay in Paris.

He broadened the scope of his personal investigation by conferring with as many Slavic and Italian representatives as possible and also by establishing a close liaison with British territorial specialists. He found that there was a substantial Anglo-American consensus, despite the fact that the British found themselves somewhat unhappily bound by secret obligations which, as a matter of honor, they had to meet, but he also learned that it was probably politically wise not to present too much of a common front because of French and Italian susceptibilities.

Seymour also increased his staff and continued to prepare reports and memoranda to be presented on call from the American Commissioners or the Council of Ten. Even so he felt the first stages of the Conference to be rather desultory in nature. There seemed to be no way of coming to a decision other than a unilateral one. The Council heard the evidence but took no action. It seemed clear to him that more organization was needed if matters were to be pushed to any conclusions.

He was by no means alone in his feelings of discontent. The French were turning on the Americans for many reasons. Incidents between nationals resulted in the necessity of bringing American military police to Paris. A belated inspection of the devastated areas by Wilson did little to help. Rumors circulated that he was so insistent on the League that the Conference simply was waiting to settle down to other necessary preliminaries until he had to return to the United States to dissolve the old Congress. In another quarter the small powers were so bitter at being excluded from the main work of the Conference that they forced a second plenary session on January 25 to vent their impatient feelings and to gain assurances of committee assignments. And the press, angered at the secrecy, turned sour on the Conference and began to criticize the Big Ten for wasting time, for failing to consult the "experts," and for anything else that could be used for a reasonably rational attack.

Near the end of January Seymour's personal work came to something of a head when he was summoned before the Council of Ten to report on Czechoslovakia. He had already concluded from his long preparation that the pledge of independent statehood made during the war could now best be fulfilled by a nation made up of Bohemia, Moravia, Silesia (the "Polish Alsace"), Slovakia, and part of Ruthenia. This was the gist of his first formal report. He had likewise concluded that Yugoslavia should not be required to surrender Fiume and other adjacent areas to Italy. He was to stick to the major outlines of these conclusions throughout the Conference.

❧

American Commission to Negotiate Peace
4 Place de la Concorde, Paris

Monday, January 20, 1919

I have had a wonderful batch of letters the last two days and it has made a lot of difference in bringing you closer to me, for this is the first reply to any of mine that I have had. I had already sent off my cable to Gladys telling her to get her passport and passage, for I note from her letters that she does not think that she can stay over for a long time. I couldn't say the month when I thought the Conference would end for I have no idea. Nor did I want to suggest that she postpone coming, for I thought she would miss most of the fun of it; and it is always on the cards that my work may be done early.

I am quite satisfied that I want to come home as soon as the work is done. Europe is no place for a vacation now; touring is impossible, living is high, and it is not right that anyone who has not some specific business should be here. And I don't feel at all like settling down for work in a library after my government work is over.

I am writing on this paper and using only one side as I understand that the French censor is cutting, and I don't want both sides of the sheet spoiled.

The Conference opened on Saturday, as you know, and we are working pretty hard, although much of what we are called on to do was foreseen ten days ago and is ready. The Commissioners are called on to present memoranda on the territorial settlements which they advocate and we are preparing the American standpoint which is to go to Wilson and the Commissioners tomorrow. The recommendations are about what we decided on two weeks ago with certain changes in form. I am doubtful about some of my recommendations, naturally, but on the whole am pretty well satisfied.

The last two days' work has been complicated by Jugoslav troubles.[1] The Conference as you know, decided not to grant the Jugoslav representatives a vote but to give two to Serbia and one to Montenegro. This is very disappointing to the Jugoslavs and plays into the hands of the Italians, who are opposed to Jugoslav unity. We have

---

1. The early history of the new Kingdom of the Serbs, Croats, and Slovenes under King Peter, formally proclaimed on December 4, 1918, was marked by internal quarrels as well as the struggle with Italy. The Serbs wanted a strongly centralized government under their control, but the Croats and Slovenes (Roman Catholics and more Westernized than the Serbs) were anxious to preserve their autonomy. Montenegro overrode and deposed King Nicholas and voted for union with the new kingdom on December 1.

felt strongly that it was contrary to the interests of peace and fairness to refuse them representation and have argued with Lansing. Today there was to be a meeting of the committee on credentials in which the matter would come up and we put the question up to White, who is the United States representative on the committee. The French, judging from Jusserand's opinion, have been willing to recognize the Jugoslavs, but the British, for some reason I don't understand, have stood with the Italians against it.[2] Thus far we have not had guts enough to come out for it.

The situation in the Adriatic is very bad. The Italians are terrorizing the people. In one town it is reported that the Italian commander told a crowd, "All who want bread hold up their hands." Naturally everyone held up his hand. They were photographed and the picture was sent to Italy as a crowd swearing love and allegiance to Italy. There have been various scraps between the Americans and the Italians, who seem to be detested by most of the Allies. The Jugoslavs are saying openly that they are ready to fight. If the impression gets around that the Conference is not going to recognize their union they will attribute it to Italian intrigue, perhaps not unjustly, and the situation will be almost unbearable.

I was too busy on Saturday afternoon to go into the Conference but I took half an hour off to see the statesmen assemble. The crowd gave Clemenceau a good reception and there were some cheers for Wilson. It is the general impression that the kind of League of Nations which Wilson is formulating will be satisfactory to us. As a matter of fact, the statesmen will begin serious consideration of the indemnities for Germany to pay at once. There is satisfaction at the businesslike way in which Clemenceau handled the meeting, and one is beginning to hope that no more time will be taken than is absolutely necessary. When Lloyd George seconded the nomination of Clemen-

2. Britain's commitment in principle to Italy's claims, as contained in the Treaty of London of 1915, was disliked by Britain's Foreign Secretary, Balfour. He would have disregarded the commitment of this and other secret treaties, if Wilson had insisted, as a price for either entering the war in 1917 or for participating in the Conference, but Wilson wavered and equivocated.

ceau for president of the Congress[3] he spoke of him as the "grand young man." The official translator read this in his translation as the "grand old man." Both Clemenceau and Lloyd George protested. Poincaré read his speech, which they said was very dull. But Wilson and Lloyd George spoke without notes.

You are probably getting fuller reports of the debates of the Conference than we, for the Paris papers are very short. And I imagine that most of the inside stuff that comes to our ears will get picked up by some enterprising reporter. It was good fun to see the statesmen come up. I had seen most of them but Foch was new to me and Pachitch of Serbia. Did I tell you the *bon mot* Clemenceau made at a meeting of the War Council at the time of the armistice? He apparently got rather tired of hearing House talk about the Fourteen Points, and finally said: "Mais le bon Dieu n'avait que dix."[4]

Yesterday I had to work all morning and part of the afternoon despite the fact that it was Sunday. But later in the afternoon Mendell and I went over to Notre Dame and listened to the singing for half an hour; then we wandered through the old narrow streets around St. Severin and went into more singing at St. Etienne. We walked to the old café du Panthéon and had a vermouth cassis. We thought that two churches and a drink made a good Sunday afternoon in Paris. We dined with Sam at the Saints-Pères and went to *Bohême* at the Opéra Comique in the evening. It was a wonderful performance and I can't wait for Gladys to hear the people they have here; she will certainly sob; I almost did myself. The soprano is well above the average in voice; not too powerful but clear and true and a marvelous actress; the tenor is superb, and the orchestra beyond comparison for this sort of production.

3. The selection of Paris as the scene of the Conference dictated that the host nation's chief representative should be the president. This gave Clemenceau added power to control the agenda.

4. Clemenceau's sarcasm was periodically reported with numerous variations on the same theme: "God gave us the Ten Commandments, and we broke them. Wilson gives us the Fourteen Points. We shall see." Or, "How can I talk to a fellow who thinks himself the first man for two thousand years who has known anything about peace on earth?" Or, "Wilson talked like Jesus Christ but acted like Lloyd George."

I have had a rest from dinners the last two days, but start in again tonight to dine with a Czech representative and have several more during the course of the week. You can't guess what a relief it is to have a dinner with friends where you don't have to talk shop. I hope that most of this will be over by the time that Gladys gets here. These diplomatic dinners seem to be for men alone.

I am chiefly interested in the fact that the Peace Conference is making hardly a ripple in the outward life of Paris. In this it is of course an absolute contrast to the Congress of Vienna, which was nothing but a round of gaiety. The papers are full of it, but away from the Quai D'Orsay there is no indication that the world is being settled. The statesmen are pretty serious and seem inclined to work and get the business over. Balls and vast state dinners are totally lacking.

Tuesday, January 21, 1919

Russia is the great topic under discussion now. The British went so far as to suggest that representatives of the Soviets be admitted to the Conference, but it doesn't look as if this idea would go through. Sazonov is in town and our old friend Bakhmetieff, who was in Washington when I was there (the former representative of the Kerensky government).[5] There is a lot of disagreement as to whether there should be any intervention. Our people are flatly opposed to sending an army to put down Bolshevism and I think are opposed pretty definitely to the idea of supporting the circle of states around Russia by sending armed forces to their support against Bolshevism. This

5. Sergei Dmitrievitch Sazonov (1866–1927) was a career diplomat under the Tsarist government, serving as Foreign Minister from 1909 until 1916 and had just been appointed ambassador to Britain in 1917 when the Russian Revolution took place. After the Conference he served briefly in the anticommunist, provisional government of Admiral Aleksander Vasilyevich Kolchak. George Bakhmetieff (d. 1928) was the last Imperial Russian ambassador to the United States, 1911–17. After the first revolution he stayed in America to represent the interim government of Alexander Feodorovitch Kerensky (b. 1881). Later he became involved in the Soviet efforts to gain possession of gold deposits once owned by the Tsarist government, and eventually became a professor of engineering in New York City.

second alternative is rather favored by the French. The third alternative is simply to let them alone, and tell them that if they will behave we will help them out economically. It's a terrible mess. The Bolsheviks have got a pretty good-sized army going and it seems to be well equipped.

Today I finished my final recommendations which went up to the Commissioners and will be put into the Conference. This, I hope, means that I am going to have some free time to work out details which thus far are in rather rough shape. I spent a large part of the afternoon in talking to the press men on the Jugoslav question. They have been in a bad hole, most of them Washington correspondents knowing American politics and how to get stories from Congressmen but totally unacquainted with European problems. Most of them a month ago didn't know what Jugoslav meant. They can't talk French, they are not used to getting stuff out of books or articles, and they don't know anybody over here; moreover there isn't enough in the French papers to orient them in the subjects which are before the Conference. They have daily interviews with Lansing, but he doesn't really know very much of the background of the subjects discussed.

They had a hard fight getting admission to the meetings of the full Conference, and they are worried by the French and British censorship which is still apparently in force. So finally they have got permission to come around to us and get talks on the various phases of the subjects the Conference takes up. Personally I am glad, for I think that the more publicity the better, and the more America learns through the press of what the decisions of the Conference mean the better chance of getting good decisions. So I was glad to spend some time explaining the main lines of the Jugoslav question and I am going to have a brief statement of the issues made out for them. I have been absolutely frank and told them everything I knew and some of it has dynamite in it; but it has to be approved by the Secretary of State before it is used. But look out for the dope in the American papers. Later we shall follow it up with stuff on the Czechs and the other new nations of Central Europe.

Last night I had dinner with a Czech, and although I complained at the idea of talking shop I really got more real stuff than I had in any one talk since I have been here. The man was not particularly distinguished, but he knows Austria and Hungary very well and has spent the last two years in Berne, which is about as good a place to pick up information as any in the world. I fired questions at him for a couple of hours after dinner. Then later in the evening I got in with a man who had had the best opportunity for studying the Italian situation and possessed very good capacity for judging it. I got from him what I gathered to be the real story of the Piave battle which led to the armistice with Austria and which was touted as such a marvelous Italian victory. The main lines of it I had heard before but this was the most coherent statement of what actually took place. I enclose a brief résumé of the story which, if it gets by, will interest you.

. . .

Story of the Piave[6]

Foch asked General Diaz to advance across the Piave. Diaz replied that he could not trust his army and considered it inadvisable to make such a move. While Diaz was in Paris the Italian papers announced publicly that the Italians were ready to advance, but that Foch considered it advisable that their advance should be deferred. Foch and Clemenceau were very angry, sent for Diaz and demanded

---

6. The Piave River marked the line at which the Italian armies halted after the disastrous defeat at Caporetto in October 1917. This emergency, coupled with the fall of Alexander Kerensky's provisional government in Russia and the disappointingly slow progress made by the British forces at Passchendaele Ridge northeast of Ypres, led in November to the formation of the Supreme War Council. Marshal Foch assumed overall military command. This step, supported by Wilson, saved Lloyd George from a motion of censure in the House of Commons but was not enough to save the French Premier, Paul Painlevé, who was replaced on November 16 by Clemenceau. The Battle of the Piave took place in June 1918 and actually started with an attempt on the part of the Austrians to cross the river.

explanations. They also demanded that Diaz should publicly deny the statement in the Italian papers. Diaz, however, refused, saying that he did not dare to do so and would surely lose his position if he did. Clemenceau then issued a denial in the French papers! This denial was never allowed to reach Italy.

The British then offered to go forward if Diaz would supply one army corps. Diaz finally consented, saying "Take the army corps, and God help you." Then the British with two divisions, the French with either two or three, and the Americans with one brigade succeeded in crossing the Piave after three days' fighting. The work of the Italian bridge builders, incidentally, was said to be very fine. The Austrians began to retreat. The Italians, however, afforded no adequate support until the British commander again made a row. Finally the Italians came up and the Austrians broke and the Italians poured through. The next day the Italian newspapers published the news that 52 Italian divisions aided by two British, two or three French, and an American brigade had won a great victory.

Wednesday, January 22, 1919

Today has been spent chiefly working on Jugoslav matters. The British have asked our government and the French to instruct our representatives at Belgrade to inform the Serbs that the United Jugoslav State would not be recognized now, that being the business of the Peace Conference. As I have written I am much opposed to this because I think that it plays into Italian imperialistic schemes and will make the Jugoslavs so sore that troubles in the Adriatic will become worse than they are, and they are bad enough. So I spent the morning in conferences and in drawing up memoranda to prevent our government from associating itself with the British in the matter. I do not know what effect my efforts will have. Lansing does not understand the situation, which is complicated by other factors. But I know that if they let this Adriatic question fester there is going to be a lot of trouble. Considering the recognition given to the Czechoslovaks they might at least recognize the *de facto* Jugoslav delegation at the Conference even if they don't want to recognize formally the existence of the state as a united entity.[7]

The weather is colder, about 40°, and there has been a thin coating of ice on the ponds. But the sun is out, and although it is not very strong, it is splendid weather. This afternoon Clive and I walked out the Bvd. Malesherbes to the Parc Monceau, coming back by way of the Wilson's house, where we dropped cards for the reception of last week. It is quite a palace. We stopped in front of Felix Potin, the Charles or the Fortnum and Mason of Paris, and studied the game exhibition. Geese are expensive and even a small scrawny chicken costs 15 francs. Prices of food are certainly high. Clothes, I should say, are about twice ours, but they look better.

Good-bye for the present and pardon a dull letter. I have heard from Lester Perrin who is loafing at Chamonix and who may come to Paris soon.[8]

Thursday, January 23, 1919

I have a few minutes before getting dressed for dinner and will start this. There is a big affair on with Victor Bérard, the Near Eastern specialist,[9] and three men from the British Foreign Office. I am not in a mood for a dinner, after the cables bringing the terribly sad news from Baltimore, but it is business and apparently I can do nothing for Clare tonight.[10] Naturally we are all very depressed. I feel just as if one of the family were gone. Thank heaven the work is press-

7. The Croats and the Slovenes were unofficially represented by Ante Trumbič and Ivan Žolger (Zholger) (1867–1925). The Kingdom of the Serbs, Croats, and Slovenes, the state's official name until 1929, was not recognized by the United States until February 7, 1919.

8. Perrin was scheduled to become secretary to Seymour's Austro-Hungarian division of the American Commission.

9. Bérard (1864–1931) was a scholarly classicist and writer on foreign policy.

10. Katharine Mendell, with whom Mrs. Seymour was to travel to France, died on January 21, 1919.

ing and one must keep one's mind on it. I can keep Clare very busy on absorbing work. It is the only thing that can help him at all.

My dinner was very interesting. Naturally I did not feel very gay but the conversation was absorbing. Bérard is one of the best-known publicists of France—a Legion of Honor man of high grade—and has written widely on international relations (on the Kaiser's policy for example) but particularly on the Near East. So we encouraged him to expound his solution of the Turkish problem, which he was ready to do. He says that he has studied it for 30 years. He does not represent the ideas of the Quai d'Orsay (French official policy) but is more liberal and, I think, in better accord with French opinion in the provinces. It is impossible to determine in Paris what is French opinion, for the newspapers of Paris are muzzled by the censorship, which is said to be worse than during the war.

Bérard says that of course Turkey as a state must disappear. (That is generally admitted.) There are two solutions as to what should be done with it: either partition it among the powers (the old method of selfish land grabbing) which would lead to trouble, jealousies, and wars, or put it under the League of Nations, each of five nations being mandatory at Constantinople; this requires less armed force than the other ports and he says that France, after her efforts in the war, is physically unable to take on heavy burdens. Greece would be the mandatory for the western coast section (largely Greek in character); Italy for the more purely Turkish section further east; the United States for Armenia; and Great Britain for the Arab section furthest east. He approves the idea of an independent Syria and an independent Arabia. A Zionist state in Palestine he considers impossible. (By the way did I tell you the Prince of the Hejaz dined here the other night?[11] I sat at the next table but did not meet him. He wore gorgeous Arabian robes and silk headdress).

11. The Hejaz is the barren province of western Arabia extending from the Gulf of Aqaba southward along the Red Sea. It has a special importance for the Islamic world since it contains Mecca and Medina. Hussein, Amir of Mecca, led a revolt against Turkish control which started in 1908. Aided by Colonel T. E. Lawrence, the revolt succeeded during World War I. The Allies recognized the independence of the Hejaz,

I doubt if our people accept Bérard's idea in toto.[12] They are opposed to Italian mandates, believing that they are totally incompetent
and corrupt, and also that Italy is on the verge of a social transforma-
tion which will keep all her energies busy at home. But it is going to
make trouble if Italian demands are refused everywhere; they can't
have Dalmatia; they mustn't get Abyssinia, and if they are shut out of
Asia Minor you can guess what language they will use. It is a difficult
problem and I am particularly interested in it because of my own
problem in the Adriatic.

Tomorrow I have rather an ordeal ahead but a very interesting
one which I rather look forward to. Mr. White is to have a very important interview and I have to be present to coach him in facts. They
will discuss the Italian claims in the Tyrol and in Istria and Dalmatia. I have been coaching myself for an hour this afternoon on the
tone I am to assume and the various ways I am to answer in case certain tricky questions are put.

The general undercurrent of opinion is that the action taken with

---

and Hussein was proclaimed King of the Arabs in 1916. He then joined the Allies, but
he had aroused the displeasure of Abd al-Aziz Ibn Saud, sultan of neighboring
Nejd. Eventually Hussein was forced to abdicate. In 1926 Ibn Saud was proclaimed
King of the Hejaz and Sultan of Nejd, which then were renamed Saudi Arabia. The
Prince of the Hejaz was presumably Ali, who occupied the throne left by his father for
a little over a year.

12. Eventually the nationalist Turks under Mustapha Kemal Pasha, more than the
Allies, defeated, in part, the plan of partition. A docile government under Damad
Ferid Pasha cooperated with the Allies by allowing occupations of Constantinople,
Adalia, and Smyrna. In the fall of 1919 a Nationalist Congress enunciated the Decla-
ration of Sivas, affirming unity of Turkish territory and self-determination, and then
set up a provisional government in Ankara, supported by Russia. The Allies nevertheless forced the sultan and Damad Ferid to sign the Treaty of Sèvres on August 10, 1920,
amid military flare-ups between the Turks and various occupation forces. By its terms
Syria was mandated to France, Mesopotamia and Palestine to Great Britain, Smyrna to
Greece for at least five years, the Dodecanese Islands and Rhodes to Italy; Armenia was
declared independent, and the Straits internationalized. Mustapha Kemal increased his
military operations against the Italians and Greeks and eventually forced Sultan Mo-
hammed VI to flee aboard a British ship. The loss of Armenia, which became a Soviet
Republic in 1921, was the price he paid for increased Russian aid, while under the
influence of "normalcy" the United States paid little attention to these distant events.
Limited Turkish military successes finally forced a revision of Sèvres by the Treaty of
Lausanne of July 24, 1923, by which Turkey recovered Eastern Thrace and some of the
Aegean Islands (but not the Dodecanese) and was released from any reparations. On
October 29 President Mustapha Kemal proclaimed the Turkish Republic.

regard to Russia was skillful.[13] If the Bolsheviks accept, something may be fixed up. Our attitude I think is correct that they may set up in Russia any government they like so long as it quits murdering and so long as it quits intriguing abroad to establish Bolshevism in Western and Central Europe. I hope the invitation to Prince's Island, if it does not settle the matter, will show them up anyway.

I must quit now. Another official dinner tonight with the British experts on Austria, Seton-Watson and Steed.

Sunday, January 26, 1919

I have been busy with interesting talks and conferences the last day and a half, and am glad to think that this is Sunday and that there is a possibility of getting caught up with the correspondence, which has accumulated in my basket. It is a bad day, the first snow I have seen this year; it is the type we get in April, rather trickling and wet, and most of it melts as soon as it touches the ground; but I dislike it as much as a real American blizzard. I had hoped that this winter I was to be spared all sight of snow.

Friday evening I had one of the most interesting dinners yet. We invited H. Wickham Steed and Seton-Watson. Steed is the foreign editor of the London *Times* and probably the foremost journalist of Europe, occupying much the position of Blowitz at the time of the Berlin Congress.[14] Seton-Watson is a publicist of means who has given up his life practically to studying Austria-Hungary, living

13. The Peace Conference was torn between opposing views as to how to treat the Bolshevist government of Russia. One extreme, represented by Winston Churchill, was direct military intervention and suppression. Another, represented by William Bullitt, was full cooperation. Wilson favored inviting the Russians to Paris but wavered in the face of Clemenceau's opposition. Eventually it was agreed to invite representatives of the contending Russian groups to a special conference on Prinkipo Island in the Aegean. The Bolshevists accepted but the counterrevolutionaries, Admiral Alexander Vasilyevich Kolchak and Anton Denikin, acting upon French advice, declined.

14. Henri Georges Stephan Adolphe de Blowitz (1825–1903), Anglo-French journalist, taught at the Tours and Marseilles Lycées, but became involved in political controversies and had to retire. He later became chief Paris correspondent for *The Times* of London and achieved numerous sensational journalistic feats, including the publication of the Treaty of Berlin at the moment of its signing.

there for many years; Steed is also a specialist on Austria. These two have done more than anyone else to help the oppressed nationalities and to bring about the revolution in Austria-Hungary. They work and live together and you could not imagine a more complete contrast: Steed is tall, elegant, distinguished in appearance, with a grey imperial beard and long silky grey hair brushed back; and with a very assured manner. Seton-Watson is a little Scotchman, hesitating in speech and insignificant in appearance, modest in his statements; in talking of Hungary which he knows better than any other Anglo-Saxon he always ends a statement "Isn't it?" or "Don't you think so?" They make a fine pair.

Steed has been in close contact with all the big men of Europe during the past five years and they have come to him constantly for advice, as one who knows the international situation better than anyone else. He said that last June Orlando had asked his advice on the Jugoslav question and that he had nearly persuaded him to recognize them, which, had it been accomplished, would have avoided the present crisis. But Orlando changed his mind during the night (Steed said that possibly Sonnino had banged him on the head) and next morning went to Clemenceau and begged him not to recognize the Jugoslavs. On another occasion the Italians had nearly been brought to the point, but backed out at the last minute. ("What swine these people are!" Balfour is reported to have said.)

Steed believes that the Sonnino policy of imperialism is bound to fail and that in two months we shall see them giving up their most extreme claims with a fine gesture; that is the moment to keep one's eyes open, for fear that they may get too much even then. He says that they hoped to "rope in" President Wilson; when they failed, Nitti, who is very shrewd, immediately resigned, to get off the ship before the wreck and in the hope of being the man to get the power when the crash came.[15]

15. Orlando was forced to resign on June 19, 1919, before he could even sign the Treaty of Versailles, and Nitti succeeded him.

Both Steed and Seton-Watson are rather disgusted at the way the Conference is starting: its slowness and its fear of taking definite decisions. They feel, as I have felt, that things are likely to linger along for about a month or so; then the people in every country will become discontented at the lack of results and demand that they do something. Then they will get down to business and hurry up. If the thing isn't finished by May, the two men think that there will be trouble. Both are pessimistic over the results of the attempt to get the various Russian parties together.

Steed had an interesting story proving German premeditation of the war. He began by telling of the activities of Schiemann, who was the Kaiser's private historian and spy.[16] Steed met him in London shortly before the war at the house of Mrs. J. R. Green, a violent Irish nationalist.[17] Schiemann was evidently working with Kuno Meyer, the professor of Gaelic,[18] studying the Irish question for the Kaiser. They traveled through Ulster together just before the war. Steed told of Meyer and Mrs. Green making a date to meet in Germany in August. After the war broke out he met Mrs. Green one day, who told him that she had an interesting card from Meyer. He went around to her house and saw it. It was dated at Berlin, July 16, 1914, and read: "We cannot meet this summer in August. By that time there will be war. Austria has just drawn up an ultimatum to Serbia which Schiemann has read and which the Kaiser has approved." All this was two weeks before the war and referred to the document which the Kaiser said he never saw. Steed said that the card is in the British Foreign Office to be used if necessary. Both he and Seton-Watson believe that there was a double plot to murder the Archduke, the first plot engineered by the police, which failed; the

16. Theodor Schiemann (1847–1921) became interested in the history of the Hohenzollerns, which led to a personal association with the Kaiser.

17. Alice Sophia Amelia Green (d. 1929) was the widow of the British historian, John Richard Green, and the authoress of numerous English and Irish histories.

18. Kuno Meyer (1858–1919), senior professor of cultural philology and history of literature at the University of Leipzig, concerned himself with Irish lexicography.

second was the Serbian plot which happened to succeed, largely because the police gave no protection.[19]

The other night I heard for the first time that when England declared war on Germany, Grey was dissatisfied with the draft of the
declaration which had been sent to Lichnowsky late in the evening.[20]
He made a new draft and sent it by Nicolson, the man I have been
dining with several times. Nicolson had great difficulty in getting in
and when he did found Lichnowsky in bed and very cross. Nicolson
explained that he had a very important message, but Lichnowsky said
that he was sleepy and could not talk business. Then Nicolson saw the
first draft lying on the bureau, unopened; he asked Lichnowsky if he
might substitute another document for the one that had come earlier
in the evening; Lichnowsky said he could do anything he wanted, so
long as he left him to sleep. So Nicolson took the first and left the
second and went back to the Foreign Office.

I had a long talk with Seton-Watson over Hungarian boundaries
and was pleased to find that his ideas were not far from ours. I must
have put up a good bluff, for he said "It's curious I never met you in
Hungary; you must have spent a long time there."

Yesterday morning I spent an hour and a half with White and
Macchi di Cellere, who brought a lot of maps and a naval captain to
explain Italy's demands.[21] We let them do most of the talking—I be-

19. Francis Ferdinand, heir to the Austro-Hungarian throne, was killed at Sarajevo
in Bosnia on June 28, 1914. The assassin was Gavrilo Princip, one of a group of young
Bosnian revolutionaries acting as agents of the Serbian terrorist organization, "The
Black Hand," founded to agitate against Austria in behalf of Serbian nationalism. Historians disagree as to the extent of the Serbian government's awareness of the plot to
murder the Archduke and of its efforts to warn Vienna. Pašić did know that the armed
youths crossed the border into Bosnia and tried to intercept them.

20. Prince Karl Max Lichnowsky (1860–1928) was the German ambassador to
Great Britain who, like Grey, tried to avert the outbreak of war. He accused his own
government of failing to support him and as a result was expelled from the Prussian
House of Lords in 1917.

21. In retrospect Seymour was to view his admittedly pro-Slavic attitude toward the
Italo-Yugoslav question, which became one of the major crises of the Conference, as "a
bit patronizing." The position of the Italians was difficult, in the first place, because they
were at the Conference arguing the destinies of their own former allies in the admittedly
uncertain triple Alliance. Next, after switching from neutrality to belligerence during
the war, they came to regard the Croats and Slovenes as pestilential enemies whereas the

THE INQUIRY: DIVISION CHIEFS IN PARIS

Seated, left to right: Charles H. Haskins, Isaiah Bowman, Sidney E. Mezes, James Brown Scott, David Hunter Miller. *Standing, left to right:* Charles Seymour, Robert H. Lord, William L. Westermann, Mark Jefferson, Colonel House, George Louis Beer, Douglas W. Johnson, Clive Day, William E. Lunt, James T. Shotwell, A. A. Young.

THE ENTIRE MEMBERSHIP OF THE AMERICAN COMMISSION TO NEGOTIATE PEACE

Seated in the first row, left to right: Colonel House, Secretary Lansing, President Wilson, Mr. White, and General Bliss. Charles Seymour is in the back row, midway between House and Lansing.

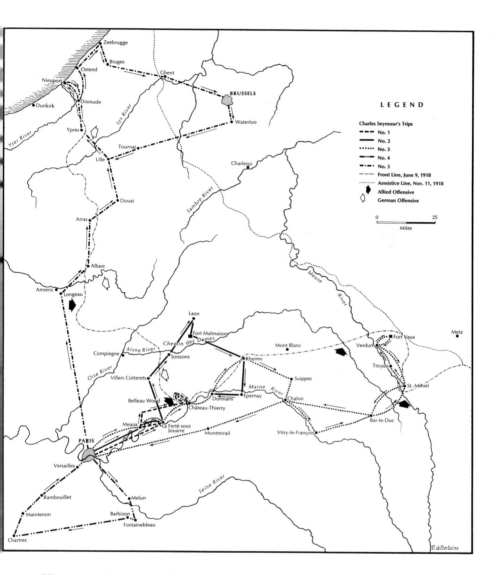

Northern France and Belgium, showing Charles Seymour's five trips in the spring of 1919 and major offensives of 1918

1. To Château-Thierry, February 2, 1919. 2. To Laon and Rheims, March 29–30, 1919. 3. To Verdun and St.-Mihiel, May 17–19, 1919. 4. To Chartres, May 25–26, 1919. 5. To Belgium, June 8–10, 1919.

Charles Seymour in 1919
(and his calling card).

Charles Seymour and his military assistants.
Left: Lester Perrin.   *Right:* Paul M. Atkins.

Sketch of Charles Seymour by his brother-in-law, John Angel, the sculptor, London, 1919.

Hôtel Crillon from the Place de la Concorde.

The Seymours, with Perrin Galpin (left) and Lester Perrin (right), Ypres, June 1919.

German tank on the Place de la Concorde.

Palace of the Peace Conference, Quai d'Orsay.

e Seymours (right), with Colonel and Mrs. Perrin Galpin
end, June 1919.

Mr. and Mrs. Seymour in Paris, 1911.

CENTRAL EUROPE IN 1919, SHOWING THE NEW STATES AND
THE SITES OF THE FOUR MAJOR TERRITORIAL DISPUTES IN
WHICH CHARLES SEYMOUR WAS INVOLVED

1. Fiume (Rijeka).   2. The Banat.   3. The Klagenfurt District.   4. Teschen (Cieszyn).

...e in front of the Palace at Versailles immediately after the signing of the peace treaty with Germany, ...e 28, 1919. *Left center:* Lloyd George, Clemenceau, and Wilson (*New York Times,* July 13, 1919).

Charles Seymour in the former House Collection Room in the Yale University Library.

cause it was my cue to speak only when spoken to, although I did ask some questions when they were lying too frankly and cynically; White because he evidently wanted to let them have their full say. It was interesting and very good fun, though it required some self-restraint not to contradict some of the things they said which were pretty far away from the facts. White whispered as they went out "Don't go, I want to talk to you." So I hung around and he said, "What do you think"? I told him that I thought that only one of their arguments was any good at all; he said he quite agreed, and that we would have to get a Serb around to put the Jugoslav side of the case. He has learned how to conceal his feelings in his diplomatic career; I was quite unable to discover how he was being affected by their arguments and felt quite nervous at times, lest he be fooled, but he evidently wasn't.

The Italians were very dramatic, waved their arms around, tears came into their eyes. They spoke quite frankly of their hatred of the French and the treachery of the Croats; Cellere said to me, "If we had not beaten the Austrians you would now be fighting the Germans and your brave soldiers would be dying on the field of battle." It was unfortunate that he had heard of me through Charles Upson Clark, and realizes that I do not sympathize with the Italian policy. It seems to me to be purely Prussian in spirit.

Yesterday noon at lunch I met Admiral Troubridge,[22] the British sailor who has command of the Allied fleet on the Danube and who is in reality dictator of Serbia, Rumania, Bulgaria, and southern

---

Americans, British, and French were prone to consider all Slavs merely as lost sheep that needed saving. Finally, in terms of security Italy had been caught short by the sudden and complete collapse of Austria-Hungary and was now concerned over the possibility of a merger between Germany and Austria, whose independence was originally established in the name of "German Austria." This eventuality would (and finally did) bring Germany to Italy's northern border. In addition, a united Yugoslavia would place another large nation of 13,000,000 to the east. Then, too, Italy was extremely sensitive to the vulnerability of its Adriatic shoreline. Cf. Nicolson, *Peacemaking, 1919*, pp. 165, 172 ff. Italy's basic difficulty with regard to Fiume, however, was that the city had been excluded from the promises of the Treaty of London.

22. Admiral Sir Ernest Charles Thomas Troubridge (1862–1926) was the descendant of a long line of British naval officers and in 1921 completed a naval career that included diplomatic, staff, and line assignments, at which time he became president of the International Commission of the Danube.

Hungary. He has charge of all waterways and as these are the only effective means of transportation he does what he likes. He told me how he is keeping industry going in Hungary by compelling the people to work mines and sugar factories and export lignite and sugar across to Serbia, and of the great fleets of barges he sends up the Danube. He is an enthusiast over water transportation, plans to connect the Black Sea with the North Sea and make this the great artery of European transportation under an international commission. He is the most magnetic man I have met over here—very handsome sea dog of about 60. He has been in the Near East for six years and knows it well; he likes the Serbs, although he considers that they are essentially agricultural in character and can never develop as the Croatians will do. He hates the Italians and thinks they have no business on the eastern coast of the Adriatic, outside of Valona which they must have "because they are like children and won't be happy until they get it."[23]

(Later Sunday evening)

This afternoon I took a long walk of two hours with Clare and Sam. We went through the Marais, down long winding narrow streets with old houses to the Place des Vosges, which is the loveliest spot in Paris. Then across to the Ile St. Louis to Notre Dame and back by way of Saint Gervais (the church hit by Bertha on Good Friday). The verger took us up to the roof, which is walled off by temporary wooden partitions, and along the gutters to the hole in the roof made by the shell. It has not yet been repaired and looks just as it did at first. Had it struck a few feet further on it would have broken the whole vaulting and the entire roof would have come down. I took a piece of the broken vaulting as a souvenir.

We have been hoping for a chance to get to the front, but it does not look as though it would be possible during these next weeks. Bets

---

23. Valona (Vione), located in Albania, was included in the territory offered Italy by the Treaty of London, but the Albanians refused to accept this settlement and drove the Italians out of the city itself to the outer reaches of the bay.

on the duration of the Conference extend from the end of March to the end of June. Somewhere between seems the most likely, although the Commissioners will have to begin to hurry up.

Tuesday, January 28, 1919

This will probably be a dull letter for I am very sleepy and don't seem to have run into much of interest, although very busy. Two months ago what seems perfectly commonplace now would have excited me enormorously; but tonight all that I really want is to be able to go comfortably into my old bed at 127 Everit Street [New Haven] and not have to worry about the fate of the nations tomorrow (not that my worrying is going to affect the fate of the nations very much). Most of my time has been spent the past two days in talking to the secretaries of the Commissioners, for as the Conference organizes, the Commissioners get put on committees and have very little time for talks with us. It is not a bad arrangement, for the secretaries are very bright men and if you want a certain fact to get to a Commissioner it is generally easier and quicker to talk to his secretary and find out exactly what is in the big man's head first. Mr. White's secretary is Chris Herter, who has been secretary of legation at Berne and is just as nice as they make them.[24] I have spent a lot of time with him today going over boundary problems and discussing the reaction of the Commissioners to our various suggestions. He knows Austrian politics very well and also general international politics; is in close touch with everything that is going on here.

The career diplomats of this type, when they are not too old, are really fine to deal with and our position is that of the "expert." They really think we know more than we do. When they find that we are not "professorish" and don't want to decide the future regardless of

24. Christian Archibald Herter (b. 1895), Harvard-trained diplomat and statesman, served in Congress from 1943 to 1953 when he became governor of Massachusetts. In 1957 he was named Under Secretary of State and succeeded John Foster Dulles as Secretary in 1959.

practical exigencies, they are very cordial. I have such men as Herter and [Allen] Dulles in mind. At the present time our group is exercising far more influence than I expected. Two quite important questions, involving our relations to other powers, were referred to me last week, and my decision, drafted in a telegram to Polk at Washington,[25] was adopted. Lord is being sent to Warsaw with Major-General Kernan as the American representative on the Commission of Inquiry in Poland; General Botha[26] is the British representative so that you see that it is a mission of importance.

I am beginning to try and dodge some of the jobs and commissions they want me to undertake. I spent most of yesterday morning in Colonel House's office discussing methods of getting into closer touch with the smaller nations. The protest of the little nations at last Saturday's Conference meeting might easily have been avoided had someone canvassed the situation beforehand and found out what was on the minds of the little states. Clemenceau certainly treats them awfully rough and our role is that of the friend and protector of the small states. Colonel House is very anxious to keep in close touch with them, but he is not very well and the Commissioners are busy

25. Frank Lyon Polk (1871–1943), Yale '94, was a lawyer, a corporation counsel, and the president of the New York Civil Service Commission (1908–09) before the war. He then served four years under Lansing as counselor for the State Department, becoming Under Secretary in 1919. When President Wilson came home after the signing of the Treaty of Versailles, Polk was appointed Commissioner to head the delegation during the six months of negotiations with the lesser Central Powers. He then returned to private practice and became one of the senior partners of the firm of Davis, Polk, Wardwell, Gardiner, and Reed.

26. General Louis Botha (1862–1919), South African soldier and statesman, was one of the two great Boer leaders, General Jan Christian Smuts being the other. They were South Africa's two Commissioners at the Conference. Veteran of the South African war of 1899–1902, Botha led the successful struggle to secure responsible government from Great Britain; his party won the first election in the Transvaal, and Botha became Premier and Minister of Native Affairs in 1907. He then turned to forming the Union of South Africa from four former colonies—Cape Colony, Natal, Orange River Colony and Transvaal—and in 1910 he became first Prime Minister of the Union. When war broke out Botha led a successful military campaign against German Southwest Africa. At the Conference he tried in vain to have this area ceded outright to the Union but could only achieve a mandate, which led to virtual annexation after World War II. It was he who persuaded Wilson to accept the mandates plan. Botha died in August 1919 and was succeeded as Prime Minister and leader of the South African Party by General Smuts.

with their various committee meetings. So apparently it is up to us to play around with the Czechs and Rumanians, even more than we have done and see what is on their mind. I have begun to make arrangements for various dinners and lunches with men like Kramář[27] and Beneš and Bratianu. Clive, fortunately, is in close touch with the Greeks. It is a job I am not particularly keen for, as I have trouble enough to keep my desk clear as it is, and these social engagements take a lot of time.

We are in very close with the British all along the line and I think that this fact alone justifies Wilson's coming over. Nothing has been said thus far about the freedom of the seas, but I know that we are in close accord on the League of Nations and on the matter of the disposition of the German colonies. The latter will not go back to Germany, and I think that the President's idea of their being given to the League, a particular power being made mandatory of the League (for instance, the Union of South Africa as protector of German Southwest Africa) is likely to be accepted. England is willing to accept this, although Australia has put up some kick. I don't think that the French like it very well. As this letter is going through American mail I can say that the French are playing politics to some extent and are not so straightforward as the British. The present government is not representative of the people as a whole, who want Alsace-Lorraine and nothing else except to get back to business.

[Nine lines censored]

Clemenceau is playing for territorial acquisitions beyond Alsace and in the Near East, which would be unfortunate. France has made

27. Karel Kramář (1860–1937), industrialist, was president of the Czechoslovak National Council in Paris, which organized a provisional government with Thomas Garrigue Masaryk (1850–1937) as President and Beneš as Foreign Minister. The latter two were the chief architects of Czechoslovak independence, declared by the Council on October 28, 1918. Kramář was chief of the new nation's delegation at the Peace Conference. Masaryk remained President until 1935. Beneš succeeded him, only to resign in 1938 after the Munich agreement. He came to the University of Chicago where he taught during World War II, returned to Czechoslovakia in 1945, and was reelected President, but could not prevent a Communist coup in 1948.

a tremendous effort and one really beyond her powers; what she ought to do now is to settle down to a period of convalescence.

Gompers is over here with strange ideas.[28] I should like to know how far he represents our working men. Anyway he doesn't know European labor. An enormous revolution has taken place here in the past few months. Socialists of the kind we feared a few years ago are now reactionaries and we might as well acknowledge the fact. If we want a lasting peace and one undisturbed by Bolshevism we have got to combine with the moderate socialists. England has already done it in essence. I don't mean that this applies to us at home in the United States, for Europe has lived with socialism 15 more years than we. I think that socialism has not begun in America; but here it is and here to stay. It is foolish to blink at the fact and if the Conference tries to, its work will be swept away in a couple of years.

I had dinner at the same table with McCormick yesterday.[29] He seems to have made a fine impression here and is the one man whom the French will listen to on the subject of indemnities. He puts the matter simply: "If you ask the indemnities you want from Germany you will kill her and will get nothing but Bolshevism; ask what she can pay from her earnings of the next 50 years and let her earn it." Baruch is in the hotel and I met him today. He is a mystery to the French; they cannot understand how a Jewish speculator can be in the position he holds.

At present I should say that Wilson is in fair control of the situa-

28. Samuel Gompers (1850–1924), British-born cigarmaker, had been connected with efforts to organize labor since he came to America at 14 years of age. In 1881 he helped found a federation of organized trades and labor unions, which five years later became the American Federation of Labor. He served as its president, except in 1895, until his death.

29. Vance C. McCormick (1872–1946), Yale '93, one-time mayor of Harrisburg, Pennsylvania (1902–05), and longtime member of the Yale Corporation (1913–36), served as chairman of the War Trade Board, a governmental agency organized to wage economic warfare. At the Conference he and Bernard Mannes Baruch (1870–1965) headed the economic section of the technical advisers to the American Commission. They were particularly involved in the reparations question. Baruch had been chairman of the War Industrial Board during World War I and later became adviser to James F. Byrnes, war mobilization director during World War II.

tion. He is showing himself a very practical politician and has the British with him and the people of all countries are absolutely behind him. What will result when he goes home it is difficult to say. It is important that the Conference begin to produce some results, for if he stalls and goes back, anything may happen.

More snow last night; I have never seen so much in Paris. It has melted today but there is still lots on the grass. I had a hasty dinner with Don Cooksey;[30] he expects to get home shortly, but it may not be before June as things go.

Thursday, January 30, 1919

I have had a very busy and a very interesting two days. Much of the work involves what we call "TNT stuff," which I hardly dare put on paper but I can talk about the associations involved which I shall be glad to remember.

Yesterday morning I was just getting ready for a peaceful day in the hope of clearing my desk of a mass of accumulated papers and was cheered by the thought of no luncheon engagement, when a call came from Bowman to pack up my available stuff on the Czechs and come right over to the Quai d'Orsay. As you will have seen by the papers the prime ministers and foreign ministers of the big five powers (the "Council of Ten" they are beginning to call them) was to consider Polish affairs and it was expected that relations with the Czechs would come up. We had very short notice which was regrettable, for I had no chance to get into "diplomatic clothes"; fortunately my fur coat was on my back, but when I got inside I felt that my trousers should have been pressed. We felt quite as though we were arbiters of the nations as we whirled into the entrance of the Quai d'Orsay through the crowd which waits to see the big men

30. Donald Cooksey (b. 1892), Yale '15 S., was a first lieutenant in the Ordnance Department. Later he became the assistant director of the Lawrence Radiation Laboratory at the University of California.

come in. Inside I found myself giving up my coat and hat to the French orderly, side by side with Mr. Balfour and General Botha. The secret conferences are held in the small room, Pichon's private office, which opens to the right off the main waiting room. I suppose there were about 20 of us in all, including the Commissioners. As we came into the room Wilson came up to us and shook hands very cordially. He is brisk and genial as ever. Lansing looks very tired; he walks very slowly and told Young yesterday that he is bothered by his heart.

Everything reminded me of a faculty committee meeting, rather than a gathering of statesmen. Proceedings opened very informally when Clemenceau suggested that the doors be closed and that they begin work. The room is about double the size of our library in the Hillhouse Avenue house.[31] It is oak with a few good carvings (cupids over the main door) and two empire commodes, a very simple fireplace, and Rubens' tapestries, copies from the Marie de Medici paintings in the Louvre; one side has two big windows looking out on the garden. There is a plain empire table in the center, at which Clemenceau sits. Almost immediately behind him is Paul Mantoux, interpreter;[32] to the latter's right, by the side of the fireplace, Pichon. He is round, bunched up, and sloppy. On Clemenceau's right is Wilson and then Lansing. Then Balfour and Botha; Lloyd George came only to the afternoon session. Then a chair for whoever is being heard by the Commissioners, in this case the Pole, Dmowski.[33] Then the two Japanese. Facing Clemenceau, Sonnino and Orlando and two or three secretaries. Bowman and I faced Clemenceau immediately behind Wilson and Lansing.

31. A reference to the Seymour home, built by Benjamin Silliman, Yale 1796. Now demolished, it stood across the avenue from the house used since 1937 by Yale presidents and served as both home and laboratory for the famed pioneer in science education.

32. Paul Joseph Mantoux (1877–1956), French historian and author, taught in Paris and London prior to the war, and afterward served in the Secretariat of the League of Nations as director of the Political Section.

33. Roman Dmowski (1864–1939), politician and writer, founded the Polish National Democratic Party in 1893 and, with Ignace Jan Paderewski, the Polish National Committee as a provisional government in Paris in 1917. After the war Dmowski became Minister of Foreign Affairs for a brief term. Paderewski (1860–1941), famed primarily as a pianist, served—also briefly—as Premier. He received the honorary doctor of music degree from Yale in 1917.

Everything was very informal, each of the men speaking when they felt like it and with very little direction from Clemenceau. The latter wore his grey gloves every moment of the session, even when writing. Most of the time his face was expressionless, even rather bored, with his long moustache covering his mouth—his heavy eyebrows in his eyes, which were generally half closed. When particularly interested, which is rare, he opens his eyes very wide and leans forward. His English is perfect grammatically, but he has a decided accent. Sonnino, on the other hand, has a perfect Oxford accent; to hear him one would swear that he was pure English. He has an attractive manner and shows the force which we know him to possess; Orlando, on the other hand, appears rather weak. In talking, Dmowski was at as much pains to impress Sonnino as he was Wilson; but he rather ignored Orlando. Botha looked his part perfectly, rather hardheaded and businesslike. He took little part in the discussion. He was there as the British commissioner to Poland I suppose. Balfour rested his head on the back of his chair and stretched his enormously long, crossed legs out in front of him and looked the image of Spy's caricature of him in the House of Commons. He never looked bored, however.

Wilson appears absolutely at home and seems to get on very well with the Europeans, speaking naturally, almost colloquially, and without affectation or any trace of didactiveness. He likes to make a humorous allusion; Balfour, Lloyd George, and Clemenceau are evidently glad of some excuse for a smile. Dmowski spoke of the qualifications of Paderewski, and particularly that he had never joined in party struggles; "fortunate man," said Clemenceau with an indescribable gesture. The session is carried on in English and French. Mantoux translates everything, very well indeed, rarely using a literal rendering but putting the idea into perfect idiom. Dmowski asked that he be allowed to translate for himself, so that Mantoux was out of a job all morning, and went to sleep for most of the time. The poor man has been translating for over a year in the Supreme War Council. Wilson and Balfour appear to be in close understanding, and in the afternoon Wilson and Lloyd George frequently whispered together. It is generally understood that so far as the League of Nations and the disposition of German colonies go, we and the British are in close accord. I suppose that Hughes[34] may put up objections and I know that Simon, the French minister of colonies,[35] is opposed; but Clemenceau has practically agreed to come with Lloyd George in supporting Wilson. The only trouble is that they don't know what they mean about mandatory powers.

The morning session lasted until after one, when Wilson said he had a luncheon engagement and suggested adjournment. "All right," said Clemenceau, "shall we meet at three?" "Half-past three," said Sonnino and everybody got up. In the afternoon session the Czechs came in, when it was half over, and for the first time I had to get down to business and stop watching proceedings as a witness. I went in late and was glad I did for while I was outside I had a very interesting talk with Lloyd George's secretary, Philip Kerr.[36] Then Mr. Wilson came out for a minute, and, seeing me there, came up to discuss the way things were going. Both he and the British are tried in their patience by the difficulty of getting down to brass tacks and are very anxious to get things started toward a preliminary settlement. He said that he had made a suggestion to Mr. Lloyd George, who had approved it, told me what it was, and asked me to take steps to put it into effect, at least in principle. I was glad that I happened to be there, for he is impulsive, had evidently spoken as a result of the long session, which was accomplishing nothing, and he might have said nothing if someone had not happened to meet him. But I think his idea is an excellent one, and can be used to expedite matters. I have been working on it much of today.

34. William Morris Hughes (1864–1952), Australian Labor Party leader, became Attorney General and Prime Minister in 1915. He embodied British patriotism and, in 1917, left the party to organize a new Nationalist Party but maintained his Cabinet post until 1923.
35. Henri Simon.
36. Philip Henry Kerr, 11th Marquess of Lothian (1882–1940), statesman and journalist, started his career in the Transvaal. In 1939 he became British ambassador to the United States.

The discouraging part of the Conference is that it seems so difficult to get an orderly program. Much matter which should be put before subordinates—details, technical disputes, etc.—comes before the Council of Ten, takes up their time, and perplexes them. They don't know any details of course. Yesterday Orlando didn't know what Austrian Silesia was.[37] The claimants, who are putting their case, cannot be restrained from going into a thousand minor points, which the Commissioners are wholly unqualified to consider. What we are working for is to have questions at issue brought before subcommittees appointed by the powers, and composed of the various experts, so-called. These are the only men who are capable of deciding the details and of presenting the matter fairly to the Commissioners. These subcommittees can be working all at the same time and make reports to the Council of Ten, which can then pass on the large question. It is the easiest and quickest way of disposing of all territorial questions and will leave the Commissioners free during the next weeks to decide on the League of Nations and International control of transportation, of labor, etc.

Of course, the Conference is working under difficulties far greater than those of the Congress of Vienna, for conditions in Central Europe are in such a state of flux, to say nothing of Russia, that it is impossible to know what the latest developments are. The Conference has to determine not merely the articles of general peace, but the details of current policy toward the Bolsheviks, Poland, the Ukrainians, the Lithuanians, the Jugoslavs, as well as how to save Hungary, Austria, Bohemia, etc., from anarchy and labor upheavals. For example, half of my work, which ought to be devoted purely to the consideration of the claims of Danubian peoples and planning for a future long ahead, is devoted to the study of measures to be taken day after tomorrow to meet an immediate and temporary crisis. Of course this can't be avoided.

37. Prior to World War I most of Silesia was in Germany along the upper reaches of the Oder River, but the southernmost part lay within the Crown Lands of Austria. Rich in coal and ore, Silesia is one of Europe's important industrial areas.

Today I have been in conference for long hours on both aspects; policy of today and preparation for the future. I have had the drafting of a very important declaration of our government with regard to the Jugoslavs. You know what I have tried to get them to do, in this quarter; two of our Commissioners have been opposed, two in favor, and one doubtful.[38] Now it seems possible that we can get put through what I have been working for; at any rate I was told to draft a statement and it might be approved. I am convinced that if it goes through, our government will get great prestige with the smaller states and that a peaceful and satisfactory compromise in the Adriatic will become more likely.

I am beginning my work as social laborer again. Dinner with Bratianu tomorrow, lunch with Italian liberals on Saturday, dinner with Serbs in the evening, and dinner with Czechoslovaks—Kramářz and Beneš—on Monday. If nothing prevents, expect to go to the front on Sunday; a brief trip—Rheims and Château-Thierry probably.

Had a good letter from Lester Perrin who has returned from Chamonix. He says to keep the socks his mother knitted, "or better still to wear them." I saw Allen Klots today;[39] he is assigned to Hoover. He has three wound stripes. I must close this to get it in the mail. I am sending it by army post, as there is no French boat this week.

38. Seymour hoped to have Yugoslavia's independence recognized.
39. Allen Trafford Klots (1899–1964), Yale '09, served as a first lieutenant in the Field Artillery, before returning to a distinguished career as a lawyer. An early associate of Henry L. Stimson, Yale '88, he became president of the Association of the Bar of the City of New York and was very active in court reform studies.

END OF THE FIRST PHASE

February 2–15, 1919

ANY GENERAL SUMMARY of the Paris Peace Conference would conclude that the distinctive and important work of its first month centered on the drafting and approval of the Covenant of the League of Nations. Even critics stress this conclusion to support assertions that Wilson's insistence prevented the accomplishment of other necessary tasks such as spelling out the terms of settlement with Germany. A measure of rebuttal is provided by Seymour's account of his own incessant labors during the same period, all aimed at reaching a just and lasting solution to the legacy of issues stemming from the disappearance of the Austro-Hungarian Empire, a settlement made complex by economic, ethnic, social, and typographical considerations.

Prior to the Conference there was a wide disparity of opinion as to the most desirable basis for the political future of Central Europe: fragmentation into completely independent units, federalism, continuation of a dualistic monarchy of the sort that actually emerged during the latter years of the old Empire, or establishment of one sizable Slavic power center, either Yugoslav or Polish, as a balance to the German and Magyar groups. The last alternative was originally favored by Seymour, who also felt that "Whatever our sympathy with the Czechs, the Poles, the Yugoslavs" any multiplication of small states would be "regrettable."[1]

These differences of opinion were partially answered by the course of events during the fall and winter of 1918–19 over which the peacemakers exercised no control. When they finally met the range of options had been

1. Gelfand, *The Inquiry*, pp. 199–208. Also Seymour, "The League of Nations," p. 37.

narrowed, but new problems had arisen. Attainment of freedom by the various nationality groups had intensified their demands, their rivalries and jealousies, their willingness to take up arms. The example of the Balkans was spreading, much to the dismay of the Western statesmen who had hoped to prevent this very possibility.

At the beginning of February the Council of Ten took a major organizational step by establishing the first of a series of territorial commissions. This arrangement seemed highly necessary to Seymour, even though he was soon to feel that the commissions suffered from limitations: narrowness of responsibility, uncertainty of authority, and exclusion of overall political considerations. Undoubtedly his reactions stemmed from a mixture of youthful impatience and confident convictions as to his own proposals. In the long run the commissions proved most useful and their recommendations were almost invariably accepted, especially when unanimous.

American Commission to Negotiate Peace
4 Place de la Concorde, Paris

Sunday, February 2, 1919

This is absolutely the first chance I have had to write since Thursday evening, and I am not sure how long I shall have now. But I ought to have lots to tell you. The great news is that yesterday noon, at 12:30 when I came in to lunch, I found a note from Law saying that he was in town on 24 hours' leave, hoping to get liberated, and that he would lunch with me at one. You can imagine my excitement. I had arranged for lunch with Borsa,[2] who is a friend of the Italian Socialist leader, Bissolati, and some of his group, for I am very anxious to get Italian public opinion; but I called it off. Fortunately there were several others going so that it was quite possible.

Law looks very well, has the most elegant uniform and fur-collared

2. Mario Borsa (1870–1952), Italian journalist and author, was the correspondent for *The Times* of London in Milan from 1918 until 1940.

coat I ever saw and is jubilant at the idea of getting out of the French army and the ease with which he had accomplished it. He has obviously been homesick and we could have talked all night if there had been a chance. But I had a conference at 8 for which I was supposed to be working all afternoon. He was enormously interested in all the things at home and really seemed anxious to get back into the coal business, though he wants to finish up the piece of writing he is now engaged in.

The other news is the arrival of letters from Gladys, hers of the 8th and the 10th of January. I have been waiting for a cable announcing plans. Clive got one from Elsie yesterday saying that she was coming with the children on March 20 to stay until September. I have had some fun with Clive over this, for we had long ago agreed that it was out of the question bringing the children and also that we didn't want to spend the summer in Europe. Now the matter seems to be taken out of his hands. He warns me that Gladys will make a similar announcement, but I doubt it and should veto it if it came. Sounds like Petruchio! I don't think it fair to Europe or to me to bring such little children and I regard it as a quite unjustified expense.

Friday was a very busy day. The morning was taken up with getting ready for the secret session of the five big powers who were to hear the Rumanians and the Serbs on their claims in the Banat, which unfortunately conflict. We received very slight warning and had not time to prepare some of the statements and maps we wanted to have for our Commissioners. Clive and I were driven over to the Quai d'Orsay soon after lunch and met the two British specialists, Nicolson and Leeper. The Conference was hearing the findings of the Polish Commission at the moment, so we talked with the British; I had another pleasant short chat with Philip Kerr, who was on hand to prompt Lloyd George.

Lord reports that the Polish Commission has a terribly hard time with the Czechs, who are unwilling to yield a thing and kicked like steers even at a temporary line of demarcation being drawn in Silesia. He said that Noulens is the life of the Commission.[3] General Kernan (our other representative beside Lord) and General Botha do not understand French and are terribly perplexed by the problem, which is bad enough in English. After a half hour's wait, the Rumanians and the Serbs (or rather as they call themselves the "representatives of the Kingdom of the Serbs, Croats, and Slovenes") were called in and we followed. Clemenceau greeted them at the door and us as well, though he can hardly know who we are.

Bratianu presented the case of Rumania; he is, as you doubtless know, Prime Minister and head of the delegation. He is large with a black beard, a rather somber-looking man with a strong nose; not so sympathetic as Jonescu, but obviously a man of a good deal of force. He presented his case very skillfully, I thought, with much restraint for a man who claims to have had the territories for which he is asking guaranteed him by the powers, before which he was arguing, in return for Rumania's participation in the war. He did not stress the treaty of 1916,[4] however, but argued on grounds of justice and future peace.

Vesnić[5] answered for the Jugoslavs, speaking with more oratory, then Bratianu again, then Trumbic again for the Jugoslavs. Pašić was there but spoke very little. The trickster is patriarchal in appearance and, except for a rather hard glitter once and a while in his rather

3. Lord was now serving as chief of the Division on Russia and Poland. Joseph Noulens, French politician and diplomat, held numerous Cabinet positions prior to becoming ambassador to Russia in 1917. At the Conference he was named head of the Inter-Allied Mission sent to Poland on January 29. Another committee, one of the first of the territorial groups, was established by the Big Ten on January 31. This was the Commission on the Duchy of Teschen, the eastern part of the economically valuable province of Silesia and the focus of a long-standing Czech-Polish dispute. Eventually it was awarded to Czechoslovakia, and then seized by Poland in 1938.

4. The Secret Treaty of Bucharest promised Rumania a part of Hungarian Transylvania and the Banat of Temesvar, which are located respectively at the northeast and southeast corners of Rumania. By a strict interpretation this treaty was abrogated when Rumania signed a separate peace in May 1918.

5. Milenko R. Vesnič (1862–1921), law professor, author, and Radical deputy, held different ministerial and diplomatic posts before coming to Paris to represent Serbia. In 1920 he became president of the Yugoslav Council of Ministers, in which capacity he signed the Treaty of Rapallo with Italy.

small eyes, looked the picture of benevolence. If Venizelos and Jonescu had only been there we should have had a complete roster of
Balkan statesmen (unless one puts Malinoff of Bulgaria in that class).

The Commissioners seemed rather puzzled by the discussion.
Lloyd George asked where the boundaries of the Banat were; I had
talked it over with Wilson on the boat, but I am not sure how much
he knows of the details; he asked for a map, and I gave him the best
I had, which didn't seem to satisfy him; so finally I made a sketch map
of the chief points (you know my skill with the pencil—it was neither greater nor less than on ordinary occasions); and this seemed
to give him more what he wanted. At least he and Lansing studied
it. I suppose Clemenceau really knew a good deal about it, but one
can tell nothing from his expression. Sonnino kept his eyes closed
during most of the talk; I think he went frankly asleep at least once;
when he opened them he scowled at the Jugoslavs; he probably doesn't
love them very much.

Only once did all the Commissioners wake up. That was when
Vesnić said that certain parts of the Banat could be shown to be Serb
by the candidacy of Serbs in the elections. Here at last was familiar
ground. "You mean to say that a majority of candidates returned in
those districts was composed of Serbs?" said Lloyd George, while
even Sonnino pricked up his ears. It was screamingly funny. Inasmuch as elections in Hungary mean less than nothing, since the majority of anti-Magyar candidates are thrown into prison by the authorities, the disappointment of the Commissioners was great when they
learned the truth—that electoral results, which they understood,
meant nothing; they had nothing familiar to guide them on their decisions. Mr. Wilson was friendly to us as always, and very genial in
his general manner. He conceals excellently his vexation at the
slow way in which things are going.

The conference lasted until half past six and we hurried back to the
hotel as we were dining with Bratianu at seven and had to dress. We
found him in his study surrounded by his associates to whom he was
telling the story of the afternoon. It is a magnificent place, must be

supported by the government, for it is a large private house on the
Champs Elysées, wonderfully furnished. He was much cast down and
worn out by the afternoon and as a result, I think, spoke more frankly
than he might otherwise have done. His thesis, and he is either a
wonderful actor or he believes it, is that Rumania has done everything to fulfill her obligations of the secret treaty of 1916 (while the
Allies failed in many of theirs); that Rumania was sold out, but
even so fought until the Allies advised her to make an armistice with
the Germans; and that the King never signed the treaty.[6]

The dinner was very elegant, quite the most chic thing we have had
in Paris. I liked the crowd that is with him. His colleague, Mišu,[7] is
extremely pleasant—a wonderful philologist (Greek) they say and a
fine linguist. Bratianu himself speaks no English and talked French to
us. He is more formal and dignified than most of the statesmen we
have met. I took good care in addressing him always to say, "M. le
Président," which is I noticed the term used by Clemenceau (short for
M. le Président du Conseil). We shall have to give him a good dinner
when we return the hospitality. He is evidently anxious to conciliate
the United States, and feels himself a little in wrong with the Europeans. I enclose a copy of a memorandum I drew up of the details of
the conversation.

. . .

Memorandum of conversation with M. Bratianu, January 31, 1919

The conversation took place before, during, and after dinner on the
evening of Friday, January 31, at the house of M. Bratianu, 77

6. When military affairs in Rumania were going badly for the Allies in 1917, General Henri Mathias Bertholet (1861–1931), French military strategist, reorganized the
Rumanian Army. (He later served on the Supreme War Council.) Even this failed to
stop a German offensive and on December 6 Rumania asked for a truce. The later
charge that the Allies did nothing to aid Rumania, at the moment of Caporetto and
the second Russian revolution, ignores the British attack at the third battle of Ypres
and the French attack at Verdun, neither of which admittedly was able to score more
than local gains. Seymour believed, however, Rumania's military collapse did prevent
the House-Grey Memorandum from becoming effective in stopping the war.
7. Nicolae Mišu (1858–1925), diplomat and politician, held numerous ambassadorial posts before the war. At Paris he was the second Rumanian delegate, Bratianu
being the first, until replaced by General Constantin Coanda.

Avenue des Champs Elysées, to which he had invited Major D. W. Johnson, Dr. Day, and Dr. Seymour.

We found M. Bratianu just returned from the conference held at the Quai d'Orsay on the question of the Banat, and we were thus able to secure his immediate reaction. He spoke frankly of the method in which the conference of the afternoon had been held. He is evidently disturbed by the fact that representatives of the smaller nationalities are being called before the representatives of the five great powers, to whom he referred constantly as his judges. He seems to feel that there is danger of the conference dividing itself into a central bureau of the Great Powers which would bring up before it the cases of the smaller nations. This is quite different from the idea of the League of Nations as the Rumanians believe it to have been conceived by President Wilson.

M. Bratianu feels that he has not been well treated by England, France, or Italy, and that they have shown little consideration toward him since his arrival in Paris. He expected to be treated as the representative of an allied power which had suffered and fought for the cause of liberty; instead he finds that Rumania is regarded as one of the litigants in a trial.

He says that the only cordial treatment he has received has been from representatives of the United States. He evidently appreciated the interview that was given him by Colonel House and says that it is the only bright moment of his stay in Paris. He did not conceal his disappointment at the fact that he was unable to see either Mr. Wilson or Mr. Lansing.

He is not willing to discuss the case of Rumania at length with France, England, or Italy, because he feels that the case was fairly presented three years ago and the justice of Rumanian claims recognized. He is ready at all times, however, to discuss the justice of the position which he has taken with the representatives of the United States, for he recognizes that their country is in a different position.

M. Bratianu like other representatives of small nations is distinctly opposed to the method of considering territorial questions which was put into force this week at the Quai d'Orsay. He feels that it is absolutely impossible to present a case fairly in a brief afternoon session, and he does not believe that the prime ministers and foreign secretaries of the five Great Powers are competent to decide the merits of any issue after such a hearing. He complains frankly that the assembled statesmen did not pay close attention. What is necessary, he said, is to have his case heard by specialists who already understand the many issues involved, who will present their conclusions to the Commissioners; but it is necessary, he went on, that the Commissioners should listen to the specialists.

It was suggested by Senator Dragicesco[8] who was present that it might be advisable to form small subcommittees composed of the experts of each power who should hear the arguments of the smaller nations interested in territorial claims. To this M. Bratianu assented as a general principle, but repeated later that he would not argue his case in full before any committee but one representing the United States.

M. Bratianu evidently felt that the Serbs had argued their case unfairly before the conference, alleging that they had introduced unimportant and unrelated details which had no direct bearing on the settlement of the Banat, and which had only the effect of confusing the Commissioners.

M. Bratianu feels that the Treaty of 1916 [Bucharest] still holds good and that France, England, and Italy are still bound by it. He says that this treaty was consummated after months of discussion and that the territorial claims of Rumania were recognized only after long negotiations at Petrograd in which Russia played the role of protector of Serbia. If those claims were recognized as good in 1916, surely there is no need of discussing them further now with the representatives of the Allied Powers. It was on the promise that Rumania should receive the territory indicated in the treaty that Rumania had entered the war, in which, incidentally, she had been left to bear the

8. Dmitrie Dragicesco, statesman and author.

brunt of the German attack, the Allies failing completely to comply with the military conditions of the treaty. Rumania had signed an armistice with Germany only after receiving advice from the Allies that this course was most favorable to the common interest. The peace negotiations with Germany had been dragged on with personal danger to the King, and the King himself had never actually signed that treaty. The moment the Rumanians learned that General Berthelot was on the Danube, they resumed the offensive against the Germans. In his opinion, therefore, the Treaty of 1916 is as good as ever.

M. Bratianu reiterated his willingness to discuss Rumania's territorial claims with the United States. However, he demands the entire Banat on the ground that it is a geographical and economic unit, and that in the Banat as a whole Rumanians are the most numerous single element. He lays great stress upon the economic necessity of the mouth of the Maros for Rumania. He says that the Maros reaches far back into Transylvania and that it is an absolutely essential means of communication between the mountains of Transylvania and Rumania proper.

He also lays stress on the fact that the Rumanians and the Serbs have always lived at peace with each other and that this results largely from the fact that they have been separated by the Danube. If the Serbs are once allowed to possess territory to the north of the Danube, conflicts between them and the Rumanians will, he fears, become inevitable. The ethnic claim of the Serbs to the Banat he regards as untenable, and he believes that they will receive in the Bačka all the agricultural and cereal land that they need.[9] To the north of the Banat and in Bukovina the Rumanian frontier, he believes, should follow the lines of the Treaty of 1916, including within Rumania such cities as Arad, Grosswardein, Békés, and Békészaba, but excluding Debrecin.[10] He disputes the accuracy of the Hungarian statistics and thus

9. The Bačka and Bukovina districts are fertile plains lying in northeastern Yugoslavia and northern Rumania, respectively.

10. The essence of the Rumanian proposal was to expand—by as much as 30 miles at the expense of Hungary and Yugoslavia—the entire arc of its western frontier. This move would have brought Rumania to the banks of the Tisza opposite Szeged in the

includes within the Rumanian frontier many districts which according to the Hungarian census are Magyar in character.

· · ·

Saturday morning was spent in conference organizing the exchange of views between ourselves and the British specialists. It was in regard to this that the President spoke to me on Wednesday and I have been working to get something started.[11] It is a matter of the utmost importance in facilitating and hastening the work of the Conference as a whole. Another thing which I have been working for is the organization of subcommissions to hear the territorial claims of the various nations. It has seemed to me so wasteful that the premiers and foreign ministers should listen to all the detail of the claims, which they cannot understand, and far better that the claims should be heard first by the specialists and then reported to the big men (or "Olympians" as the British, and now we, call them).

I heard tonight that this plan seems to have been approved and that the Conference (technically the "Commissioners of the Five Powers") has appointed a commission to hear the Rumanian claims. Clive and I have been appointed to represent the United States. It means a big advance toward doing real business. Saturday evening, from 8 until 1, I passed in conference considering British proposals. We hold a meeting with their specialists on Monday morning.

Today we have spent visiting the American battlefields, Château-Thierry, Belleau Wood, Vaux. We have had a splendid day, both in weather and interest. We started at 8, in an army automobile with

---

center of the arc, and of the Danube opposite Belgrade, Yugoslavia, at the southern extremity. Eventually this proposal was rejected and the Banat was divided, approximately one-third going to Yugoslavia and two-thirds to Rumania. As is so often the case, this compromise satisfied neither disputant but their mutual enmity abated in common disgust at the Conference and in common interests against Hungary.

11. This suggestion of correlation of studies with the British was one of the origins of the territorial commissions which postdated the commissions on the League of Nations, responsibility for the war, international labor legislation, etc., most of which were organized at the January 25 session. Wilson's suggestion was acted upon only informally in light of the establishment of the Commission on Czechoslovakia on February 5. A similar group to handle Rumanian, and later Yugoslav, affairs was organized on February 1 and enlarged on February 18.

my friend Lieutenant Waters in charge. There were three of us, Clive, Lybyer, and myself, and they asked us if we would mind taking a lady correspondent for the *Christian Herald* along. As the army furnishes the trip we could hardly refuse, and she turned out to be a very good sport, young and not at all bad looking. It is cold, of course, very cold for Paris, it seemed to me, and the snow of last week is about an inch or so deep. Also the army chauffeurs drive like Jehu, which on narrow and slippery roads, with cows and pedestrians who instinctively choose the path the automobile is taking, makes it nervous work.

We drove out the main road to Châlons, and in less than an hour were at Claye, which was the furthest point reached by the Germans in 1914. Thence to La Ferté sous Jouarre where Sir John French[12] turned them back definitely, and on to Meaux. There for the first time we found signs of heavy shellfire. But earlier, within an hour of Paris, the trees have been cut down to give the artillery free range, and just out of Meaux there are the trenches which were dug last July in preparation for a retreat; all the tactical points, such as woods and farms, points to be used as machine-gun nests, are strung around with wire. About a quarter of an hour out of Meaux we reached the headquarters of General Bundy.[13]

Very soon after, we came to Torcy, which is the point where the Americans held the line—thence south to Vaux. Here the houses are badly shattered by shellfire, many absolutely crushed, many with their walls fallen, showing the furnished rooms, some with round holes about six feet in diameter in them. The ground is all pockmarked with shell-holes, from three to ten feet across. The road runs down a shallow valley for half a mile or so and one sees on the right a wooded hill, rising very sharply, about half the height of East Rock [New Haven], steep but not precipitous. This is Belleau Wood. We got out of the car here and went up it. It is almost impossible to be-

12. Sir John Denton Pinkstone French, first Earl of Ypres (1862–1925), was commander-in-chief of the Home Forces and, in 1918, became Lord Lieutenant of Ireland.
13. General Omar Bundy (1861–1940) commanded the 2nd Division, American Expeditionary Force, and was one of the heroes of Belleau Wood.

lieve that our men could have stormed it, considering the steepness
and the thickness of the undergrowth. Even now in winter it is hard
climbing except on more or less beaten paths, and there are the worst
brambles I have ever seen, with thorns half an inch long—worse than
barbed wire.

There are all sorts of evidences of fighting. The rain has washed
away the earth in places and almost our first sight was the skeleton of
a German; in other places feet were sticking out of shallow graves.
There were lots of unexploded hand grenades, which we left alone,
and all sorts of bits and pieces of equipment. I picked up several
things, mindful of Gladys' advice to get relics for the children—part
of a German gas mask, a small splinter of shell from a tree, a German
drinking cup, and a Springfield rifle. The fact that they came from
Belleau alone makes them interesting. The saplings are all cut down
to five feet by shellfire and only the big trees and the undergrowth is
standing. Our losses were terrible, we were told, and there are at
least four American cemeteries standing in the vicinity; but it was
worth it, for the Germans were consolidating here and, if they had
held, could have dominated the valley on July 15, whereas our capture of it made possible our advance on July 18. One cemetery was
made up of men of the New England Division, mostly of the 104th,
but some of the 102nd (New Haven's old 2nd Regiment.) H., you
remember, was in the 104th.[14]

We went down the road to Bouresches and Vaux. This road lay in
no-man's-land between the lines, but most of the shells went over it
and it has been repaired. The foxholes where the Germans dug themselves in, covered with branches, are still in perfect shape. The Germans held the railroad embankment along the side of the road at
Bouresches until the big advance, and their holes are on one side,
while on the other are the foxholes made by the Americans, either in
their raids in no-man's-land or when they started the advance. Waters
was not in this fight (he was with General Gouraud, up the Marne),

14. Harold Ludington Hemingway (1893–1918), Yale '14, was an infantry captain killed on October 21 in France. He was Samuel B. Hemingway's cousin.

but he told us of the advance behind the barrage at very slow walk, and the rushing of the enemy position when the drumfire lifted.

We motored through Vaux on to Château-Thierry where we got an excellent lunch at a hotel I remember from 17 years back; after lunch we went over the bridge where the Americans covered the retreat of the French in June with their machine-gun fire until the French had crossed the river, when it was blown up; there is a temporary bridge there now. Opposite the bridge the houses are pitted by machine-gun and 75 mm. fire. La Fontaine has a bit of his leg shot off;[15] further on in the square the houses are a mass of ruins. It was up this street that the Americans had to fight when they took the whole town on July 21. The Germans had cut a hole in the clock of the Hôtel de Ville and put a machine gun there which swept the square and street for a quarter of a mile. In the hotel dining room the walls are filled with rifle and machine-gun holes, and a shell came through the second story.

We motored up on the hills to the north to get a view of the Marne Valley, and found great captured dumps of munitions. Most of the shells were unexploded but we explored some old German gun emplacements and picked up a lot of exploded 77 shell cases, and took them along. They will serve for vases, if you want, although they are of steel and not brass. We came back to Vaux which is an absolute ruin. They say there are two families living in it now, but I don't know where. The Americans concentrated heavy artillery on it for 24 hours, then rushed it with infantry and before the Germans could come out from the cellars had it, with losses of 7 men and 25 captured. The town is a mass of ruins, all simply caved in, nothing left. It is the most striking picture of what artillery does that I have seen. We explored some ruins, found remains of German bullets, bits of equipment, etc.

We left Belleau on one side coming back (you remember that it

15. Jean de LaFontaine (1621–1695) was the famed French poet and author whose statute stands in Château-Thierry, his birthplace.

was at Belleau Wood that John Overton was killed)[16] and came on to
the line followed by Kluck in 1914. There are still many trenches of
those early days of the first German advance, cut in the formal style,
the German echelon fashion and the French zigzag, very shallow, and
quite out of date we were told. It was very interesting to follow the
country down which the Germans advanced, but naturally far less
so than the earlier part of the day. We got back at five, just at dark.

Forgive this hastily written letter, which I am too tired to correct
carefully. I am going to bed at once, for last night was late and I have
lots of stuff on for tomorrow.

Saturday, February 8, 1919

I am ashamed indeed that I have allowed all this time to go by without writing, but it seems to be the first chance that I have had all
week. It has been the busiest week of my life; and there have been
various worries resulting from an attempt to knife me on the part of
a person I won't name here, which took a good deal of time. I am
glad to say that my worries about the underground fight are all over,
and that my position has been strengthened by the incident.

I suppose that I can now call myself a sort of diplomatist, since
most of my work this week has been in the exchange of views with
representatives of other powers. Monday was entirely taken up with
an initial conference with the representatives of the British Foreign
Office. Our relations with the British, who are the only people here
who are not playing chauvinistic politics (a fact that it took Wilson
about a week to discover), are so close that we are exchanging views
with absolute frankness on the territorial settlement of Europe. This
does not mean that we are forming any arrangements to support the
policies of each other without reserve; but simply that we come as
close to agreement as possible on every question and push the Conference to act as rapidly as possible.

16. John Williams Overton (1894–1918), Yale '17, was a marine lieutenant; in
college he was an outstanding runner.

I think that Clemenceau is playing the honest game. The French Foreign Office, however, is not trustworthy and the Italians decide nothing without a view to their own particular selfish interests. The British, like ourselves, are trying to get an arrangement which will offer the best chance of long peace; if we can work together, there is a good chance of getting the best possible settlement. This is the point of view taken by Wilson and Lloyd George, and we very soon found that it was not only possible but very pleasant to work with the British.

The men we met with on Monday are permanent officials of the British Foreign Office. I had always heard that they represented much that was best in the British system of government, and after meeting with them this week I am much impressed by their capacity, strength of character, and honesty. Their pride in the tradition of honesty in British foreign relations is one of their chief characteristics. We met with Sir William Tyrrell, who is K.C.M.G., C.B., etc., and chief assistant to the superintending ambassador; Sir Eyre Crowe, also K.C.M.G., etc., Sir Esme Howard, Sir Louis Mallet, Headlam-Morley, and Akers-Douglas.[17] It seemed rather ridiculous for amateurs like ourselves to sit with these professionals; but we seem to be the best that the United States government has been able to produce. As a matter of fact both Haskins and Day are as good as any of them, though not familiar with diplomatic procedure.

The British were as cordial as an experienced Newfoundland to a puppy, and we were able to get down to business at once. We sepa-

17. William George Tyrrell, 1st Baron of Avon (1868–1947), a career diplomat, was private secretary to Sir Edward Grey in the Foreign Office. From 1919 to 1928 he served as assistant, then Permanent Under-Secretary of State at the Foreign Office, and then went to Paris as the British ambassador. Sir Eyre Crowe (1864–1925) was another career diplomat who preceded Tyrrell as Permanent Under-Secretary, 1920–25. At Paris Harold Nicolson served directly under him. Esme William Howard, 1st Baron of Penrith (1883–1939), had already completed a long succession of diplomatic assignments at home and abroad before the war. Afterward he became ambassador to Spain, 1919–24, and to the United States, 1924–30. Sir Louis dePan Mallet (1864–1936) preceded Tyrrell as Grey's secretary and served briefly as ambassador to Turkey. Sir James Wycliffe Headlam-Morley (1863–1929) was an educator who entered the Political Intelligence Bureau during the war. Arestas Akers-Douglas (1876–1947) was Lord Curzon's diplomatic secretary. Later he served as Great Britain's ambassador to Russia and is credited with establishing a successful *modus vivendi* with the Soviet leaders.

rated into small groups, each man discussing different areas with his opposites. The plan has been to set first the ideal boundaries of the enemy countries, Germany, German-Austria, Hungary, and Bulgaria, then Turkey (which is going to have pretty restricted boundaries).

So far as German boundaries are concerned I am responsible for only a small line, that separating Germany from Bohemia, and this has been very easily fixed up. When it comes to the boundaries of German-Austria, however, there is an enormous stretch of territory to be considered; and as for Hungary, her boundaries bring in the question of the frontiers of the Slovaks, Rumanians, and Jugoslavs. It has been regarded as important to finish up our conferences and get our reports finished and recommendations made before Wilson goes back next week; so there has been need for hurry and constant labor. Of course these conferences with the British are unofficial in character and their results will not be presented to the big conference; they will only affect (we hope) the attitude of the American and British Commissioners.

Wednesday morning I was busy getting ready for the secret session of the premiers and foreign ministers in the afternoon which I was told to attend.[18] Beneš and Kramárz were to present the Czech case. We had lunch with Beneš before we went over to the Quai d'Orsay. He is a delightful little chap, just as friendly and as moderate as one could wish. The only question is whether he will be able to last, because he is caught at home between the extreme chauvinists who want to grab everything in sight and have been making bad trouble with the Poles, and the socialists and labor leaders.

We went over to the Quai d'Orsay right after lunch. I sat immediately behind Wilson and Lansing, having discovered that it is convenient to prompt them when the man talking is making absurd statements and to give them maps and statistics explanatory of the material that is being discussed. I had been warned that they did not

18. To hear the Czechs state their case. For Seymour's views on the background, see his "Austria-Hungary in 1914," *Saturday Review of Literature, 3* (April 16, 1927), 370.

like to have too much told them; but I found them very grateful for everything that I said and very genial. Once Wilson got up and called me into a corner to explain a point; Lansing turned around several times to ask me a question. Once it was very humorous, for he asked me to point out something on the map before him; I had to stand up between him and Wilson, and Lloyd George leaned over and said: "I say, what's that?" So I had to repeat in a fairly loud voice; there was Beneš talking to the Commission and there was I six feet away from him explaining to Wilson, Lansing, and Lloyd George. You would have been amused.

I have as good a souvenir of the secret sessions as one could want. Lansing draws all the time the session goes on, with his left hand, caricatures and grotesque figures, really very well done. When one is finished he drops it on the floor and begins another. I picked up a couple and gave one to Dulles, to get him to sign it as done during the conference. Lloyd George was filled with admiration for the drawings: "I say," he said, "could I have one of those; they're awfully good." So Lansing gave him one and he folded it carefully and put it in his pocket with gratitude.

Lloyd George is really the best fun of these conferences; very alert, not knowing much about things in exact terms; passing comments in a loud undertone without cessation, regardless of whether they are complimentary or not. He reminds me of a very businesslike bird. He is much shorter and fatter than I had realized. Balfour is "diplomatic" in manner, rather "sweet," apt to be very sleepy. Of course the translator, Mantoux, is always a joy. He puts more spirit into his translations than the principal puts into his original speech. Mantoux never says, "Mr. Beneš claims this territory on the ground of historic rights." He says, "We feel by virtue of our noble history, etc.," with his voice shaking with emotion and fervor.

Beneš presented his case very well, I thought, but it took three hours, and poor Kramář, who wanted to speak, was not allowed to. When he asked for half an hour, Clemenceau said, "O, we'll appoint a special commission and you can talk to them for a couple of hours.

Now we had better have a cup of tea." Of course this rather irritated the delegates of the little powers. Bratianu said to me: "The fact that our case is of the greatest importance does not prevent the big men from going to sleep, and the fact that they go to sleep will not prevent them from judging."

In the evening we had the Rumanian delegation to dinner at the Crillon. They are a very genial lot, and I confess that their case seems much stronger than I had thought a fortnight ago. It is the only instance where I have been clearly influenced in favor of claims after personal contact with the claimants. Generally, I have been prejudiced against them by their extravagance. But I fear that considering the excited state of mind of the Serbs and the concessions which the latter will have to make to the Italians in the Slovene and Dalmatian area, the Rumanians cannot hope to get what they want in the Banat. Did you see that our government has recognized the Jugoslavs? As you know, I have been working for this since Christmas, and am very much pleased that it has gone through. The text of the declaration is exactly as we drew it up in this office. Clare came to dinner with the Rumanians, as he has been working on the Banat, and I think that he enjoyed it.

Thursday I was in conference with the British all day, taking lunch with Sir Eyre Crowe and Leeper at their hotel. Crowe is a delightful man. He has been in the Foreign Office for a long time, possibly all his career, and told us interesting things. He does not haggle over details, goes right to the heart of the issue, and is very tolerant of a differing point of view. As I said, the British are most objective in their attitude toward all territorial questions on the continent except one: the cession of the south bank of the Scheldt to Belgium; this they consider would endanger their safety, should Belgium again fall under the control of a first-class power. They don't like the French way of doing things and from what I know from various sources, I think that they are right. French politicians and functionaries as a class are absolutely selfish in their national aims and unscrupulous in their methods; and the influence of finance and business in politics, while concealed, is enormous and at times disgusting.

Friday morning I was busy preparing my reports on the boundaries we had discussed with the British, a work of some difficulty, for they have to be concise and yet fairly comprehensive. In the afternoon Clive and I went up to their headquarters again to talk over final points. We have now settled all the points on which we agree and disagree in the matter of the boundaries of Germany, German-Austria, and Hungary. We also exchanged views on the matter of Rumania frontiers, in order to be ready for the first meeting of the commission to consider Rumanian claims, which is to take place Saturday.

Sunday, February 9, 1919

We had the first meeting of the Rumanian Commission yesterday afternoon. Clive and I represented the United States, Sir Eyre Crowe and Leeper the British Empire, Tardieu and Laroche France, and Martino and Count Vannutelli Italy.[19] It was held in the big banquet hall of the Quai d'Orsay. Everything was very correct to be in harmony with the gilt and marble, mirrors and tapestries of the place. Each power was allowed to bring a private secretary; I hope that if Law has to wait here for a boat that I can use him as secretary in the meetings. I think that he would enjoy it and his French would be useful, for we insist on the bilingual principle in the meetings, the British and we speaking English and the French and Italians French. There are two interpreters, who translate as we talk, not so cleverly as Mantoux, but very well.

19. Jules Laroche (b. 1872), a French career diplomat, later headed the Commission for Revision of Treaties, then went to Poland in 1925 and to Belgium in 1935 as ambassador. Giacomo DeMartino (1868–1957) was head of the Italian Foreign Office and secretary-general of the Italian delegation. After the Conference he too held a series of ambassadorial appointments: Berlin, London, Tokyo, and Washington (1925–32). Count Louis Vannutelli-Rey (b. 1880) was secretary of the Italian Embassy in London and served later in numerous ambassadorial posts. In 1957 he became vice-president of the Center for International Reconciliation in Rome.

I was surprised to find how well my remarks, which sounded very crude in English, sounded when translated into French; there is a secretariat which makes notes and draws up a *procès-verbal* of the proceedings; it is rather terrifying that every word one speaks will go into the documentary report of the Peace Conference. There was a good deal of jockeying to begin with and a good deal of rather dirty work in maneuvering for position, so to speak. The British stood firmly with us in killing this and in getting down to honest work.

Tardieu was chosen chairman but had to go away, so the Italian, as vice-chairman, took his place. He began by assuming that we should start by collecting all the treaties upon which the Rumanian claims were based and discuss their validity. You see Italy wants to get the validity of the Rumanian secret treaty of 1916 brought forward and if possible recognized, so that her own secret treaty of 1915 will have a precedent for recognition. The Italian was supported by the French. Of course we Americans at once said that we could not enter into any discussion of the treaty whatsoever, that we had no official knowledge of its existence and could take no part in any commission which claimed to discuss its validity. This rather took the Italian's breath away, for I think that he thought we should be simple and as amateurs allow him to put through anything. He blustered a little (all in the most polite language), but we held to the fact that we had no instructions from our government and couldn't consider it.

Sir Eyre Crowe stood by us nobly (of course we were careful not to appear to be working together) and argued that if the treaty were valid no commission would have been appointed. The Conference would simply have decided that the treaty was good and Rumania's claims would have been recognized, ipso facto. After some talk the Italian said that he would pass over the question, reserving the right to return to it. (Clive and I, now that we regard ourselves as real diplomats, never make a statement to each other without "reserving the right to change our minds and having it clearly understood that we make no sacrifice of a general principle." So if I ask him to pass me a cigarette he will do so "reserving the right to refuse such assist-

ance upon a future occasion and insisting on the principle of his full
liberty in the matter of giving and refusing cigarettes.")

Thus we took the first trick, which we were sure of unless we had
been absolutely blind. But I mention the incident to show how one
must be on one's guard and how these Italians play politics. We then
proceeded to the discussion of definite territorial claims and really
got through quite a bit of work. The Frenchman Laroche made me
sore, for he didn't know much about the facts of the case and he insisted on making long and flowery speeches to go into the *procès-
verbal* on matters on which we were all quite agreed. On one point
we (the Americans) were in a minority which rather pleased me as
showing the others that we knew what we wanted to do. The only
trouble was that I had to represent our side of the case and it was a
side of which I personally disapproved, but had been overpersuaded
by Day, Johnson, and Lord.

We talked until nearly 6, when we adjourned into the next room to
take tea with real and very rich macaroons. What was my delight as
I took my cup to see, on the sofa on the other side of the room, Marshal Foch and his chief of staff who had been called in to advise the
War Council,[20] which was sitting in the room next to us. He has a
wonderful face—I watched him closely for ten minutes—is short,
rather heavy, and rather sloppy in appearance, slightly bald with thin
tousled hair, and smokes a very disreputable short cigar. The sleeves
of his uniform are covered with stars (the marshal's) but at a distance
of 15 feet one would never pick him for the generalissimo. I never
expected to be taking tea in the same room with Foch. I was not presented and did not like to ask to be, as he was waiting to to in to the
War Council. Later we happened to go out together, putting on our
coats at the same table. He attracts more attention than any other figure, even Wilson. I had a nice time with Count Vannutelli, who is
probably a trickster, being Italian, but is young and friendly. The

20. The Allied Supreme War Council continued to act on all matters of military
policy until January 10, 1920. General Bliss was the American representative; General
Sackville-West the British. Foch (1851–1929) was not a member.

Frenchman, Laroche, and I did not get along very well. Otherwise tea was very pleasant.

I suppose that the secret conferences of the Big Ten are at an end;[21] they have been good fun and I shall look back on them with pleasure. I forgot to say that two times I suggested points to Wilson which he used very skillfully.

Yesterday I had lunch with Coromilas, the Greek minister to Italy and formerly Venizelos' Foreign Minister.[22] He is a diplomat of the old type—very courtly, flattering and epigrammatic. Speaking of Clive he said (knowing that I would repeat it): "Ah, Day. Yes, he is clever, very clever." This delighted me, for he had said on another occasion knowing that Clive would tell me: "Ah, Seymour. Yes, he is very clever." There was no sense in having me to lunch, for I have no interest in Greek claims, but I think his business is officially to jolly Americans.

Of course I am delighted that Gladys is planning to come over at once. I think that territorial matters will be settled in time for us to get home in good season. Our weather has been cold this week and we have had more snow, but I hope that things moderate soon.

Saturday, February 15, 1919

Another week has nearly gone by without my sitting down to let you know how things are going. Everyone has a cold here, and the Paris cold seems to take it out of one more than any I have known. I

---

21. The occasion for this observation is not clear. The Council of Ten persisted until March, having met 72 times. By then the Ten seemed too cumbersome and too susceptible to press leaks, and at Clemenceau's behest the heads of government split away into a Council of Four (Japan choosing to sit in only when the discussion dealt with the Far East). This left the foreign ministers to meet as a Council of Five. The Five met 39 times; the Four (or Three while Orlando temporarily left the Conference) met 145 times. By contrast there were 7 plenary sessions and 1,646 meetings of the various commissions.

22. Lambros A. Coromilas (1854–1923), member of the Greek Peace Commission, had served before the war as minister to the United States. Afterward he represented Greece at the League of Nations and served as Minister of Finance under Venizelos.

am all right now and quite chipper, but yesterday I felt as shaky as if I had had typhoid. It is not influenza with me in any form, but a sort of bronchial trouble which is very vexing as it wakes me up several times during the night with the coughing. The military doctor here is a cheerful soul who asks if "you have been spitting blood" and if you have not, decides that you are all right, sends around salts and cough mixture and tells you to get well. He has one advantage, namely that he advocates the smoking of cigarettes—says it is good for all kinds of sickness. The weather has been abnormally cold for Paris and I think that accounts for my trouble.

Yesterday I had Gladys' cable saying that she was sailing on the 15th on the *Espagne*. I was naturally much upset at the difficulty she had with her passport. The whole business is absolutely typical of the State Department. As you may have gathered from my letters, the Inquiry has been put in charge here of matters relative to advice of Commissioners, and only Inquiry men have been put on commissions, such as the Rumanian and Greek. This has been a thorn in the flesh of the State Department people and they have got back at us in petty ways. This question of the wives' passports evidently offered them the chance they were looking for and they took advantage of it. We were told the passports would be furnished within 72 hours. Some underling with spite in his soul simply omitted the names of all wives except those of State Department officials. The incapacity, the pettiness, and the red tape of our government institutions, whether military or civil, combined with the favoritism, simply passes comprehension. I have had to give up being sore at it, or I should be a mere bundle of nerves.

You would not believe the waste and inefficiency going on here connected with the Commission. Routine offices of little importance are vastly overmanned with proportionate expense, while important divisions are left without adequate clerical assistance. The cost is so great that an investigation is being started; but instead of sending home some of the army of military do-nothings they are giving us cheaper correspondence paper and firing stenographers.

All I can say is that I thank the Lord that I belong to a college faculty whose methods are perhaps unscientific but who don't get snarled up in red tape, and who can accomplish things with decent economy and efficiency. Well, I mustn't get in a state over it, for I have all the help I need here and am allowed to play far more of a part in the work of the Conference than I ever expected would be the case.

Just now all my time is being given to the commission to hear Rumanian claims. We had our second meeting on Tuesday, with Tardieu presiding, and thrashed out the question of the boundary of Transylvania. We couldn't hope to finish it up, of course, but we found out each other's views and have arrived at a fairly close approximation of where we think the line ought to be drawn. It is I and not Clive who has studied this part of the line particularly closely, so I had to do most of the talking. Our point of view is that all the land that is really Magyar in character ought to be left to the Hungarians; the French admit our principle in general but would give Rumania far more than we propose in order to include certain railroad lines which they think Rumania needs. The British stand about half-way between us. The Italians have not yet shown their hand clearly. The discussions are interesting as we all of us know the question pretty well and on this part of the field I think the French and probably the Italians have no national interests and are playing fair.

One has to be far more polite and diplomatic than in an ordinary committee. If the French make a proposition which is perfectly rotten and the chairman asks your opinion, you can't say "I don't like it," but rather: "At the present moment I feel that my government would have some hesitation in accepting the proposition of the French without reserve; may I suggest that a modification in the following sense would perhaps provide for a settlement which might, in the eyes of the inhabitants concerned, appear more equitable." I find that I am losing all capacity to say just plain "no" or "yes"; it has to be, "I should be rather slow to agree," or, "at the present moment I should feel inclined to concur."

We are now ready to get down to brass tacks and study the details of our proposals, and I hope that we can finish up in ten days. There was to have been a meeting this afternoon, but Tardieu had to go away and Martino, the Italian, was sick; so it was postponed until Monday. Tardieu makes an excellent chairman, very anxious to avoid all unnecessary talk, and businesslike in his procedure. He and I had a pleasant chat on Yale, where he got an honorary degree in 1917. He is one of the big men of France now, and I should say one of the strongest of the younger men. The Americans who have come in close contact with him in his capacity as Commissioner for Franco-American Affairs say that he is too clever and has stung us on various economic deals, but he is very cordial and delightful in manner.

I find that membership on the Commission has conferred a public distinction which was hitherto lacking. You see it is the first international appointment for me. The State Department people are much vexed to see these jobs go to the amateurs, but really our system of government is such that there are no State Department people who could hold their own when it comes to command of facts; this sounds rather egotistic, but the small roster of regulars simply doesn't know enough.

Wilson left last night. The carrying through of the League of Nations was a great triumph for him, and, considering the difficulties which he faced on arrival, really a great piece of diplomacy.[23] It would never have been carried had he himself not come over, and the feeling here is that it will be hard to put through a satisfactory peace treaty unless he comes back. Of course the assistance of the British was invaluable and in many ways the League, as drafted, was largely the work of Lord Robert Cecil, who is a very strong man. Wilson's prestige is on the whole as high or higher than two months ago, although he has drawn down upon himself the wrath of the French official class and of the French imperialist business interests. With them the United States is not popular now. We are fighting their exaggerated claims for an impossible indemnity from Germany,

23. The third plenary session approved the initial draft of the Covenant of the League on February 14.

which would lead to complete economic collapse in Germany, and their demands for a boycott of German trade until the devastated districts of France are built up again.

One thing sticks in my gorge and that is that the French are still holding up the large supplies of food collected for Germany. If they are sent in they will be paid for in gold, and there will be so much less gold left for an indemnity; so the French refuse to let it go in. This strikes me as calculated barbarism and you would think so if you could read the telegrams I do of starving women and children. Bullitt has just come back from Berne where he saw what he calls the most pathetic sight of his life: 500 children of Vienna sent to Switzerland for three weeks to get food and a decent living. All the children of Berne were down at the station to meet them. He said the Austrians were mere skeletons, absolutely green from undernutrition. We have lots of stuff to send in to Austria, but the French won't let it go in. I have the most pitiful letters from Walter Davis, who is in Vienna with the Coolidge Mission, of the conditions there; lots of luxuries, but not a bit of coal or much bread or cotton cloth; in the maternity hospitals they have to put the babies, just born, in old newspapers.

It is the merest luck that I am not now on my way to Poland. I was called up the other day to be told that the President had appointed me to the commission which is to settle the scrap between the Poles and Czechs in Teschen. I didn't mind particularly until I remembered that this commission was instructed to proceed to the spot, which is just west of Cracow and if you look it up on your map you will find that it is quite a way from Paris, in fact on the frontier of what was Russia in 1914. This didn't please me much, with Gladys about to arrive; I pointed out that I was already on the Rumanian Commission, but they told me that a substitute could be found for that; but that I was the only man who knew anything about Teschen and would have to go. It really looked serious for a time; it would have been an interesting and important job, but I wanted to stay in Paris. Furthermore, the work that I am doing here is more interesting and more important. I had to put up rather strenuous protest to get out of the commission for Teschen, but I finally managed it.

I think that I see a let-up in the work coming. The Rumanian Commission should have its report ready soon. There is a Czechoslovak commission to be appointed and a Jugoslav commission and of course if I am on either of those I shall continue to be busy. But if not, when the Rumanian Commission finishes its report I shall not have much beyond ordinary routine to do and shall take things easy. We have got to hurry up and sign a treaty pretty soon and get the enemy delegates here; when they arrive I shall be very busy with the counterclaims they will undoubtedly put up, but which I think we shall dispose of rather summarily. If I were guessing I should say that the preliminary treaty ought to be settled by then; of course no one can guess now how long they are going to bicker over economic questions or the international control of rivers and railways, and colonial matters. But the commissions are working hard over these and will be forced to come to some decision within a decent length of time. I think that Wilson's return will hurry things up.

It has become so much milder these last two days that I can almost smell spring when I put my nose out of the window. And spring days in Paris, at least when the sun shines, are—as I remember—wonderful. I am hoping that I can take a rest now from seeing people. I have met most of the interesting personalities with whom I could hope to get in touch, have shaken hands with the various prime ministers and foreign ministers and shall probably never get further. Venizelos is the one man I look forward to seeing and talking to. Of course I am now cut off from close personal relations with the Rumanians, by reason of being on the commission to adjudicate their claims. And the last two weeks have been so busy that I have not had time to see other nationalities.

THE BUSY INTERIM

February 22—March 16, 1919

EVEN BEFORE President Wilson sailed for America, Lloyd George went to London to handle domestic problems in the form of labor riots. A few days later Clemenceau was temporarily incapacitated by an attempt on his life. Despite the absence of the "Big Three" the work of the Conference seemed to accelerate markedly during late February and early March. One cause was the growing realization that settlement with Germany could not be postponed indefinitely. The third renewal of the armistice in mid-March and the tightening of the screws on Germany by the Supreme Council, out of concern over the purposes of the Weimar government, brought this awareness to sharp focus. Another cause, of course, was that the Conference had at long last discovered a reasonable working organization in the many commissions.

During this period the idea of a preliminary peace with Germany, something akin to the French suggestion which Wilson had ignored, once more came to the fore. Now it seemed even more logical and desirable to settle with the principal enemy before trying to solve all of the large and complicated questions which had emerged from the war and which threatened to push the German question to the side. By mid-March military terms had been drawn up and tentative decisions on two major territorial issues had even been reached: there would not be a separate Rhineland republic and there would be a Polish corridor. But on many other related issues, notably reparations, agreement seemed almost unobtainable.

The full-scale operation of the commissions on a scheduled basis and with established objectives meant a change toward some order in Seymour's personal routine—previously he had to jump from one rush job to another probably unrelated one—but it also meant, if anything, more intensive labors. This fact and the arrival of Mrs. Seymour in France meant that he had less time for letter writing. The frequency of his correspondence decreased markedly. The new emphasis on Germany itself made him very much aware of the difficulty of reaching any fair or, in the American tradition, generous peace as long as the spirit of hatred was alive. "We were hampered," he later wrote," by the atmosphere of Paris, where German guilt was assumed as a proved fact. Everyone was afraid of being called a pro-German."

Back in Washington the new Senate was given something quite concrete to discuss when Wilson arrived with a copy of the draft Covenant. It lost little time in voicing its displeasure. Wilson met with the Foreign Relations Committee, but confident and intransigent as always he made no effort to compromise beyond the possibility of seeking to insert a reservation regarding the Monroe Doctrine into the final draft. Far from gaining Senate support his visit produced the "Round-Robin" signed by 39 Senators who declared that the establishment of peace should be separated from, and completed before, the creation of the League. Wilson did, however, receive favorable endorsements for the League from 34 of 36 state legislatures and 33 governors. Buttressed by this evidence, on the eve of his return voyage to France he defied the senators and asserted once again that peace and the League were inseparable.

American Commission to Negotiate Peace
4 Place de la Concorde, Paris

Saturday, February 22, 1919

I made a bad guess when I counted on finishing up the bulk of my work this week, for things are getting more rather than less complicated. The Big Ten decided on Monday that Jugoslav claims should be referred to our Rumanian Commission, which really makes of this commission the body to turn in recommendations on most of the Balkan boundaries. Then yesterday I received word that I was senior (!) American delegate on the commission to hear Czechoslovak claims. So I shall have my hands full for a good three weeks. Fortunately for me, though unfortunately for justice, the Italians refused to allow the contest between themselves and the Jugoslavs to be fought out anywhere except before the Big Ten; so our commission is spared that difficulty. As it is, my work seems cut out for me, for I am now on the commissions which report on the boundaries of Rumania, Czechoslovakia, Serbia, Hungary, and German-Austria, all those boundaries being included in the mandates of the two commissions. It is far more important than any work I expected to be called upon to do over here, and I am naturally much pleased, although it involves a certain nervous strain.

All the other first delegates (of Great Britain, Italy, and France) have the rank of ministers plenipotentiary, and as I am now on a diplomatic equality with them, I regard myself as a "person of no little importance." Second delegates (I am second delegate on the Rumanian Commission) have the rank of counsellors of embassy in the other countries. I do not yet know the composition of the French and Italian representation on the Czechoslovak Commission. The British first delegate is Sir Joseph Cook, former Prime Minister of New South Wales;[1] and the second delegate my friend Harold Nicolson. Our first meeting is on Wednesday, but I have had to prepare much material for it and this is my chief excuse for delaying my letter for so long. I am going to have Lester Perrin appointed as United States secretary to the Czechoslovak Commission.

Naturally everyone has been much upset by the attack on Clemenceau and although the news is good, we are still nervous.[2] His loss would be a disaster, for he is the one strong man who can hold power in France now and I believe that he has been working sincerely and honestly for a just peace. In certain matters his opinion has naturally

1. Sir Joseph Cook (1860–1947), English-born statesman and Liberal politician, held numerous governmental posts in his adopted Australia, starting in 1894. He served as both Prime Minister and Minister of Home Affairs from 1913 to 1914. While representing Australia at the Conference he was Minister of the Navy; later he was senior delegate to the League of Nations.
2. Clemenceau (1841–1929) was shot and seriously wounded on February 19. The would-be assassin, Emile Cottin, an unbalanced youth with communist ties, was sentenced to death. President Poincaré commuted this penalty to ten years of solitary confinement.

been different from ours; but he was straight, and most of the French politicians are not. In essential matters I think that he had come around largely to our point of view. Tardieu told me this morning that he was doing well, but had overtired himself trying to work and could not see people. I talked with a soldier who came on the scene just after the shots were fired, and said that the anarchist was nearly lynched. It shows the robustness of the man when you remember his age and consider that apparently the shock of the attack has not affected him at all.

He was on his way, when shot, to a conference here with Balfour and House, to try and arrange a speeding up of affairs. Things are going rather more rapidly, but so much time was lost in January through unbusinesslike procedure that some decided effort must be made to work at lightning speed now. House came around yesterday to tell us of the necessity of haste. They are anxious to get all the reports of the committees whose work concerns Germany finished up in two weeks' time. That will give a week or so to polish them up before Wilson comes back in the middle of March, and they want to call the German delegates in before the end of March. I don't see how this is possible, but I still believe that the treaty with Germany can be signed by the middle of April, unless unforeseen circumstances arise.

Le Havre, France

Monday, February 24, 1919

I was stopped, and here I am at Le Havre waiting for Gladys. Forgive the pencil, but I am keeping a carbon copy of my letters so as to have some sort of record here. The *Espagne* is due to come in this afternoon, but so far they have not received word of the exact hour of her landing; I hope to know by noon and trust that it will be early enough to let us get to Paris tonight. I have commission meetings tomorrow and the next day; I can be away tomorrow, if necessary, but ought to be at the first Czechoslovak meeting on Wednesday morning.

I have had several pleasant and interesting dinners this past week, largely owing to the fact that now that I am sitting on these commissions I don't have to see the representatives of the little nationalities as often as I did last month. We are judging their case and therefore wouldn't want to be seen too much with them. Thursday night I had dinner with Trubee Davison, who came up from Cannes with his father, who is planning a great development of the International Red Cross. I talked with Mr. Davison on the phone for a minute; he was very cordial and asked Gladys and me to come and visit them at Cannes. I wish we could! Trubee told me all about his father's plans for putting a glass case over the old gentlemen who now hibernate at Geneva in charge of the International Red Cross and of establishing a live board which will be the clearing-house for all the medical, sanitary, and surgical experiments made in any country of the world. It is a great conception and I told Trubee that I thought it would do more to foster an international spirit and prevent war than the League of Nations. He evidently told his father, for I had a letter from Mr. Davison asking me to give him my opinion of his plan in writing.

Friday night I dined with Phil Platt.[3] He is to organize a course of lectures on public health throughout the big cities of France and seems very enthusiastic over the prospect. He is quite bald and very old in manner. It was difficult to believe that I used to teach him history (back in 1912). He had with him a bottle of sparkling Sauterne which he brought into the dining room and which seemed the best wine I had ever tasted; but it gave me the worst indigestion I ever had (for about half an hour).

Yesterday I had lunch with Mr. Lansing and Vance McCormick, at the Ritz, on Allen Dulles' invitation. I find it hard to make up my

3. Philip Skinner Platt (b. 1889), Yale '12, served first with the Belgian Relief Commission and in 1917 was assigned to Petrograd to assist in prisoner-of-war relief. He then transferred to the American Red Cross in Paris. Next he was commissioned a lieutenant in the Sanitary Corps and became an instructor in the A.E.F. University of Beaune. Back in civilian life he became executive director of the Palama Settlement of Honolulu and of the Lighthouse of the New York Association for the Blind.

mind about Lansing; he has seemed to me stupid and to take no interest in having an effective department, and he certainly knew little or nothing of conditions over here when he came over.[4] But I will say that somehow or other he seems to have picked up a general idea of what everything is about. He has not been well. He was very genial. He said that the Germans were planning to come to Versailles with demands for enormous indemnities for the loss incurred in Germany as a result of illegal blockade! McCormick favors taking all the art treasures of Berlin, Dresden, and Vienna and holding them as collateral. He believes that Germany must not be pushed too hard now because of the danger of anarchy; he also thinks that she is certain to get economic control of Russia in the future, unless we Americans make a very bold, decided, and intelligent bid. I talked with him on reorganization at Yale for some time; he is on the Corporation. He is a very fine man and very intelligent, but I think it unfortunate that men who know so little about a university or college should have the power to reorganize Yale so completely at the present time.

Saturday I had lunch with the British Foreign Office people, and we drew up the terms to be incorporated in the treaty with Germany regarding her frontier. The treaty as a whole is now being drafted. If boundaries were all that had to be considered we could call in the German delegates next week. Unfortunately economic questions are far from being decided. The fight has been as to whether Germany should pay the total cost of the war or only for the damage caused by her aggression. I think that Balfour and House have broken the deadlock. House told the Reparations Commission to stop quibbling over a definition. The French could call it an "indemnity," the British "war-costs," and the Belgians "reparations." The important thing, seeing that Germany has only so much she can pay, was to find out how much that is and then decide how it is to be distributed.

Of course the delegates from German-Austria and Hungary cannot be called in before our various commissions have reported. The Ger-

4. These observations, wrote Seymour later, reflected "unconscious arrogance."

man delegates will probably come first and alone. In any case German-Austria will not be allowed to unite with Germany before peace
treaties are signed. We are not going to let Germany have anything
to say on the matter of any boundaries but her own. It is difficult to
guess how much opportunity will be given the Germans to discuss
the conditions we propose to them. I am inclined to believe that they
will be permitted to protest and may even secure relaxation of terms
on certain points which are not regarded as vital.[5]

We had three meetings of the Rumanian Commission this last
weekend; I think we are making progress. Monday we proposed certain modifications in one line, in order to help Rumanian transportation conditions upon which the French and the British lay great stress.
But we could not accept their proposals in toto, which would include
far too many Hungarians in Rumania. Tardieu asked us to meet
their economic and strategic expert, General Le Rond, and their
ethnic expert, de Martonne, in special conference.[6] So we spent Tuesday afternoon at the Quai d'Orsay. We found General Le Rond very
genial, although he could not advance any new arguments. But he
drew a new line, which represented a very serious concession and
went a long way toward meeting our point of view and indicated a
good possibility of our getting together. This we discussed at our
Wednesday meeting, when we agreed to study the concessions and see
how far we could meet them on our side.

In the meantime the Italians had not disclosed their hand at all,
and we did not know whether they would back us or the British and
French. But on Tuesday Count Vanutelli-Rey asked me if he could
come around for a talk; he appeared on Wednesday and told me that
his government had decided that we were absolutely right and that
they would support us. And in the afternoon session of the Commission Martino said he thought the American proposal the better one.

5. In principle this prophecy proved correct, but in fact only token attention was
given to the German protests.
6. Major General Le Rond, aide to Marshal Foch, served as military adviser to the
French delegation. Emmanuel de Martonne (1873–1955), geographer and author,
taught at numerous Italian universities and was a member of the Academy of Science.

We are not certain of the reason for their attitude. It may be that they are going to ask for our support in another and more vital part of the field (in which case they will get fooled, as we are not doing any bargaining). Or they may have made a secret agreement with the Hungarians in order to play them off against the Jugoslavs. In any case our hand in the Rumanian Commission is strengthened. I have drawn up a new line, conceding a little more and assuring Rumania good railroad connections, but one which does not sacrifice any vital Hungarian interests. I think the French will accept this. I am not sure about the British, who are honest but a little stupid and obstinate.[7]

Saturday we heard Bratianu in a discussion of critical issues. Tardieu put the questions which we had formulated beforehand and was skillful. He had to put them in such a way that Bratianu could not guess in what direction our decisions were tending. Tardieu was very polite (French lends itself to extreme diplomatic politeness) and kept the Rumanian, who is rather testy and morose, in a good temper. But he always held control of the situation and never let Bratianu get on the track of rhetorical platitudes, the way the Commissioners are apt to in the Council of Ten.

Tomorrow the Commission is going to hear the Serbs. I know their arguments pretty well and so can afford not to be there if the *Espagne* does not get in today. It is clearly going to be impossible to satisfy both Rumanians and Serbs, and I think that both are going to be pretty sore. Tardieu said to me, "You and I will not be able to travel either in Rumania, or Serbia, or Hungary, after this commission has finished."

I left Paris last night at 5 and had a comfortable trip down. I had reserved a seat, which was lucky as the train was fearfully crowded, although it was very long. We got in at 9. Le Havre was a British port during the war and it is filled with Britishers now. My impression is that these here are inferior to the Americans I have seen. I haven't seen so many drunken soldiers since I got to France. The feel-

7. This comment was "way off the track." (C.S.)

ing between the French and the Allied troops is tense, and the latter ought to be taken out of France as soon as possible. As I came into the hotel here an incident of an illuminating character occurred. Right behind me was a French major. As we came in the door, a young British officer who had been drinking tried to push through. The major protested at his rudeness and quite a little altercation took place. The Frenchman said, "Oh, these Americans are insupportable." I butted in and said, "Pardon, my major, but that was not an American; it was an Englishman." "Well," he said, "Englishmen then. They are all just as bad as the others."

4 Place de la Concorde, Paris

Sunday, March 16, 1919

I fear that it is a disgracefully long time since I have written. The only excuse I have is that business has crowded in thick and fast the past ten days; and that since Gladys' arrival time goes so fast that one doesn't realize how the days are flying.

Most of the important part of my work here is now over, I think, although no one knows how much longer it is going to take to finish up the details and get the Germans, Austrians, and Hungarians in to sign up. We have finished the draft of our report on the boundaries of Czechoslovakia and meet with the legal experts tomorrow to draw up the articles to be inserted in the treaties with the enemy powers.[8] The Rumanian and Jugoslav report is behindhand. We are still fussing over certain changes in the boundaries we want put in, and I doubt if the articles for the treaties are done before the end of the week. But even so we are so much ahead of the commissions

8. "Report Submitted to the Supreme Council by the Committee on Tchecho-Slovak Questions" (March 12, 1919). A signed copy is in the Yale Library. The full membership of the committee included the following: United States—Seymour and Dulles; Great Britain—Cook, Nicolson, and Crowe (technical adviser); France—Cambon, Laroche, and Le Rond (technical adviser); Italy—Raggi and Stranieri.

which are deciding indemnities and financial questions that our delays are not holding up matters.

Most of my work of the past ten days has been on the Czech Commission. We started late and have had to go at rapid speed. Jules Cambon is chairman of the Commission and it has been interesting to work with him and see him at close range.[9] He was, as you doubtless know, French ambassador at Berlin before the war, and knows Germany and German politics, from the French point of view, as well as any man alive. He is old, short and fat, with white mustache, rather bent and near-sighted. His charm lies in his very genial smile and quaint expressions of humor. In some ways he reminds me of old President Dwight[10] when about to make a funny remark. He is far less businesslike than Tardieu, more of a gentleman in the old-school sense of the word, but extremely clever in the way he expresses the sentiments of the Commission and equally clever in never losing sight of the French point of view.

We have opposed the French constantly in the Commission, as they have wanted to give far more to the Czechoslovaks than we have believed to be fair or even wise for their welfare. As first American delegate I have had constantly to take the lead in opposing Cambon, and have been always struck by the politeness with which he heard my remarks and his perfect fairness in debate. The Italian first delegate, Salvago Raggi, is one of their big five (like Cambon and Tardieu for the French).[11] He is the typical diplomat of the old school, very suave, outdoing himself in politeness, playing his hand very carefully and never letting any of us know what stand he would take

9. Jules Martin Cambon (1845–1935) entered government service in 1871 and served in numerous diplomatic posts, including that of ambassador to the United States, 1897–1902 (when he mediated peace preliminaries to end the Spanish-American War) and to Spain, 1902–07. During the war period he was the general secretary of the Ministry of Foreign Affairs, and then was France's fifth Commissioner at the Conference. Later he presided over the Conference of Ambassadors, the successor group to the Supreme War Council and the Council of Ten.

10. Timothy Dwight (1828–1916) was president of Yale from 1886 to 1898. He was namesake and grandson of another Yale president who served from 1795 to 1817.

11. Marquis G. F. Salvago Raggi, former ambassador to Berlin.

until we had shown our position. For example, when Cambon asked
him to explain Italy's position, he would say, "I ask myself whether it
is not wiser, at this stage, to put at least two possibilities before ourselves," and then say nothing. If he wanted to delay matters he would
say, "I don't quite understand," and use up 15 minutes in having
explained to him what was perfectly evident from the start. And all
this with the most magnetic and friendly manner. He is a fine-looking
man, tall and grey. He had been Italian ambassador at Berlin and
thus Cambon's colleague.

The British first delegate was the Prime Minister from the Antip-
odes, Sir Joseph Cook. He and I struck up a great friendship from
the start although we were always diametrically opposed to each
other in debate. He is blissfully ignorant of everything European
and practically every word of our discussion was Greek to him. Sir
Eyre Crowe comes in to tell him what is what and generally whispers
over his shoulder what to say; but sometimes Sir Joseph thinks that
he has a good idea of his own and will fight like a steer for it. My
whole line of argument in the Commission has been that the fewer
Germans and Magyars in the Czech state the better for it; but Sir
Joseph insists that our duty is to reward the Czechs for what they
have done in the war by giving them all the population possible, regardless of whether or not it wants to be Czech citizens. His simplicity
rather worries Sir Eyre and Nicolson, who is the second British delegate.

We have been able to work faster in the Czech than in the Rumanian Commission, as we delegated a lot of the detail work to a
subcommission which worked out on the map the principles we decided on in the main commission. I put Dulles, who is the second
American delegate, on the subcommission, and thus found time for
the enormous amount of work that I had to put in on the report of
the Rumanian Commission, where I was second delegate. The game
is, as you may gather, for the second delegate to do the work and the
first delegate to make the noble speeches. As a matter of fact, we had

less difficulty on the Czech than on the Rumanian Commission, for all of us were pretty well agreed as to what we thought were the best frontiers. The Italians, who are, perhaps, thinking of a future alliance with Hungary, would have liked to fight some of the points, but Raggi was far too clever a man to get in wrong by entering into a useless struggle, and very gracefully entered into complete accord with the others. We have drawn up our report, a copy of which I enclose. The last two meetings have been spent in writing articles to be inserted in the treaties with Germany, Austria, and Hungary. These took a lot of discussion with the legal experts, who quibble over every word and phrase.

Cambon gave a delightful dinner to the Commission last week, at a very recherché club, which I enjoyed immensely. I was amused by the careful formality of it. Cambon, after general talk before dinner, gathered the three other first delegates, Raggi, Sir Joseph, and myself, and led us out to dinner, while the rest of the party, about 15, followed. Then at the end of the dinner we four went out first, while the others stood to let us pass. I sat between the two British delegates, which was comfortable, as it spared me the necessity of making small talk in French.[12] After dinner I had an interesting talk with Cambon and his secretary about Berlin, and principally about the conditions under which they left it when war was declared in 1914.

I had another interesting chat with General Le Rond, who is the chief French technical adviser at the Conference. He has had an extraordinary career in French Africa, Tonkin, Japan, and is aide to Foch. We talked about the military policy of the United States. I have worked constantly with him on both commissions. He is very keen, but always fair, though we have had several rather hot arguments. I had a short talk with one of the Japanese representatives. They are rather gloomy, as they are not particularly interested in what is going on, don't speak French with facility, and don't understand

12. The author's later reflection was that this was "perhaps shrewd."

very much. Le Rond told me that at another commission the other day there was a tie vote two against two, which could be broken by the Japanese. The president asked the Japanese which side he would support. "Yes," was all the reply given.

One of the interesting developments in the life here is tea at the Quai d'Orsay. All the distinguished people in the building generally gather at 4:30 and we have an opportunity to see them and even sometimes to speak to them. I was talking to Le Rond the other day when Foch came up to him, and Le Rond introduced me to him. The marshal is certainly not distinguished looking at any distance, but he has a remarkable face, lined and with fine expression. I think that he looks with distrust on all civilians connected with the Conference, believing that they are not going to make the most of the victory that he has given them. Clemenceau is about and looking just the same as ever.

The news, which is only whispered about as yet, is that Orlando and Sonnino have definitely split, and that Orlando is making all kinds of overtures to Wilson for the Italian acquisition of Fiume.[13] I cannot believe that Wilson will consider them, although certainly it would be very convenient to have the Italians back the League of Nations with enthusiasm. The question of Fiume is precisely the one in which we (I mean the men of the former Inquiry) cannot exercise much influence, inasmuch as there is no commission organized to decide this point and it is to be decided by the Council of Ten. But we are taking no chances and are bombarding our five Commissioners with memoranda on the subject, all of them designed to prove that if Italy got Fiume every one of Wilson's points would have been violated. We must be permitted a little exaggeration once in a while. I don't

13. Prime Minister Orlando, a liberal at heart, felt he could achieve Italian objectives by political bargaining with Colonel House, notably by offering Italian support for the League. Baron Sonnino, the Foreign Minister, insisted on independence of Italian action. He demanded full British and French compliance with the Treaty of London, and more, no matter what the consequences for the principles of nationality and self-determination. He was frank to admit that strategic considerations and prospective economic advantages led Italy to expand its claims beyond the promises of the Treaty of London and to insist upon the acquisition of Fiume, specifically excluded from the Treaty.

think that any of us are really worried but the issue at stake is so large that we shall not be comfortable until the matter is decided. For this is a question that affects the future peace of the world vitally.

Italy is the great stumbling block to the success of the Conference. Another is the anarchy in Central Europe. The third, which we cannot understand, is the opposition to the League of Nations at home. Thus far we have seen no logical ground for the opposition. If it is the discussion of the League that is holding up the signing of peace, that is ridiculous. It is impossible to sign peace until it is decided what boundaries the states of Central Europe are to have and what indemnities they are to pay, and that can't be done before our commissions have finished their work and turned in their reports; and I assure you we have worked at lightning speed. All the work that is being done on the League is being done simultaneously and is not holding up the peace for a minute.

If the objection to the League is based on the Monroe Doctrine and the nonparticipation of the United States in world and European affairs, all I can say is that that is based on complete ignorance of the situation over here. Unless the United States undertakes the burden of helping to keep peace over here, another war is inevitable, and the past three years prove that we are vitally concerned in any European war. It is simply a question as to whether we wish to pay insurance against the horrors and the expenses of the last years. Of course it is not certain that the League will prove to be effective insurance, but it is the opinion of the leading European statesmen that there is no other insurance which promises any hope whatever of being effective.

What people at home seem to fail to realize is that the war has brought Europe, and with her the world, to the very brink of complete demoralization; you can't realize it until you come here, and read the telegrams from Central Europe. It is far worse than after any war of recent or even medieval history because of the interdependence of nations at the beginning of the twentieth century. Now no new frontiers however good (and these that we are drawing are not good, although I think they are the best possible in the circumstances), and no covenants to keep treaties or to avoid labor wars or to provide for laboring classes, are going to be sufficient to tide over the world crisis which is certain to last for years. It is absolutely necessary that some sort of world governmental organization be developed to see that elements of discord are eliminated so far as possible and that some sort of positive reorganization is effected.

I don't see that anything else can do this except the League of Nations in some form or other. Of course the present draft can be criticized in details and because of its lack of details. But the important thing is to avoid elaborating mechanism at present, for the attempt would prolong and possibly break up the Conference. If the general principles can be accepted and written into the peace treaty the points of detail can be arranged later. I can understand that the League was not very skillfully presented by Wilson on his return to the States, but what I can't see is that the senators should set up their own judgment of the necessities of Europe and the world against that of Lloyd George and Clemenceau, who are certainly hardheaded men and who have come around to Wilson's point of view. Another thing to remember is that the League as drawn up is largely the work of Lord Robert Cecil and that many of the ideas of Léon Bourgeois[14] have been incorporated; so it is by no means an American fad.

I mean to write strongly about this because I believe that should the opposition of Republicans to the work of Wilson at the Conference bring into question the ratification of the treaty of peace by the Senate, we shall have approached a world disaster. This would play into the hands of the Italians and the intriguers and go far to neutralize whatever help we brought to the cause of civilization in the war. I think that intelligent people here regard it as impossible to reach a satisfactory settlement of Europe at the Conference; but the Conference is on the whole, considering the difficulties, doing fairly well. Purely destructive criticism is not going to help.

14. Léon Victor Auguste Bourgeois (1851–1925), Socialist statesman and author, was one-time Premier of France (1895–96) and held several other Cabinet posts.

I have asked myself whether I am affected in my attitude by any other factors than those of pure reason, and I have come to the conclusion that I may reason badly, but at least I am not greatly affected by emotion. No one hitherto ever accused me of being a Wilson man and I don't think that my judgment has been touched by the cordiality of his manner. I began to approve his foreign policy as far back as last September, and for no reason that I can see except that it seemed to me to be right. I am certainly not an "administration" man, for I have made plain what I think of our government officials and the way they do business, and it is not as if I had anything to expect personally from the government, for I expect to go back to college in the fall. I am pro-Wilson at present because, seeing things as we do from somewhere near the center, his policy seems to me to be the only wise and farseeing one. An example of his influence is shown by the fact that the French, who two weeks ago were wobbling on several points, are now coming back again.[15]

If you get a chance tell some of your friends that many of us here who have always voted Republican and should like to vote Republican in 1920 and who are not so far blinded but that they retain their freedom of opinion on our American representation in Paris, nevertheless believe that Wilson has played a great part in Paris and one deserving of support by intelligent and patriotic Americans whatever their party. (This is the opinion of very cool-headed men who have seen things—Walter Davis, Day, Bowman, and all of my British friends, and above all of Thomas Lamont.[16])

It has been the greatest fun having Lester Perrin in the office. He has served as secretary of the American delegation in the Czech Com-

15. Seymour's position on the Wilsonian program was echoed in his article, "The League of Nations," published in 1919, and in many of his subsequent writings and speeches, especially at the beginning of World War II. See "The Power of Public Opinion," *Vital Speeches, 5* (July 15, 1939), 602–04, and "University Ideals and Democracy," *Vital Speeches, 7* (March 1, 1941), 311–13.

16. Thomas William Lamont (1870–1948), Harvard-trained banker, was a member of J. P. Morgan & Co. Representing the Treasury Department on the Peace Commission, he was assigned to the Finance Section and the Reparations Commission. Long active in international finance he helped formulate the Young Plan of 1929 to reduce reparations.

mission and has also come into the Rumanian Commission as secretary. I fear that it has been rather hard for him to get on to some of the technicalities of debate in the commission meetings; but he has done his job very well and mixed wonderfully with the other secretaries, most of whom are professional diplomats. He has unquestionably enjoyed going over to the Quai d'Orsay and seeing the big people there. Then these last ten days Walter Davis has been here. He had an interesting experience in Vienna and came back with very good ideas, but rather too late to get them applied in the territorial settlements.

Gladys has doubtless written you of our various amusements. As I had hoped the work has not been so hard these last ten days and we have had a good deal of time together; going out to Versailles for Sunday, taking in several operas, luncheon and dinner parties, and several fine long walks. The other night we went to a reception given by the Houses. We got in rather late, and the very big people, for the most part, had left, but we had a very good time. Today we had lunch with Miss Lansing, sister of the Secretary, and as she has charge of the Red Cross at Epernay, we hope to have the arrangements for our trip to the front, which we expect to make on Sunday and Monday, much simplified through her assistance.

Things are now nearly ready for the enemy delegates and I do not see why they should not be called in by the first of April. In the meantime our work is likely to be slack. I think that the Germans will haggle longer than people expect and that during that period we may have a good deal of work to do. On the other hand, having received the terms they may want to go home and think them over. If so I hope that Gladys and I could take that time for a visit to England. Every day when my work does not fill every hour I kick myself for not being over there. But everything is very indefinite. If things go well the preliminary treaty may be signed by the middle of May, possibly earlier. I do not suppose that the final treaty will be signed for six months or a year. We are making the articles of the preliminary treaties very complete so that they will serve as a basis for a final treaty essentially unaltered, we hope.

CRISES AND DECISIONS

March 24–April 28, 1919

WHEN WILSON RETURNED to Paris he changed his residence from the Villa Murat to the Place des États Unis on the rue Nitot. Physically this brought him nearer Lloyd George; symbolically he continued to stand alone, for his return quickly ended discussion of a preliminary peace without the League. Colonel House's growing concern over specific problems involving Germany failed to move the President, who remained convinced that the League must be the heart and foundation of any enduring peace, or any peace that would differ from those attempted before. The result was the beginning of the end of their friendship. As the pace of the Conference increased during April and as necessary compromise solutions were reached, Wilson became even more adamant in his view, although he did consent to a few minor concessions insisted upon by the Senate.

External events and the President's rigidity combined to produce the Conference's darkest hours. A revolution took place in Hungary and the peacemakers suddenly found themselves debating military operations. Their expectations regarding the Bolshevist government in Russia proved unreliable; instead of collapsing, it was gaining strength, and Allied military expeditions were sent to several Russian ports on varying and confused reasons, including the protection of military supplies, the rescue of Czechoslovak troops, and—in the case of Japan—the expansion of military control. In Munich a local upheaval put a Soviet government in power for three confusing weeks. These current activities all directly affected the work of the Conference, and also increased the virulence of the attacks from the press, based on the failure to act decisively.

Eventually the logjam was broken by further organizational changes. The creation of the Council of Four did little to advance democratic procedures, but it did provide a means of decision-making. The appointment of a Central Commission on Territorial Questions with Tardieu as chairman—he also presided over five of the ten area commissions—and Mezes as the American representative provided a logical channel for reconciling views of the different smaller commissions and for reviewing and settling contested recommendations prior to submission to the Big Four. Aided by these changes and faced with the sheer necessity of action, the Big Four did resolve some of the major issues. In a dramatic showdown with Clemenceau, Wilson held to his previous position opposing France's desire to create a new state in the Rhineland. The mandate system was revised for final approval. The main outlines of the territorial questions, with the major exception of Fiume, were approved, leaving only minor, last-minute details to be ironed out. The final draft of the League Covenant was approved at the fourth plenary session on April 28. The reparations question, however, remained unsolved.

Seymour's work on the two territorial commissions seemed almost completed, and he found time to engage in more and more social activities with Mrs. Seymour, also to take one trip to the battlefields. Then unexpectedly he became involved in the very center of one of the most intensive debates of the many that marked the Conference. Acting on the urgent pleas of some of his territorial experts, Wilson decided that one compromise with principle was enough for the Italians. Having yielded on the question of the Tyrol province, he refused to heed further importunities with regard to Fiume and once more spoke boldly of his principles. This led to the dramatic moment when Orlando, perhaps taking note of Wilson's similar earlier threat, walked out of the Conference, at least temporarily.

This departure produced several results. Japan seized the moment to renew its claim to the Shantung Peninsula. Wilson feared another defection from the League and reluctantly agreed, thereby leading to China's refusal to sign the treaty. On the other hand, the President's affirmation of his idealistic beliefs seemed to clear the atmosphere. The press—save for the Italian papers—rallied to his support, and the impression made on many of his young associates was strong and lasting. For them it was a renewal of faith.

❧

American Commission to Negotiate Peace
4 Place de la Concorde, Paris

Monday, March 24, 1919

I suppose that I shall be stopped after writing two sentences, but I do want to start this letter. My life is rather unsettled as I am on call at any moment, on account of the revolution in Budapest.[1] We have sent to the Commissioners recommendations for action and are liable to be called up any second to explain and defend them. Thus far we have not heard whether they are ready to act or not. We knew that conditions in Hungary were dangerous, but have been unable to get anyone here to take them seriously and send out either a mission or an Allied force to occupy Budapest. Now it is possibly too late.

But we have recommended that the Rumanian and Czech troops be allowed to advance their line of demarcation and that Allied troops be sent to hold Budapest. If that is done promptly the Bolshevik movement in Hungary may be checked and held. It is possible to do this there, because of the centralization of life in Hungary; if the Bolsheviks do not hold the capital they are helpless. But if no prompt action is taken it looks as if Vienna would be the next to go Bolshevik and after that probably Prague. It is a difficult situation, for pretty soon there will be no organized authorities with which we can deal or sign peace. And, of course, the more the movement spreads, the greater the danger that it will really get hold of Germany.

We got news of the revolution on Saturday night at Le Rond's dinner. This was a very sporty affair at the Cercle Interallié, which is one of the old houses on the Faubourg St. Honoré next to the British Embassy with beautiful gardens opening out on the Champs Elysées. There must have been about 20 there, and I was amused as I came into the room (I was rather late) to find that I knew every one of the group, British, French, and Italians. I sat between the British Colonel Cornwall and the Italian, Stranieri.[2] Cornwall is a very interesting man, was practically chief of the field intelligence service during the last year of the war. I have worked with him at the Quai d'Orsay and found him, like most of the British professional soldiers, charming. He said that the lowest moment for the British army dur-

1. The Communist-led uprising that followed Count Károlyi's resignation, which may or may not have been authentic. Belá Kun then came to temporary power.
2. Lt. Col. J. H. M. Cornwall. Augusto Stranieri, a young officer of the Foreign Office, had served in consular posts and was a member of the Italian delegation to the Conference.

ing the whole war was immediately after the battle of the Somme
(1916)[3]: they had been superior to the Germans in everything and
yet they had been unable to do more than make a dent in the line. It
seemed to them as if the war would never end. Of course the most
dangerous moment was in April 1918, when the Germans were
within an ace of separating the British and the French.[4]

He agreed that had the Germans driven on Amiens in May they
would have won the war. He said the tanks were an absolute failure
in 1916, although they justified their existence later. He gave me
details on the French mutiny. Stranieri was polite and laid himself
out to give me a good time, as the Italians are doing all in their power
to conciliate us at present, but was rather dull. After dinner I
talked with Nicolson,[5] to see if there were no means to come to an
agreement on the report of the Greek Commission, which is divided.
I am not directly concerned in this, but I know that Clive agrees with
the British and it is only a question of persuading Westermann, the
other American delegate, to change his point of view on Asia Minor.
Then I talked with Le Rond on the revolutionary situation in Hungary and on the necessity of signing peace at least with Germany at
once. He agrees in the abstract, of course. But it was impossible to
talk frankly, inasmuch as it is the French who are holding the peace
up, no matter what their government-inspired newspapers say. They

3. The Western Front changed little during 1916. The Germans pushed back the
Verdun salient a few miles; the British offensive along the Somme River north of Paris
showed equally small gains—five miles or so along a 25-mile sector—as a result of
heavy fighting for four and a half months during which tanks were used by the British, but in such small numbers that they were ineffective.

4. Gen. Ludendorff's first offensive of 1918 also took place along the Somme River.
Between March 21 and April 5 the Germans gained up to 30 miles along a 50-mile
front in a battle hailed as "the greatest artillery duel in world history," during which
the Paris Gun bombarded the French capital and Marshal Foch was given overall Allied
command. The Germans moved too fast for their own strength, however, and fell back
exhausted.

5. As the association between the Americans and British developed, Nicolson wrote
in his diary that he liked "the scholarly sort, such as Coolidge, Seymour, Day and Allen
Dulles, because they are quiet and scholarly and because they like the truth." *Peacemaking, 1919*, p. 310. He also commented that the Crillon "is like an American battleship
and smells odd" (p. 225).

refuse to name the extent of their financial claims on Germany and, of course, until they do it is impossible to sign.[6]

Yesterday Gladys and I had planned to go to the front with the Bowmans, spending the night at Château-Thierry or Epernay and going on Monday (today) to Reims and the Chemin des Dames. But both Bowman's and my plans had been so indefinite that we had not got the car in time, and there was none left to take us. So the trip was postponed. I was not sorry for it will be warmer later. Only we don't want to put off these trips too long, for if the treaty should not be signed all these areas will be closed up again. We had a late breakfast and took a walk up the Champs Elysées before lunch, which we took with the Days. We have been so busy that we have hardly seen Elsie since her arrival. I have not had dinner in the Crillon for nearly a week. In the afternoon we went to the Madeleine, where there was lovely music—Gregorian chants beautifully sung—and a very long but interesting sermon. We got out at 4:30 and walked for an hour, ending up at Latinville's on the rue la Boëtie, where one gets about as good cakes as are now to be had in Paris.

In the evening we went out to dinner with Phil Goodwin[7] and [Allen] Dulles. Goodwin has a delightful apartment up by the Étoile and it was fine being in a private homelike place once more and having dinner served by a maid, and going into a private drawing room for coffee before an open fire. He has been in Budapest with the Coolidge mission for the last three months, leaving just three days

6. The argument over reparations was one of the bitterest that took place. It involved many factors: categories to be included in assessing costs; estimates of value; Germany's capacity to pay and categories of payment; Europe's capacity to absorb payments without disrupting normal trade; division of payments among the victors; length of time for payments, etc. France obviously wanted to collect as much as possible but was deterred by American arguments as to Germany's limited capacity and by further disagreements on how payments should be divided. Another question was the relationship to interallied war debts, a relationship the Americans persistently denied.

7. Philip Lippincott Goodwin (1885–1958), Yale '07, an architect, came to France with the Red Cross and then enlisted in the army and was commissioned an infantry lieutenant. His services in the Intelligence Section led to his being attached to the Peace Commission and to trips to Budapest, Galicia, and the Banat to secure information. After the war he designed, among others, the New York Museum of Modern Art, and became a valued patron of the Yale Art Gallery.

before the revolution. He was full of interesting stories about Hungary and was very gloomy about the prospect. He blames the Peace Conference chiefly for the situation, because it has not sent enough food and assistance to the Hungarians and because the new boundaries are unfair to Hungary. The Conference is caught between two stools. Either it is too hard on the defeated enemy and makes it desperate, or, as is the feeling in the French papers and at home, I judge, it is too lenient and encourages the enemy to raise its head bumptiously.

Monday morning we had a meeting of our Czech Commission to consider the situation in Hungary and to make recommendations to the Council of Ten, which has now become the Council of Four—Wilson, Lloyd George, Clemenceau, and Orlando. We agreed to recommend the advance of the Czech line of demarcation to permit better railroad communication serving anti-Bolshevik operations; but took no steps to advise the sending of Allied troops. Both Cambon and Raggi regard the situation as almost desperate and think that it will have to be fought out between the Hungarians and the Czechs and Rumanians. Cambon said, "these boundaries we are fixing up are like putting brass rails on a ship that has already sunk." As soon as I got back I started to draw up a memorandum for our Commissioners advising that an Allied force be sent immediately to occupy Budapest and preferably Vienna. I have been opposed to military action in Russia for I believe that the country is too large and too decentralized. But I believe that a small Allied force holding Budapest could control the situation, for that is the center from which everything radiates.

Thursday, March 27, 1919

My recommendation for the sending of Allied troops to Budapest has been turned down. General Bliss, who exercises great influence in matters of policy, is firmly opposed to the use of American soldiers in Central and Southeastern Europe. He does not see the difference between this case and that of Russia. I am discouraged, for I think that if the Conference simply sits back when we have a legal right to interfere, according to the armistice terms, the trouble is likely to spread and soon we shall have no one with whom we can sign a treaty.

I think that the Conference is approaching the moment of crisis. Desperate efforts are being made to hurry things up and there is no doubt but that the new committee of the four heads of states can settle the vital matters rapidly. Doubtless much that we hoped to put into the preliminary treaty will have to be left out; but if the financial articles can be settled the territorial boundaries are ready and a treaty can be signed with Germany soon. If that is done, the treaties with Austria can wait a few weeks, and the one with Hungary until that situation is calm. It is probable that the Hungarians, if they want to make a fight of it, can go on for two or three months unless the Conference takes decided action. The revolution is only partly Bolshevik; it is also national and a protest against the partitioning of Hungary among the new or the smaller states. It started because they had got word at Budapest of what was being discussed in our commissions here at Paris.

Monday evening Gladys, Lester, and I went to the theater—*Phi-Phi*, a light comic opera. It was beautifully done with very pretty music and a good deal of fun, with a classical background, Phi-Phi being Phidias and Pericles and Aspasia, all prominent Athenian characters. But I must admit that if I had realized how very Parisian the humor was going to be in parts, I should have hesitated to take Gladys. Tuesday who should appear but Don Hemingway, on three days' leave. He is in the army of occupation, not far from Coblentz, and is pretty miserable. He gets enough to eat but there is little to do and he doesn't like the people; no danger of fraternizing for him. He was very glad to see us and has spent the last two days with us, lunching and dining regularly.

Yesterday Jim Thornton also turned up on his way to Biarritz for ten days. He lunched with us and in the late afternoon he took us all, including Lester and Don, to tea at a place new to me, next door to Ciro's where one gets very bad tea and execrable cakes at an exorbitant price; I think that Thornton paid 35 francs for five of us. But it is beautifully furnished and filled with the most elegant ladies I have thus far seen, and there were no Americans; one must pay for all that! Today we had lunch with the Foster Dulles',[8] who asked us to meet a French couple. He was lecturer at Cambridge University before the war (now he is a captain) and very charming, as is his wife. Gladys went off with Mrs. Dulles to the Chamber of Deputies after lunch and had a very amusing time. This Dulles is older than my colleague on the Czech Commission and is acting as counsel to the Reparations Commission.

Saturday, March 28, 1919

I never seem to have a moment to finish this letter and I shall have to leave unsaid many things which were in my mind when I began it. Thursday night we had dinner with the Steve Philbins, who have a nice apartment just off the Ave. de Bois de Boulogne. She is an attractive girl, who has been nursing here for a year and more. They had in Birch Helms,[9] who is now a major and taking General Churchill's work on the Commission—not a very important job but better done by the major than by the general. He agrees with me that it is time to take some decided action in Central Europe, but fears that noth-

8. John Foster Dulles (1888–1959), brother of Allen, was an international lawyer and statesman. During World War I he served on the War Trade Board as an assistant to McCormick and then became a representative on the short-lived Supreme Economic Council and the Reparations Commission at the Conference. In his later years he was instrumental in founding the United Nations and negotiated the United States Treaty of Peace with Japan in 1951. He served as Secretary of State from 1952 until his death.

9. Birch Helms (1886–1940), Yale '09, an infantry officer, served in the Military Intelligence Division and then was assigned to the Peace Commission to assume responsibility for military attachés and the investigating commissions for Central and Eastern Europe and Asia Minor. After the war he went into the international banking business with Blair and Co.

ing will be done. I had a long talk with Coolidge, just back from Vienna, in the afternoon. He thinks that our commissions have made a great mistake in planning to give so much territory which is Hungarian in character to the new or enlarged states and believes that it will make trouble for the future, even if the present crisis is safely passed.

He also thinks that we are paying no attention to the Fourteen Points and that there is much justification for the enemy contention that we are planning an "imperialistic" treaty. But he is ready to perceive that there was nothing for us Americans on the Commission to do but compromise with the French and British, who wanted to give the Czechs and Rumanians more than we; if we had refused to play with them, the result would have been the breakup of the Conference and political chaos; and even so we are getting a pretty good balance between "just and practical" terms which in the matter of territorial settlements are nearly mutually exclusive. I am much pleased by the President's attitude on the Adriatic settlement. We were worried last week lest he be fooled by false counsel, but it is pretty clear now that he will fight for any line that we (I mean the specialists in our section) tell him is right.[10]

Yesterday Gladys and I took a good long walk across the river and then up to the rue du Vieux Colombier, where we found a wonderful present for Charles Jr., which you can tell him is his birthday present from me. We walked on beyond St. Sulpice and into the Luxembourg Gardens where we watched the old men and poilus playing croquet! In the evening we had early dinner with Lester in our room and went to *Louise* at the Opéra Comique. Today we had the Mezes to lunch to meet Elsie and Clive. Elsie's uncle is trustee of the College

10. The Americans involved with the reshaping of Austria-Hungary had taken a firm position against Italian demands for Fiume, demands Italy strengthened by sending troops to the city shortly after the armistice and by creating a pro-Italian City Council. In particular, Mendell—prior to his departure—had delivered to Wilson a memorandum flatly rejecting the Italian position. Although he had yielded to Italy with regard to the Tyrol, Wilson had accepted this advice and was opposing Orlando on Fiume.

of the City of New York, so she was interested in meeting him but found him rather dull.

This morning we had our final meeting of the Rumanian Commission with the legal experts to go over the articles of the treaty setting out the boundaries.[11] It is rather embarrassing because part of the frontiers abut on Russia and the Ukraine, and there is no one there with whom we can sign a treaty. If the Hungarian business develops into a definite open break we shall have the same difficulty for all of our boundaries except the Jugoslav.

Tomorrow we are planning to start our trip to the front, going with the Bowmans. If the weather is good it ought to be a fine trip, and even if it is not perfect we shall be all right as we have got a closed car. Bowman has doped out the best route and the proper places to stop with the military men and I know that Gladys will enjoy it.

I hope that my next letter will be more optimistic. Every peace congress in history, I remind myself, has always had moments when it seemed as if everything was wrong and as if nothing could be arranged. Matters were far worse than this at the Congress of Vienna. I hope that by the end of next week we can see a little light.

Monday, April 7, 1919

I have been fooled again in thinking that work was going to ease up, for the past week has been about as busy as any. I got back from our trip to the front a week ago to find that a part of our Czechoslovak report which we had thought was all finished had to be reconsidered, and it has required a solid week to come to a decision. This was concerned with the question of Teschen, which is claimed both by Poland and the Czechoslovaks. Since our report was made

---

11. "Report No. 1" (with Annexes) was presented to the Supreme Council on April 6 by the Committee for the Study of Territorial Questions Relating to Rumania and Yugoslavia. The Committee consisted of the following: United States—Day and Seymour; Great Britain—Crowe and Leeper; France—Tardieu (chairman) and LaRoche; Italy—de Martino and Vannutelli-Rey. Numerous other assistants took part in the work of the Commission. A signed copy is in the Yale Library.

Lord has come back from Warsaw and Dubois[12] from Teschen and both expressed extreme dissatisfaction with what we had proposed as frontiers. They insisted on a reconsideration and were able to secure it as the first decision was reached without certain new information which they brought. So we had joint meetings of the Polish and Czech commissions every day, and long private discussions between ourselves nearly every evening, which lasted until midnight or thereafter.

Finally on Saturday afternoon we reached a compromise solution which was approved by ourselves, the British, French, and Japanese, with only the Italians disagreeing. After agreeing on the principle we had another meeting yesterday morning to settle the details. The final solution reached is satisfactory to me, but Lord does not like it as it is unfavorable to Poland. But I finally got him to accept it, by picturing the kind of settlement which might result if we sent up a divided report and the Big Four, with nothing definite to guide them, should throw up a coin to decide, or pick out a worse compromise of their own.

The Big Four are rushing things fast and some of the difficulties which seemed so serious a week ago are apparently disappearing. They have settled the principle of German indemnities and hope that it will not take long to finish the details necessary for the preliminaries. They have settled the Czechoslovak–German frontier, not following the proposals of our Commission exactly, but accepting the principle and avoiding some of our detailed suggestions.[13] They are evidently going in for settlements on large general lines, and some of the labored hours we have spent in working out details may go for nothing. But we don't object strongly so long as they realize the necessity for speed. Everything is now in the hands of the Four, and so far as England and the United States are concerned the only people that count are Lloyd George and Wilson. Except in two or

12. Presumably Louis Dubois, French official who later became chairman of the Reparation Commission, or General Pierre Dubois (1852–1924), who commanded the French Sixth Army in 1916 and then was placed in charge of the Saint-Nazaire and Brest areas of American bases.

13. The Commission recommendations included a corridor connecting Czechoslovakia and Yugoslavia, which the Big Four rejected.

three spots they are accepting the Commission reports, which on the whole seem to me to present about as good a solution as can be found.

As regards Italian claims there is no commission and everything is being settled by the Four. The result is that Italy is going to get more than she ought, but not so much as she claims. The worst injustice will be done to the German Austrians in the Tyrol; Italy will probably not get Fiume, but I fear that they will try to make it a free city, which is a bad solution unless it is also applied to Trieste, which the Italians will not permit. But Italy will not get Dalmatia, unless present indications are all wrong.[14]

The truth is that Wilson does not care about smaller territorial arrangements in comparison with the success of the organization of the League. He is willing to accept minor injustices of frontier if he can avoid a fight, believing that the League can later take care of any troubles or complaints.[15] He may be right. It hurts me to see some of the territorial arrangements that are about to be made, but it is certain that Europe cannot wait very much longer. What is needed more than anything is some sort of a peace, regardless of details of injustice. The Italians can probably spill a lot of trouble and hinder the League if they want; hence they have to be conciliated.

Last week I was much depressed over the situation; but I have come to the conclusion that it must be accepted; the best must be made of the situation by every government accepting the responsibilities that come with the League, realizing that the international crisis will not be over when the preliminaries of peace are signed and that everyone will have to work just as hard on these international problems for a number of years as they have been doing these past five months. United States cooperation is necessary and what I fear is our unwill-

14. After Wilson committed himself on the question of the Tyrol, the Inquiry experts proposed that Trieste be internationalized and that Fiume be annexed to Yugoslavia.

15. The author was unaware at this time that Wilson had refused to yield to Clemenceau on the creation of a buffer state in the Rhineland and had gone so far as to order the *George Washington* to prepare to sail.

ingness to come in and also our total ignorance of the factors involved.

Of course it is possible that some final hitch may develop in settling reparations or frontiers and that the League may not be successfully worked out. But while the Big Four have had their difficulties these last ten days, it is believed that a solution can be arranged. The President is to sail, probably on May 5, on the *George Washington*, which indicates that it is believed that main issues will be settled by then, although the treaties will probably not be signed until later. I talked to Colonel House on Saturday morning, and he said that he thought we could get away by June 1. Gladys and I are still hoping that we can get over to England for a fortnight at the end of April, perhaps at Eastertime; if we can't go then we may have to wait until the end of the Conference, in which case we shall sail from England.

I suppose that Gladys will have told you all about our trip to the front. We missed Law as we covered some of the ground he must have fought over, and it would have been wonderful to have had his explanation. We started Sunday morning at 7, going out to Meaux, then turned north up the valley of the Ourcq through La Ferté and Villers Cotterets. So we had the whole field of one of the most important parts of the Battle of the Marne for an hour, and could see traces of the fighting of five years ago. At La Ferté we got our first real touch of the fighting of last year. The village is badly knocked to pieces, a lot of the houses entirely destroyed. The sides of the road are full of dugouts, most of which are evidently now being used for German prisoners who are working on the roads and in the fields. We didn't get out of the car until we reached the forest of Villers Cotterets, where we wanted to go through some dugouts which evidently served as sleeping quarters for troops in the first line of reserve. There must have been heavy shellfire here last year, for the trees along the road are knocked all to pieces; trees two feet through, and more, are cut short and hardly a tree of any size is left standing.

It is a scene of terrible desolation. Beyond Villers Cotterets we reached the line where the Franco-American advance of July 18, 1918, began.[16] We could place this fairly accurately from the German graves, which were pretty thick, scattered through the trees and fields, all dated July 18. A good deal of material is strewn along the road, which has not yet been cleaned up. Gladys found a battered German helmet and we came on no end of empty shellcases, gas masks, etc. There are considerable dumps of both German and French munitions. We picked out brand new fuses from the boxes, Mrs. Bowman saying that they would be lovely playthings for the children! We later learned that the smaller ones had fulminate of mercury and the larger ones T.N.T. caps, so we decided not to throw them away but to place them very carefully in a soft spot in an unfrequented ditch. Most interesting were three French tanks which had been put out of action southwest of Soissons and were stranded in a field filled with German graves. We climbed in them, my first entrance into a tank, and investigated the engines, which were largely intact. Two had been hit head on by what must have been a pretty high explosive shell, for it had torn the armor all to bits.

We stopped on the heights southwest of Soissons to take in the lay of the land and study the bastion which the Germans held while the rest of their line to the south pivoted around, and where so many of our men were killed. I thought of how we read the news last summer and of what it meant when the word came that the Germans had been driven back of the Soissons–Château-Thierry road. The road here is covered at the side with all sorts of material. The ride into and through Soissons is terribly depressing because of the destruction, although it was less than what we were to see, and I felt very badly about the cathedral. I had not realized the extent of its ruin. There is a great pile of rubble in front, about 15 feet high, and I got some of the stained glass from the cathedral still in its lead and some pretty pieces of tile work.

16. The first Allied counteroffensive of 1919 pushed Germany back from the Marne to the Vesle River, eliminating the gains made by Gen. Ludendorff's third offensive.

We pushed on up the road to Laon. As one goes north the desolation becomes almost complete. Of course this ground was fought over several times between 1914 and 1918, and there is little left of the villages. The ground is like the surface of the moon through a telescope, simply a mass of shell-holes, merging into each other, with the subsoil churned up. We went on past Fort Malmaison at the western end of the Chemin des Dames, and to Chavignon where the permanent trench line ran at the time of the German advance a year ago. The whole territory has been no-man's-land at one time or another and is nothing but craters and masses of tangled wire. I suppose that some of the craters must have come from mines as they are at least 25 feet in diameter.

We got out frequently to go into the trenches, which are falling in fast, and into the abris. One of these was enormous, said to hold several thousand men. We went in quite a way, as far as we dared, with lights. It is made of infinite galleries, all far underground, part of it out of a quarry. It is whitewashed, electric-wired, with large halls and small sleeping quarters; beds made out of boards and chicken wire, or simply masses of straw. I took a sign, "Galerie Maud'huy," showing that the French had evidently held it last or for the greater part of the time; but there was some German equipment left. Horse bones were in what looked like the stable, with cavalry equipment; and several kitchens, from which we took a poker for Chatham. We also took some entrenching tools from the outside trenches for the children. We had lunch just opposite Fort Malmaison. It was without exception the most desolate spot I ever visited; for minutes at a time absolute dead silence, not a bird of any kind; only the reports of shells or hand grenades which are being fired by the Annamites, who are just beginning to clean up.

We came south again and then east onto the Chemin des Dames; here we got out and stayed for an hour or so going through the German abris, which are in excellent condition. German graves showed that the abris were held until the middle of last September. They are much more elaborate than the French, almost invariably lined with whitewashed boards and with many lights. The entrances are camouflaged skillfully, so that often it was difficult to spot the entrance even from close at hand. Most interesting of all were the arbors, behind rocks and mounds, but with some sort of a view up or down the valley, which probably served the officers as pleasant outdoor salons. They are festooned with camouflage, but quite open-air and fitted up in the style of beer gardens.

Some of the dugouts are lined with a sort of canvas which has all the air of grass cloth and is as clean as a drawing room. Some of them have doors and windows made out of munition boxes with oiled paper instead of glass. The dugouts were full of all sorts of stuff most of which we did not like to touch as we were not sure whether or not they might be traps. We picked up all the German helmets we could carry, got some new gas masks, bayonets, etc., and I found some German paper-covered novels and a German army hymn book. The French had evidently taken the real prizes such as field glasses and revolvers. The place was thick with hand grenades and I hope they send some one to clean it up before some crazy people blow themselves to pieces.

We went back to the main Soissons-Laon road and down to the Vesle, through Fismes where the Americans were fighting in August; Jim Thornton and Curt Platt[17] were in this and a good many more of our friends. We got to Rheims about 6. The town is certainly in terrible shape, but is beginning to show some life; they say that nearly ten thousand are back of the hundred and more thousand who lived there before the war. For street after street every house is in ruins; then one comes on a row that seems in good shape, although often the houses are only shells. The Lion d'Or where I stayed 17 years ago is flat as a table, with nothing but rubble left to mark it. This is directly in front of the cathedral, which retains all its main lines— towers, buttresses, and traceries, but which looks terribly battered.

17. Joseph Curtis Platt (1887–1950), Yale '10, brother of Philip Platt, was an artillery lieutenant who served in the Oise-Aisne offensive. He returned to Scranton and entered the banking business, becoming president and chairman of the board of the Lackawanna Trust Co.

It is this battered aspect which changes the character of the building; formerly it was perfect. Much of the sculpture is left, but badly mutilated. It seems to me to be spoiled absolutely for what it was; it is now a lovely ruin.

We motored up over the mountain of Rheims, past the trenches the Germans dug in July in their advance south, and, with the most beautiful sunset, down into the valley of the Marne, with Epernay at our feet. It was one of the loveliest sights I ever saw; there had been snow flurries during the day and the hills were white, the sun was reflected in the winding Marne, and the broad vineyards were green. We had wired for rooms and were well received at a plain but very comfortable hotel, where they put hot-water bottles in our bed, and gave us an excellent bottle of Moët and Chandon for ourselves. The hotel had been pretty well smashed last year but our room was newly rebuilt and very clean; across the narrow street from our bedroom window was a ruined house knocked in by a German shell last July. Everything brought us very close to the fighting.

Monday morning we came down the Marne Valley through Dormans to Château-Thierry. I had not realized before the intensity of the German attack in the sector. The villages are not the absolute ruins one sees north of Soissons, but they are pretty well shattered. We stopped in Château-Thierry and again in Vaux, which our men shelled and captured in July, where some 20 people of the two thousand have come back. We talked to some of them, and I take my hat off to their courage, philosophy, and cheerfulness. At Soissons we Americans are not very popular. But in the Marne Valley everyone waves to the American car. One old man we talked to showed us things left by the Germans in his cellar and offered us a German rifle. He refused absolutely to take anything for it. "It is not mine," he said. "What would you? The Americans drove the Germans out, and it belongs to them. You are Americans. Take it." It is a pity that the feeling like this is not general, and also that our American troops feel as they do. Our chauffeur refused to stop to help a French car which was in trouble. When we made him stop he complained bitterly: "Many a time my camion has been in trouble and never have the 'frogs' raised a finger to help me."

We stopped at Belleau Wood for an hour or so, and took our picnic lunch on the side of the hill from which the 26th Division advanced on July 18, Gladys digging up shrapnel from the ground as we ate. We got back comfortably in the middle of the afternoon, in time for our Commission meeting at 5. I had not meant to write so much about our trip, but really we are getting a little weary of conference politics, which is "shop" and this trip stands out as a wonderful experience. I hope that we shall be able to get to Verdun and the Argonne.

Tuesday, April 8, 1919

A very sad thing has happened. Donald Frary, who was a Yale instructor in history and who collaborated with me in writing my last book, and whom I got appointed as assistant librarian to the Commission, died on Sunday of pneumonia. I was closely associated with him and very much interested in him as he seemed to me to be the most promising of our younger historians. He had a cold, went to the front on the same day that we did, went to bed on Wednesday; the next day he went to the hospital, very few even knowing that he was ill. Pneumonia came on on Saturday and he died at noon on Sunday. He was unmarried, an only son, and for his age had shown great intellectual strength. Without his help I never could have finished the book. We shall miss him sadly at Yale and his loss will weaken the department immediately. I could count on him absolutely in my recent European history work and think that he would have made a fine scholar; as a teacher he had in two years established himself soundly. We had funeral services this afternoon. They were in the church on the Ave. de l'Alma, and the church was filled. Colonel House and Lansing have cabled to his family and I think they have a right to be proud of him.

Last week social and affairs of recreation were at a discount owing
to the pressure of work. But Sunday afternoon Gladys and I went out
to St. Denis to see the lovely abbey church and the tombs of the kings
of France and yesterday we spent an hour in the Bois, sitting under
the trees; it was like a summer day. I forgot to say that Jim Thornton turned up on Saturday and we spent a gay evening, going to
Larue's for a wonderful dinner and then to the Nouveau Cirque. I
believe that Gladys and Elsie are going to tea at Mrs. Wilson's tomorrow (they threaten to take Clive and me, but we count on getting
out), and we have dinner or theater engagements for every night of
the week except Saturday, so the gay life seems to be on. Now that
the commissions are over we have to begin to pay back some of our
social debts; the quiet monastic life which I love is still in the distant
future. Forgive my failure to give interesting news of the Conference;
I am sick of it this week, but shall hope to be more *en train* next.

Sunday, April 13, 1919

Really the last week has had almost the air of a *fin de la saison*. No
more commission meetings, very few conferences, a great deal of
dope as to what was being decided by the Big Four and a general
clearing up of offices. We even had warnings to get our maps in order
so that arrangements could be made at short notice to get them packed
up, and a request to begin the reports to the American Commission
on the activities of our various divisions—reports which are to form
part of the permanent records of the Peace Conference. I have spent
a lot of time going through my papers, books, and manuscripts choosing what I thought I should like to have in my library at home, or
rather what I should have space enough to take home.

This doesn't mean that we are going home at once or that the Conference is over. But it does mean that the most important questions
are settled in their broad lines, and that if Europe doesn't break up on
our hands the rest is largely a matter of details. As I wrote last week

the questions that touch upon the treaty with Germany are about settled, so much so that the German delegates are being sent for and I judge should be here before the end of the month. There is no telling how long it will take them to sign the treaty; but the hope is that they will be given only a limited period. Then will come the ratification of the treaty at Weimar and by the legislatures of the Allied states. That will take possibly a month.

I take it that it is felt that the treaties with the smaller states— Austria, Hungary, Turkey, Bulgaria—ought not to hold up the dissolution of the Conference. After the treaty with Germany is signed and the main lines of the other settlements are fixed, the Conference can go home. Then the League of Nations can organize, take over the work of the Conference and prepare the treaties with the smaller states. It is impossible to get those treaties fixed up immediately, because of the unsettled state of affairs in Central Europe, and the Council of the League is just as capable, or more so, to carry them through as the present Conference. Everyone feels that the main necessity is to sign with Germany and send the Conference home, after which we shall have, at least nominally, a condition of peace, and international conditions will have reached as stable a condition as is possible in the present circumstances.

It is impossible to guess at dates, but I should say that this conference could leave by the end of May. Unless I can get to England before then, which is still possible though not probable, my plan is to go over then and sail from England, both because it is more simple to get passage, and because time would be saved.

Wednesday, April 16, 1919

Since I wrote the above, President Wilson has come out with the statement that the German delegates are expected here by April 25, and as this will be in your papers you know as much as I do about the situation. Yesterday and today we have been working over the Adri-

atic situation trying to find some settlement which will save the faces of
the Italians and let them down easy with their people at home and yet
give the Jugoslavs what they really ought to have. I have been so busy
on Czech and Rumanian matters that I have left the handling of Jugo-
slav-Italian matters to Johnson and Lunt. They have worked very
hard and fed a lot of memoranda to Wilson and House. We are all of
us agreed that the Italian claim to Fiume and northern Dalmatia is in
the nature of a hold-up game; they have no justified rights there and
if the claim is granted even under nominal form, it is going to make
serious trouble for the future.

We have been confident that Wilson would stand out firmly against
the threat that Italy would not come into the League unless her claims
were granted; but during the last day or so the prospect has become
rather terrifying. It looks as if the President had in mind some kind of
a compromise and the French and British would follow suit. If the
matter is not decided correctly I feel that all the work that Wilson has
done to get a settlement based on justice will be largely nullified. The
claim of the Italians is made simply so that they may go home with
sufficient loot to please their constituents. Italian sovereignty over
Fiume or any part of Dalmatia would be a glaring injustice to the
Jugoslavs. Any acquiescence in this injustice by the United States
would make clear that we have failed to keep our pledge of protecting
the rights of the small nations. The principle that "there shall be no
bartering of peoples" would be publicly and cynically thrown aside.
Italian sovereignty over Fiume would signify to the world that the
League of Nations accepts the doctrine of Talleyrand and Metternich
that the threats of a strong nation are more worthy of respect than the
rights of a weak nation.

No League of Nations which begins its career with an unjust bribe
can enjoy the confidence of the common people which is essential to
its success. Better a League without Italy than a League based on
Italian participation bought at a price. If Italy gets Fiume as the price
of supporting the League, she will have brought the League down to
her level. It becomes a coalition to maintain an unjust settlement. The

world will see that it pays a big power to use the old methods: secret treaties, shameless demands, selfish oppression. If Jugoslavia loses Fiume, war will follow sooner or later, for she will not submit and she ought not to submit. When it comes, the League will be fighting on the wrong side; ought we to hope that it will be strong enough to win?

I think that the President never had such an opportunity in his career for striking a death blow to the discredited methods of Old World diplomacy. He has the privilege of going down in history as the statesman who destroyed by a clean-cut decision against an infamous treaty the last vestige of the old order.[18] I am very much afraid that he is going to take the shortsighted view and court Italian support of the League with some compromise in a place where any compromise is immoral. This will kill his prestige with the French and British liberals. It will also mean that many of us who have felt that he was playing a really great part over here will go home believing that, at the critical moment, he was untrue to his principles and ideals.

We have all of us been busy as bees during the last three days since we received indications that the decision might be taken at any moment and in the wrong sense. Yesterday afternoon Johnson, Lunt, Day, Bowman, Young, and myself met for three hours and finally drew up a personal letter to Wilson stating our position perfectly frankly, quite as frankly as I have in this letter to you.[19] This we sent up to him in the evening and by great good luck the matter had not been settled by the Four during the afternoon. We made a dent, for this morning we found instructions to consider another compromise, which was not so disastrous as the one nearly accepted yesterday. We have discussed that this morning and are returning it with the comment that we cannot advise any compromise. Johnson is seeing House

18. Nicolson, *Peacemaking: 1919*, quotes these sentences almost verbatim but without identifying any source (pp. 181–82).

19. In pressing for Fiume to be awarded to Yugoslavia, the six signers based their arguments on ethnography, self-determination, economics, and history. They pointed out that since 1890 Hungary had deliberately encouraged Italian settlement in Fiume as a move to block Slav nationalism. It should be noted that the experts were not entirely in accord, for Mezes, Beer, Miller, and Shotwell disagreed with the conclusions of their associates. See Paul Birdsall, *Versailles Twenty Years After* (New York, 1941), pp. 275–86.

now. The trouble is that the President will not take advice unless he asks for it and even with the unanimous opinion of all the experts in the field is liable to follow his own judgment of the situation. I had a long talk with Leeper of the British Foreign Office last night and he expressed great fear and great disappointment both that Wilson was not standing more firmly and also that Lloyd George and Balfour were not stiffening him up more, even though England is bound by the treaty of 1915. Well, we ought to know soon how the matter comes out.

As to Danzig and the Saar District I personally think that the decision made, which is the result of Lloyd George's and Wilson's unwillingness to take a lot of Germans out of Germany and put them under foreign rule, is right, although it was not recommended by our experts, who advised making Danzig Polish.[20]

Friday, April 18, 1919

I never get time to finish a letter, but hope to do so today, which, being Good Friday, we have declared a holiday for our office. I am dividing it between clearing up my desk, easing my epistolary conscience, and, if possible, going to some church with Gladys to hear some good music. Last night we had the Days and our British colleagues on two commissions, Nicolson and Leeper, to dinner. We have been given a large salon on the first floor to use as a reception room for guests after dinner, so it is going to be easier to entertain. It is a fine room, in fact was to have been Secretary Baker's salon; but he has gone to another hotel.

Nicolson was very amusing telling of Foreign Office life during the war and particularly of the British intelligence service; he confirmed

20. Danzig was made a free state within a Polish customs union. The Saar was to be placed under an international administration for 15 years during which time the French had the privilege of working the coal mines as repayment for the destruction of French mines. A plebiscite held in 1935 favored by a 90 per cent vote a return to Germany and marked the first step in Hitler's program of expansion.

my opinion that it was very good—much better than that of the Germans. He had one friend who assumed the place of a German spy who had been shot without the knowledge of the Germans and who sent letters for seven months to German headquarters full of information. He drew his pay regularly and made a lot of money from the German intelligence fund; once and a while he would go to the British War Office and say, "My people are getting uneasy; can't you give me something spicy for them." Then they would hand out a good piece of real information, after which he would send on some more misinformation. The Germans finally got on to him and sent him a letter asking him what was the address of his sister in Brussels. As he did not know whether he even had a sister he had to stop.

I was interested to see how little animosity against the Germans these Britishers have. They had been in touch with the man who captured von Rintelen,[21] for whom they had a good deal of respect. They refused to call him a spy. A spy is only one who sells his services for money; if he works for patriotism or love of adventure he is "an intelligence officer."

Saturday, April 19, 1919

I did not get very far with the letter yesterday for I was called into another conference over Fiume. The President had received our personal letter protesting against any compromise which would give it to the Italians even under nominal form, and sent us a very cordial answer. But it was rather vague. He thanked us for "reinforcing his judgment," but didn't say that he approved our advice. The situation is complex. The three Commissioners—Lansing, White, and Bliss—are kept out of the matter entirely. They feel very strongly against

21. Captain Franz von Rintelen (1877–1949) was chief of German naval intelligence and master of the spy system in the United States whose assignment was to prevent munitions from reaching the Allies. He was seized in 1915 and imprisoned. After the war he settled in England and became a wealthy socialite and author.

granting Italian sovereignty over Fiume and yesterday sent a memorandum to Wilson to this effect. But whether or not this will have any impact remains to be seen. Actually, they are exercising little more influence on events than we are, if as much. House claims that he agrees with us in principle, but that his hands are tied. Actually, I think that he is behind the President in making any sacrifice in order to get full support from Italy for the League.

So you have Wilson and House deciding everything, the six of us territorial specialists and the three Commissioners being bitterly opposed to yielding. The French and British are simply waiting on Wilson's decision. I must confess that I finally take back what I said some months ago about Bliss. He is a man of very interesting ideas and I think in the main very good ones. But he lacks the force to put them over, or perhaps I should say the peculiar power of influencing the President; and the President is all-powerful. The General also lacks the power of organization. Hence his influence here has been practically negligible. White is as nice as ever, but too old.

Lansing has a strong critical sense, but no constructive power and is stupid about catching the relative importance of things. I had occasion to have a talk with him over Czech boundaries last week and was irritated as well as amused; he is perfectly genial but rather testy at having to be told the meaning of things, and yet he has to be told. At the meeting of the five secretaries at the Quai d'Orsay in the afternoon, where I sat just behind him, he showed that he remembered a lot of what I told him, but he never knew when he was on strong or on weak ground. He argued with great vehemence; he failed, however, to catch the important nuances in the different questions and always confused the debate. I kept trying to put him right with whispers to his left ear, much to the amusement of Tardieu who was sitting just to the left. They call the five foreign secretaries the "Little Five" in contradistinction to the "Big Four," while the three Commissioners who do not get into things—Bliss, Lansing, and White—they call the "Lesser Three."

Easter Sunday, April 20, 1919

The Adriatic question is still unsettled, thanks perhaps to our personal letter to the President which has evidently stiffened him against Italian claims. Whether or not it will break Italian demands I don't know; but this much is certain, that if there is a compromise, it will not be so bad a compromise as it would have been before we sent our protest. The "Lesser Three" are with us. It is a curious situation, for we who are the creation of Colonel House are in this case opposing what I must believe to be his policy. He was not overpleased at the memorandum of the "Lesser Three" and Auchincloss was furious.

We went to the Madeleine this morning to hear high mass; it was a beautiful service, a Mozart *Kyrie* and *Sanctus,* with two organs, orchestra, and perfectly harmonized voices. As a religious experience it does not touch me as deeply as a British cathedral service; but it was the finest Roman service I ever heard. Easter means so much to these people, and this, the first Easter after the war, was doubly joyful.

It was the really warm perfect day that one expects here at Easter. This afternoon we started to listen to a concert in the Tuileries, but it turned cold so we went into the Louvre, where they have opened new galleries with the best-known pictures—Leonardo, Titian, Raphael, Rubens—three or four of each. It was too crowded to enjoy it much, but it was nice to take a glance at them again. As we came out an army car stopped in front of us, and we saw the Davisons. I was very glad to have Gladys meet Mr. and Mrs. Davison, and hope that they will ask us to dinner.

One day last week Gladys and I went over to the Left Bank and bought all the postcards which I have been wanting to get—pictures of the French generals and all the diplomats that I had met. I missed Cambon and Tardieu, but shall hope to get them later. As souvenirs I am going to have the *procès-verbaux* and reports of our commissions bound up and signed by Tardieu, Cambon, Raggi, and Crowe.

We are not dining out very much, but get lots of company from the men and women in our section of the Commission. Last Monday we had young Stoica in;[22] he is a delightful Rumanian captain, a favorite of the Queen, who spent last year in Washington where I met him. He is a Transylvanian and was in the Hungarian army, but escaped while on leave and went into the Rumanian intelligence service.

I have been unable to get leave for a fortnight to go over to England, and at present it looks as if we should not be able to get there until the Conference breaks up. My bet is that I can get off the first of June; then we shall go to England and sail from there.

Friday, April 25, 1919

We are thinking about little except the declaration of the President on the Adriatic and the withdrawal of the Italians from the Conference.[23] I am hoping that you have enough facts about the problem at home to get the right and wrong of it; but everything that I have seen in the press is so confused that I am worried as to public opinion in America.

As I wrote last week, the gist of the matter is that the Italians have tried to blackmail the Conference into granting unjust demands which

22. Vasile Stoica, diplomatist and writer, was a member of the Rumanian delegation at the Conference, later was a delegate to the League of Nations. He became minister to Albania in 1930, to Bulgaria in 1932, and to Great Britain in 1936.

23. The Italians walked out of the Conference on April 24 after Wilson, having informed Orlando in advance, made a unilateral public statement in which he tried to set straight the record on Fiume. It had not been included in the pledges made to Italy in the Treaty of London; it was not essential to the strategic control of the Adriatic; the population was almost evenly divided; the President refused to "barter peoples," especially since Italy refused to sanction a plebiscite. Orlando's departure was actually calculated to rally support from the Italian people for a position that was becoming increasingly obnoxious to the Big Three. In the end, the Conference failed to settle the status of Fiume but awarded the South Tyrol and Trieste to Italy. In September 1919, the poet Gabriele D'Annunzio seized Fiume for Italy. No one took action, but in 1920 Italy and Yugoslavia signed the Treaty of Rapallo which created a nominally independent Fiume and confirmed possession of strategic islands off Dalmatia by Italy. Then in 1924 Mussolini annexed Fiume. See Seymour, "The Struggle for the Adriatic," *Yale Review,* 9 (April 1920), 462–81.

if approved would certainly lead to war with the Jugoslavs. Part of the Italian claims had been promised in the Treaty of London by France and England, and they have to keep to their promise, although their representatives have told us that they regard the bargain as iniquitous and hoped that we could get them out of it. Fiume was not included in the promise and France and England are standing with us in refusing it to Italy; but they are letting us take all the blame for the trouble with Italy. Still this cannot be helped and I am glad that our nation is the one that takes its public stand for what is right. I wrote so much last week as to the feelings of all of us who have studied the question that I have nothing more to say; all of the French and British specialists who have studied this question for years agree absolutely with us.[24]

Yesterday I had calls from a Frenchman who is working for Tardieu and from an Englishman who is working for Balfour, and both of them congratulated me on the stand which Wilson had taken in the name of fair treatment for the small nations.[25] We Americans are so absolutely disinterested in this matter that I do not see how anyone can suspect that we are not standing for what is absolutely right, unless they think that we are stupid. The Italian complaint that we spoiled a compromise that was on the point of being arranged is not true; we had already compromised by giving them the greater part of the Treaty of London in the Tyrol and Gorizia, territory which includes over a quarter of a million Germans and a quarter of a million Jugoslavs. Sonnino's policy is bound to lead to disaster for Italy; it seems to

24. Faithful to his shipboard pledge, "Tell me what's right and I'll fight for it," Wilson also made it clear in his *ex parte* statement that he was taking the advice of his experts, the members of the Inquiry, who argued against any kind of political compromise that might save face for the Italians. The latter was Col. House's objective, and was opposed by Bowman, Seymour, and their associates.

25. Upon his return to America, the author received a letter dated July 4, 1919, from Ivan Ritter von Žolger (Zholger) of the Yugoslav delegation thanking him for the work done on Yugoslavia. "I am convinced," it said, "that you will help to promote among the American public the sympathies for our young country and you will preserve us a kind memory, as we will to you." Seymour later became a director of the American-Yugoslav Society.

me a clear example of *quem deus perdere vult prius dementat*. But what is to be feared is whether he will not involve the Conference in the disaster.

We in our group feel responsibility since Wilson's action is what we advised and pressed upon him. It seemed to us that in a case of this kind, where the issue between right and wrong was so clear-cut, Wilson could not do anything else but follow Luther's example and say, "Here I take my stand, I can do nothing else." Looking back on the Conference, the only criticism that I have heard any expert give is that the public statement was not made earlier. The Italian statement that their departure was caused by the sudden publicity of the statement is hardly true. Both Clemenceau and Lloyd George had seen it and approved it. Orlando had been told about it and knew what it contained. What I fear is that Clemenceau and Lloyd George will let us take all the blame for the confusion, although on Fiume they stand absolutely with us.[26]

The Germans are expected on Tuesday. I believe that some of their forerunners, secretaries, etc., are already on the way.

Saturday, April 26, 1919

We are going on with our work busily, although it is a question how much use it will be in case the Italians refuse to sign with Germany, and France and England refuse to sign without her. The Italians are working their people up to a tremendous pitch of nationalistic excitement and there seems to be no doubt but that Orlando will get a great ovation and an overwhelming vote of confidence in the Italian Chamber. Then he will come back here claiming that the whole nation is behind his policy and insist that the Conference give him the

26. This was precisely what took place. The author later was to comment on the large extent to which Wilson had sold his idealism to the "young enthusiasts," and to characterize his own attitude during the hectic period of the debate over Fiume as marked by "dogmatism and inconsistency."

Treaty of London line as well as Fiume, which the Treaty left for the Croats. I don't see the answer at present.

In the meantime we are pleased to have the support of the best of the British press; it was hardly to be expected that the *Chronicle* or *Daily News* or *Morning Post* would support Wilson. More encouraging still is the turnover of the French press, which has been pro-Italian and anti-Wilson. Of course this does not mean that French opinion is strong, for the French press changed its attitude at the direct command of Pichon, who called in the editors and hinted strongly that France stood with Wilson in this matter although no official statement of this could be made. It is humorous to note the change in the *Temps* since this interview.

Clemenceau had a talk with an Italian delegate yesterday morning before the change in the French press; the Italian said, "Well, I see that your press is behind us." "Yes," said Clemenceau, "but you know as well as I do what that means. I have a list here of the French papers which have been purchased by the Italian propagandist bureau, and the price paid for each paper." The American correspondents whom I have talked with are, for the first time, thoroughly enthusiastic over Wilson and I hope are sending home good stuff. They say that this is the first "man-sized" stroke of the Conference and are pleased that the President has come out into the open in a difference where the rights and wrongs seem clear to them.

My work on Teschen still continues. We are now trying to get Beneš and Paderewski to come to an agreement by themselves. It is almost hopeless, but it seems worthwhile to try, since the matter is not pressing, a decision not being needed for the German treaty. There was a meeting of the "Little Five" the other afternoon which I attended to discuss it. Lansing was not well and his place was taken by White. The latter was as dear and sweet as could be but, knowing nothing about Teschen, very uneasy. I primed him for a statement and after making it he turned around almost pitifully and said to me: "Was that all right?" Personally I do not approve entirely of trying to get the parties interested to come to a compromise, for I think that their constituents will be dissatisfied and claim that Beneš had sold out to Paddy, while the Poles will claim that the latter sold out to Beneš; whereas if the Conference imposes a settlement of its own both countries will be dissatisfied, but not so much with each other as with the Conference, which has so much contumely to bear that a little bit more will make no material difference.

Thursday afternoon we had a spree, going to the Opéra to hear *Cavalleria* and *Bohême*. The former was not done too well but the latter was perfect, if one excepts slight defects in singing. The setting, the orchestra, and the acting of any Puccini opera here in Paris is wonderful. My conscience was eased to find Westermann and his chief assistant sitting in front of us, also taking a vacation. We went to a café afterwards to discuss the crisis, read the papers, and watch the Frenchmen.

Mrs. Lansing's reception the other night was good fun. As Gladys said, the Conference is like a ship's voyage where everyone is very stiff and standoffish at first, but the last day suddenly melts in the friendliest fashion and becomes very intimate. At any rate this party was very different from Mrs. House's where everything was stiff and formal; people seemed to be out for a good time and the ladies certainly enjoyed themselves; every time I looked around Gladys was surrounded by a group of five or six including the duc de Montmorency(!),[27] several colonels from Bliss's staff, and young secretaries of legation.

I had an interesting talk with Bullitt, who is disgusted with American unwillingness to patch up a truce with the Bolsheviks.[28] Lansing

27. Napoleon-Louis-Eugène-Alexandre-Anne-Emmanuel de Talleyrand-Perigord, comte de Perigord, duc de Montmorency, officer of the Legion of Honor.

28. During Wilson's absence from Paris, Bullitt was assigned a special mission to investigate the confused and chaotic situation in Russia. He became convinced of the permanence of the Lenin government and returned to urge recognition and assistance. When his advice was ignored, Bullitt angrily left the Conference. Later he was to serve as the first American ambassador to the Soviet Union.

came around and said to Herter, with whom I was talking: "Have you heard what 'The Four' decided about Fiume?" Herter said that he had not. "Well," said Lansing, "snoop around a bit and see if you can find out." This shows how well our Secretary of State is kept informed of what is going on. He feels more strongly than the President about the question of the Adriatic. House believes that the President is on strong ground, but he is by nature a diplomat and wants to arrange the matter by friendly negotiation, even if it means a compromise which the rest of us believe would be unjust to the Jugoslavs.

Today Gladys and I have been out to lunch with René Versein, who was on the French High Commission in Washington, and came over on the *Espagne* with Gladys; he brought a very Parisian friend, who was so beautifully made up that Gladys and I were a bit shocked when they appeared. But she turned out to be delightful. Versein is a pleasant fellow who knows a good many things, but thus far I have not been able to get him to talk freely.

Monday, April 28, 1919

This is Monday morning and we are beginnning to clean up our offices in earnest. I am getting the more important pamphlets and books which have been sent to me ready to go home at once. We have very distinctly the impression that we shall not need them any more and that except for incidental conferences our work here is done. News on Fiume is contradictory but in sum not so bad. Of course we expected to have the demonstrations in Italy, for the government had worked the people up into a frenzy of nationalism. On the other hand we get congratulatory messages from all the smaller nations. The leader of the Ukrainians said on Friday: "We were going home disgusted. Now, after what the President has said, we are willing to abide by *any* decision that he and the American experts come to." The same thing was said by the Greeks.

Yesterday was cold and windy and we gave up all plans for a Sunday in the country. We took a short walk by the Seine in the morning and in the afternoon went to see the international boat race, in which the American crew, chiefly a Yale, Harvard, and Cornell aggregation, was just beaten by the New Zealanders. It was long waiting, but we were well repaid by an aeroplane which came down and did stunts over the Seine right in front of our eyes, flying down to below the level of the bridge and then shooting straight up and looping slowly, not a hundred yards from us. We came back to the hotel to get warm, and spent the evening talking Conference gossip with Bowman, most of which is so filled with T.N.T. that I don't dare write it. Gladys and Elsie picked up something of the same kind the day before, which I hope we can remember to tell you personally.[29]

It looks now as if we should go home about the middle of May. In these circumstances I am going to make a strong attempt to get permission to go over to England almost immediately, staying as long as possible there, and coming back here to sail. Of course this is, as always, indefinite; but we will cable as soon as we know anything. There is much of interest behind the decision to come home a fortnight earlier than we had expected, but we don't yet know everything, and what we do know does not bear putting on paper.[30]

We shall have to hustle to do the various things that we had promised ourselves in Paris before going. I still hope to get to Verdun and hope that Gladys can go with me to Lille, Arras, and Ypres. But if it proves impossible we have seen enough to know pretty well what the country that was fought over looks like, and have seen elaborate trench systems.

What remains to be done in the peace settlement will have to be done by the few big men at the top, and I think that they may want

---

29. The "T.N.T." may have been the report that the Italians planned to seize Fiume by force and present the Conference with a fait accompli, but the personal tone also suggests the first evidence of the break between Wilson and House.

30. The six signers of the letter to Wilson rather expected to be discharged from their duties.

us out of the way in order not to embarrass them by obtruding our consciences when they feel it necessary to make a deal.

We are going to *Faust* tonight and, if there is no revolutionary disturbance on the first of May, hope to go again then.

✤ 8 ✤

ALARMS AND A MAJOR EXCURSION

May 1–21, 1919

AT THE END OF APRIL the German representatives were summoned to Paris to receive a copy of the treaty. They were placed behind barbed wire and, in keeping with the confusion and delay that frequently characterized the Conference, they were kept waiting for over a week. Finally, in an apparent spirit of revenge they were handed the lengthy document, approved the day before by a plenary session, on May 7, the anniversary of the sinking of the *Lusitania*, and in the Palace at Versailles where William I was proclaimed Emperor of Germany in 1871. Meanwhile the Italians, fearful of overplaying their demands for territorial loot, returned to the Conference.

The Germans were not unexpectedly dismayed at the terms, which they at once announced to the waiting world. A few minor American representatives left Paris in protest, and Senator Knox introduced a resolution calling for separation of the League from the treaty. Lloyd George, who shared a common British concern that Wilson was not going to be able to lead the United States into full support of treaty obligations, began to have second thoughts and to seek means of softening the treaty, but Clemenceau would not budge. Surprisingly enough Wilson now backed Clemenceau on the basis that it was too late to undo the work already finished.

The Conference then turned its full attention to completion of the settlement with Austria-Hungary. For Seymour this meant a flurry of last-minute meetings with regard to boundary details. Generally the Council of Four approved unanimous commission recommendations—Teschen and, later, Klagenfurt being two exceptions; questions of ethnically mixed or virtually inseparable provinces were resolved in favor of the former governments, the Tyrol and Bohemia again being the most notable exceptions. Consequently, when the Austrians were called to Paris in mid-May they were presented with detailed maps of the new successor states. The two of primary interest to Seymour were, of course, Czechoslovakia and Yugoslavia. The former was to be a composite of national cultures formed by the union of three major provinces—Bohemia, Moravia, and Slovakia —in addition to parts of Silesia (Polish) and Ruthenia (Magyar). The inclusion of German Bohemia was dictated by both economic and strategic reasons; it would give Czechoslovakia a sound industrial basis and would also provide a military wedge to apply against Germany if necessary. The projected map of Yugoslavia seemed even more piecemeal; it was put together by linking the already united Serbia and Montenegro with parts or all of eight other provinces of the former Austro-Hungarian Empire, each of them peopled by Slavic groups but some of them still disputed by Italy.

The terms of the German treaty and the Adriatic question were clearly the central issues throughout the month of May, but they were not the only ones. Disposition of the German colonies under the mandate system brought protests. The Supreme Economic Council renewed the blockade. Plans for the disposition of the Baltic states were discussed. Proposals for the settlement of Asia Minor created violent dissension. In short, the prospect for a comprehensive agreement still seemed remote.

American Commission to Negotiate Peace
4 Place de la Concorde, Paris

Thursday, May 1, 1919

This being May Day everyone in Paris is doing no work and although we could have forced our office force, which is chiefly composed of the A.E.F., to appear, we decided to "chômer"[1] also, there being little or nothing to do. A good deal of excitement is in the air, for the advanced Reds of Paris have promised to make trouble. The labor federations agreed with the government not to make any manifesta-

1. Cease work.

tions; but semi-Bolshevik elements arranged for a monster mass-
meeting on the Place de la Concorde and a march through the boulevards to the Place de la République. This was forbidden by the government and everyone wondered what would happen. American soldiers
were warned not to appear on the street unless it was necessary and
there was some electricity in the atmosphere.

This morning everything was quiet, and up to 2 o'clock the streets
were dead. All the shops are closed, the métro is not running and there
are no taxicabs. When I went to the offices after lunch I saw two whole
squadrons of cavalry coming from the Tuileries out on to the Place and
a battalion of infantry over the river. They scattered to all the strategic
points on the Place and up the side streets, three platoons of cavalry
going up the rue Royale, where they formed across the street; the
space in front of the Madeleine was filled with cavalry which came in
from another direction. Over in the Tuileries they had machine guns
ready to be brought out. Between the platoons of cavalry were lines
of *sergents de ville*.[2]

All this time, up to about 3, there were very few people around.
Knots would sift through the cavalry, who paid no attention to them,
form groups on the Place, and then be scattered by the cavalry who
walked their horses against them. About 3, however, looking out
from my office window up towards the Madeleine, I saw a great mass
of people, filling the street from side to side, yelling, and with large
red flags. They got through the first line of cavalry by the Madeleine
without much trouble; the cavalry let about 500 through, evidently
wanting to separate the crowd, then they closed up. These 500
came down the street where they met the two platoons of cavalry almost under my windows. There was quite a struggle, the cavalry evidently preferring to let a man get by rather than hurt him.

But those who got by, generally in groups of ten and a dozen, had a
hard time, for they ran into the line of *sergents de ville*, who outnumbered each group two to one, and who set on the people with
ferocity; there was no joke about their fighting; the *sergents* ham-

2. Policemen.

mered them about the heads, got them on the ground and kicked them. An ambulance came up and we saw several, pretty badly wounded. An American M.P. told me that four men had been killed, but this has yet to be confirmed, and will never get in the papers; certainly the fighting for ten minutes was fierce enough. The cavalry finally charged with the flats of their sabers and cleared enough of a space to permit a fire engine to come in from the rue St. Honoré; this used the hose on the mob and broke it up. Altogether the thing was handled skillfully, for the troops managed to separate the crowd into groups which were always outnumbered, and which finally slunk away in twos or threes. One of the soldiers in our office, a courier, was an ex-policeman from Boston and was full of admiration for the way the crowd was broken up.

To an American it seems foolish to prohibit a mass labor parade, and when one sees the brutal manner in which the *sergents de ville* treat the crowd one's sympathies are with the latter. A fairly well-dressed man under our windows, after the real fighting was over, simply spoke to a *sergent* and got two hard punches on the jaw which sent him sprawling. But they say that if they don't keep the crowd thoroughly cowed and let them get out of hand, anything might happen.

I asked a French officer why have any troops on the streets, and why let the *sergents* be so provocative. He said that if they had not broken it up when it started, there would have been 50,000 on the streets in an hour and that they could have started a good second-class revolution. But with the troops occupying all the strategic points nothing could possibly succeed. Most of the troops evidently were good-natured but did not sympathize with the manifestants who looked pretty Bolshevik. They all had red rosettes. I shall never forget the sight of that black crowd coming down the street waving its red flags at the moment it ran into the troops. It might have been Petrograd, or the Revolution of 1848, which started close to here and in very much the same manner. They say there were various fights in other parts of

Paris. Gladys came over to see the later part of the fuss, the passageway from the Crillon to the office running behind bars and the gates being closed.

Tonight we are having dinner with the two Polish delegates—Paderewski and Dmowski—with flowers, cigars, and wines, inasmuch as it is a "state dinner."

Thus far we have not had any contact with the German delegates, who are kept strictly to themselves at Versailles and not allowed to go outside fenced-in limits. It is quite possible that we may never see them, inasmuch as they meet in public only when they receive the treaty and when they sign it. We had lunch today with the Herters; he is White's secretary and, as White is on the credentials committee, is going out to Versailles to get their credentials. The Germans refused to furnish their credentials except in exchange for the credentials of the Allied delegates, which is technically correct but rather amusing. I talked with Major Tyler,[3] who is our liaison officer with the Germans, and he says that they know they are representatives of a defeated power. Brockdorff-Rantzau, he says, is the only gentleman in the lot.[4] Their experts are all businessmen and it is likely that they are going to put up the chief objection to the treaty on economic grounds.

Fiume has sunk a little into the background and the Italian press is rather more conciliatory. I am afraid that they will get some sort of a compromise in exchange for coming back to Paris. Colonel House is optimistic and thinks that they cannot stay away for long. He is more of a negotiator than the President. Clemenceau is reported to have said to Colonel House: "You and I could settle anything; but I don't understand President Wilson very well; I could talk just as

3. Major Royall Tyler, field observer for the Commission.
4. Count Ulrich von Brockdorff-Rantzau (1869–1928) was a career diplomatist who led the German delegation at the Conference. He protested against the Treaty on two major grounds: its terms were not in keeping with the conditions of surrender, and many were impossible of fulfillment. The first Cabinet of the Weimar Republic, led by Philip Scheidemann, resigned rather than sign. Scheidemann was succeeded by Gustav Bauer on June 23, and Brockdorff-Rantzau became Foreign Minister. Later he served as ambassador to Moscow.

easily to Jesus Christ." I have his remark on very good authority.[5] We think that the Italians showed so much obstinacy last week because they thought that the American experts were at odds. Several of our men had had long interviews with the Italians and were not so strongly opposed to their claims; but all the experts who were responsible for the particular area were united in their opinion and it was their opinion, evidently, that counted with the President.

Friday, May 2, 1919

Our dinner last night was a great success. Elsie sat next to Paderewski and Gladys next to Dmowski, who is really the bigger man politically, though not so picturesque. Paddy was simply delightful, all smiles and apparently really delighted to be in a pure American dinner. He said he loved America more than anything after his own Poland and had thought of becoming an American citizen often, but had waited in the dim hope that some day he might have an independent country of his own. He was as cordial as could be, shaking hands with a very strong grip, joking, and making pleasant speeches. He seemed naïve. "I am popular just now at home," he said; "I think it is because I waited to become a Polish citizen."

I asked him how he liked addressing crowds and he said "Oh, I am used to them; I used to play the piano, and people were kind enough to come in large numbers." I said that I had had the pleasure of hearing him, and he said, "You are very good indeed to call it a pleasure." When I spoke of Horatio Parker in New Haven, he shook my hand again, and spoke with the greatest enthusiasm of Yale, which had given him a degree in 1917. He said that he had literally not touched a piano since 1916, and Mme. Paderewski said the same thing later. His hair is getting thin in front but is still thick behind. He looks more intellectual than he used to. I was surprised to notice the

5. This remark was verified by Col. House.

benevolence of his eyes, not expecting that in a temperamental genius. I was also surprised to see that his hands are large, not tapering, the fingers not very long and very thick. They are obviously muscular.

After dinner I talked for a long time with Dmowski, who is a rather cold politician, but, I think, sincere. He says that Poland is now the only bulwark against Bolshevism and is going to be the only block to German control of Russia.[6] He feels that war between Poland and Germany is inevitable; that Germany will never give up Silesia and Posen. He feels that England had not supported Poland as she should and that she will regret it later. He talked for a long time on the absolute ignorance of everyone in Western Europe of Russia and her problems. The revolution there, he says, was assisted by Englishmen, who failed to understand that any revolution which caught the army, as did that of 1917, was bound to lead to anarchy. Mme. Paderewski is short and fat, black and shrewish looking.[7] She is said to be a woman of great force and looks after her husband as a lioness her cubs.

We are planning to go over to England on Sunday and stay for about a week. I managed to persuade the people higher up that I was not needed while the purely formal matter of handing the treaty over to the Germans was going on, inasmuch as they will probably not put in any answer for two weeks, and most of our work is at a standstill. So I have permission and we start on Sunday morning. I now think that it is very likely that we shall sail for home in about three weeks. I am glad, for everything that I am concerned in is settled, except the Adriatic, and that is obviously going to be settled on the basis of some sort of a deal.

The weather has been abominable, cold and rainy. On Monday afternoon we went to the Mint with the Days to get some of the war medals which have been struck off by the government.

Stopped suddenly—forced to send this without finishing—will write from England.

6. Dmowski was somewhat inconsistent. (C.S.)
7. Despite appearances, Mme. Paderewski was not shrewish. (C.S.)

Wednesday, May 14, 1919

Here we are back in Paris again after a wonderful rest and the best sort of good time with Beth and her family.[8] We had planned to come back on Sunday or Monday anyway, as I was not supposed officially to be away and feared that something might come up of importance. Then came a telegram on Saturday from the Commission asking me to be back for Monday. It seems that they had decided to push the Austrian treaty through as rapidly as possible and that the old Council of Ten, which had not met for weeks, was to consider the recommendations made by the Rumanian and Czech commissions and settle the boundaries of Austria and Hungary. It was really important that I should be there, for the big people might take exception to some of our proposals which ought to be explained to them and defended.

It was fun to go into Pichon's study again and see all the big men, the "grosses légumes,"[9] they call them. It was the first time I had seen the Italians since their return a week ago.[10] Orlando looks very white and worn and says very little and without much pep. He looks ten years older. Sonnino is unchanged in appearance and preserves some truculence of manner, but is not aggressive. He put up many objections in debate, but invariably gave in, sometimes gracefully and sometimes not; he was rather disingenuous in manner and did not make a very good impression. It seems likely that they are going to take anything that is given them in order not to lose everything.

8. During this absence from Paris all of the members of the American Commission were warned of bomb plots against them and of the need to be suspicious of packages received in the mail. In particular, any bearing the label of Gimbel Brothers were to be examined carefully.

9. The bigwigs.

10. The Italians returned on May 5, after being wildly applauded at home, but without having disrupted the "Big Three." Lloyd George and Clemenceau backed Wilson's statement but by permitting him to make it alone they avoided any of the Italian public hostility. They did send a message to the Italian Commissioners, however, stressing the point that Fiume was excluded from the Treaty of London promises. Fear that the entire Treaty might be cast aside and that Italy would be denied any reparations brought Orlando and Sonnino back.

It is said that they returned to Paris just in time; France and England were on the point of sending them an official note to the effect that their withdrawal and abstention from the Conference was to be regarded as a breach of the Pact of London[11] and the Treaty of London, and that peace with Germany would be signed without them and the Adriatic question settled on its merits without regard to the Treaty of London. They may have had advance news of this. At any rate they seemed scared. If matters turn out as we now hope Wilson's policy and his action in publishing openly the American point of view will be fully justified. Some arrangement may be made for Fiume which will allow them to surrender gracefully and save their faces.

It is suggested that Fiume be left under the League of Nations but within the Jugoslav customs orbit until Italy can turn Buccari into a port with equal facilities as regards docks, moles, railroads, etc. As this is absolutely impossible, or at least seems so, it would be tantamount to leaving Fiume to Jugoslavia but with political local autonomy, which would be fair. Even this arrangement would be made only if a plebiscite in Fiume indicated the desire of the town to be left outside Jugoslavia, which is doubtful. The President has said definitely that he will not approve any compromise.

Clemenceau was irritable and brusque, evidently in a hurry and unwilling to let matters drag, which pleased us all. When Sonnino evaded questions Clemenceau pinned him down brutally. "You must want one thing or the other M. le Baron Sonnino," said Clemenceau, when Sonnino was trying to postpone a decision; "are you in favor of the proposal made by M. Tardieu and the Commission, *oui ou non?*" At one time matters became tense and Sonnino said that in view of the universal hostility shown to Italian interests he saw no use in continuing the discussion; but Orlando and Balfour calmed him down.

Clemenceau treated Tardieu with irritable impatience; the latter

11. The Pact of London of September 4, 1914, bound the Allies not to seek a separate peace. A later Pact of London was a military convention stemming from the Treaty of London. It provided for Allied protection of Italy against Austria.

rose to whisper to Sir Eyre Crowe, who sat behind Balfour; this ob-
scured Clemenceau's view of the Italians; he rapped sharply on the
table, motioning Tardieu back and snarling, "S'il vous plait, Mon-
sieur." The gesture was so peremptory that Tardieu, who is himself a
Commissioner Plenipotentiary, was obviously offended. He looked
like a sulky pupil who doesn't dare refuse to obey the master but who
wants to be treated more carefully; he moved back with great dig-
nity and assumed carelessness, but I saw his eyes flash. Maybe he
already regards himself as almost in Clemenceau's shoes.

A little later I myself drew Clemenceau's wrath. The interpreter,
Mantoux, next to whom I was sitting, asked me a question about a
map; I leaned over his table and spoke in a low tone, only a foot or so
away from Clemenceau. The latter turned suddenly on me with a loud
and fierce "ssh." It came so abruptly and Clemenceau's eyes were filled
with such irritation that I realized why they call him the "Tiger" and
lost no time in shutting up and sitting down.

Wilson looks tired but has not lost his debonair manner or good humor in debate. As I have written, there can be no real understanding
between Clemenceau and Wilson but they are enough men of the
world to make it seem as if they were on the closest terms. Wilson was
very genial to me, when I explained the various points of importance,
and contrary to our fears raised no objections. The President is temperamental. At times, as you know, he works regardless of any advice; this has happened here, notably in the cases of Danzig and the
Saar. At other times he accepts absolutely the advice given him by the
men whom he thinks are capable and objective. That was true in the
case of Fiume. Monday he was in the latter mood and took all our
recommendations without question. "If anyone who knows about this
will tell me what to do, I will do it," were his very words. As usual
he was very quick to understand the points at issue. In this respect
he stands head and shoulders above the majority of his colleagues.

Lloyd George did not take much part in the discussion. Did I tell
the *bon mot* that is passing about with regard to the big Britishers;

it comes from one of their own men; "Bonar Law[12] cares but doesn't know; Balfour knows but doesn't care; Lloyd George neither knows nor cares." Forgive me if I have written this before; it is good, and I want to remember it. As a matter of fact on Monday Balfour had been very carefully coached and was very good, explaining when misunderstandings arose and smoothing down incipient acerbities. Fifteen years ago he would have been wonderful. Today he still has the best mind here.

I talked with Tardieu and Cambon after the meeting and they, as chairmen of the commissions on Czechoslovakia and on Rumania and Jugoslavia, respectively, were both very happy men. This means that I have very little real work left to do. I suppose that I must stay until the terms are presented to the Austrians who come this week; the treaty should be ready next. The Hungarians may be delayed, inasmuch as we do not want to recognize the Bela Kun government and should prefer other representatives; but I may be able to get away before they come. The proposal that six of us should go home this week, a proposal made by Mezes, has been refused by the Commissioners. Therein lies a very little story, which I hope you will remind me to tell you when we get home.[13] I have asked for passage about June 1 and within a week hope to know with some definiteness. I am now anxious to get back; I feel that I have given all that I can and have received all that I can. I would not willingly have missed this last meeting of the great; it was quite a picture to see the three most important men in the world whispering over a table, after the meeting.

Bowman went back yesterday with his wife. We gave him a dinner Monday night where we discussed the history of the Inquiry and the

12. Andrew Bonar Law (1858–1923), Lord Privy Seal and British Peace Commissioner, was leader of the Unionist Party and had served in Parliament and as Chancellor of the Exchequer (1916–18). In 1919 he became Lord Rector of Glasgow University, and in 1922 he led the overthrow of the wartime coalition government and served a short term as Prime Minister.

13. The story that the six signers of the letter to Wilson were being punished was subsequently denied by both Mezes and House.

way it had developed and the part it had played here. Bowman may justly be proud, for he did much to avoid the various pitfalls and is largely responsible for the fact that the Inquiry has put through its program, in the main, and has done the big job here. There were 14 of us, of whom 9 have served on commissions in some form or other and had direct contact with the President. Of the 14, only 5 called themselves Democrats and they were of the Mugwump variety. But it was interesting to notice that everyone, including the strongest Republicans, were unanimous in the belief that Wilson was the only man in America who could have handled our foreign relations effectively since last summer. I think that all of us feel that his policy up to the beginning of the Conference was practically flawless, with the possible exception of not allowing the war to continue a fortnight longer; but that responsibility, with the terrible loss of life that would have come, would have been heavy. All of us feel that no one living in America could have secured what Wilson has secured at the Conference, although some of us feel that Roosevelt in his prime would have done better. Of course it was too much to expect that we could have preserved our prestige everywhere as it was last January. It is now very high in Central and Southeastern Europe and, I think, England. It has inevitably been lowered in France and Italy.

I think the chief criticisms passed on the President were, first, that he has a one-track mind and that this fact slowed up the Conference. Instead of making an immediate and very general peace, purely preliminary in character, once he got on a subject he would not leave it until some sort of a definite solution had been arrived at; this accounts for the amount of time lost at the start. The other powers were not strong enough to insist upon an immediate general settlement. With the consequent delay the value of the cards which we held in January diminished. A second criticism was that, as at home, he kept himself isolated. He should have lived at the Crillon and kept in closer personal touch with his own Commissioners and those of other powers. Fortunately Colonel House acted as intermediary and thus indirectly kept the President in touch with all the currents. There was some disagreement as to whether or not the time spent on the League of Nations had held up the Conference. Personally I think not.[14]

Bowman told of a very satisfactory interview he had just had with Lansing, who said that he wanted to speak with him about the Inquiry. Lansing said that at first he had not understood what it was nor what kind of men were in it (as a matter of fact I suppose he did not like it because it had been organized by House). But that during the work of the commissions and in the Council of Ten and of Five he had come to see that the men were very strong and that the work they had done was indispensable. It is pleasant to get this as we had all felt that when we arrived we were looked on with some suspicion, possibly as a fad of Colonel House.

I have said nothing about our week in England. It was most satisfactory in every way; we found John so congenial and Lawrence delightful.[15] We did very little except shop and be with Beth and John all we could. On Friday they had a tea for us and invited their closest friends that were in town. We were greatly pleased that our old friend Sir John Biles[16] came up to see us. He had tried to get us to lunch with him and Sir Ernest Shackleton, the Arctic explorer, but could not reach us in time. He reiterated the invitation that Lady Biles had sent us, to come and visit them in Scotland—but it seems

14. The author strongly reiterated this view in his article, "The League of Nations." He also vigorously attacked one of Wilson's detractors, whose book on the Peace Conference he called "an imaginative travesty" and "pernicious." See Seymour, "A Great Opportunity Missed" (review of John Maynard Keynes, *The Economic Consequences of the Peace*), *Yale Review*, 9 (July 1920), 857–61. Accusing Keynes of missing an opportunity to make his total analysis as sound as his criticism of the economic clauses of the Treaty of Versailles—the same criticism made by the American delegates—he wrote: "It is more truthful to say that the President, discovering that a peace of reconciliation was impossible (and no one abroad last spring could fail to see this fact), decided to save what was nearest his heart by a series of compromises. The word is detested by doctrinaires, but we have the authority of Gladstone for believing that it forms the essence of statesmanship."

15. John Angel, Seymour's brother-in-law, and his son, now a noted anthropologist and a curator at the Smithsonian.

16. Sir John Harvard Biles (1854–1933), mariner, naval architect, and author.

clear that we cannot accept. That evening we went around to the house of one of John's friends, a painter and saw his work.[17]

Saturday we went to the Academy to see John's "St. George," which seemed to us one of the finest items in the exhibition. The sensation of the Academy paintings is Sargent's "Gassed"—a horrible thing.[18] Altogether we found the London Academy much more interesting than the Paris salon, which we saw the week before.

Our trip back to Paris on Sunday was comfortable from beginning to end; we had an early start, breakfast on the train to Folkstone, the Channel like Lake Whitney,[19] and an easy ride to Paris. The road was the one the Germans tried to cut last year and a good part of the way there were evidences of warfare: lots of shell-holes, support trenches and dugouts, half-ruined villages, etc.

Here the weather has turned into summer and we are taking every chance of getting out into the open. Almost the nicest thing in Paris is our balcony, these hot days, looking up to the Etoile and over the trees of the Champs Elysées, with the music from the Ambassadeurs floating up to us.

Tuesday, May 21, 1919

I am enclosing a hurried unsatisfactory description of our trip; I have not had time to write out myself the impressions made by it, so I simply dictated hastily the main facts. If I had had no other experience over here, this trip alone would have been worth the time it took.

.   .   .

17. The painter was Frank Salisbury, who later did the portrait of Mrs. Edward S. Harkness, wife of one of Yale's most munificent benefactors. It hangs in the Yale Library.

18. John Singer Sargent (1856–1925) was the famed American painter best known for his portraits.

19. Body of water just north of New Haven where Yale crews practiced.

Notes on Trip to Verdun Front—May 17–19, 1919

We left Paris Saturday morning, May 17, at 8 o'clock, in perfectly dry weather, not very much dust, going out east on the main road to Meaux. Everything was quite different from the trip in March when we started in a snowstorm and had to ride inside a closed car, seeing far less of the country. This time our car, a Hotchkiss, was so arranged as to let the top down, and we were in perfectly open air, although well protected from the dust behind. My plan, which I had worked out with Major Johnson, was to go first to Rheims, and spend the first day on the Champagne front, and the night in Bar-le-Duc.

The chauffeur, however, had failed to understand that we wanted to go to Rheims, which he knew we had already visited, and it was only after passing through La Ferté-sous-Jouairre that I noticed that he was on the direct road to Montmirail and Chalons, which would have given us a pretty ride and an excellent view of the battlefields of 1814, but nothing of the last war; we stopped him and after consultation turned up across country, north to Château-Thierry. Mrs. Scranton[20] had not visited here before, and we spent half an hour going through the streets from which the debris had been cleared but which still presents as completely a ruined aspect as in January.

We went up to the Marne to Dormans where we crossed the river and followed the main road to Ville-en-Tardenois. This was a ride which I had long wanted to take, as it represented one of the two main lines of retreat of the Crown Prince's army last July, when the Germans were trying to get themselves and their supplies out of the pocket, and where their retreat was threatened by the French, British, and Italian attack between Epernay and Dormans and the French attack on the northwest near Soissons. The villages were badly battered, some of them completely destroyed, and Ville-en-Tardenois itself

---

20. Mrs. William W. Scranton, grandmother of Gov. Scranton of Pennsylvania, Yale '39, accompanied the Seymours. She was a volunteer worker in the canteen established in Paris by Ann Morgan, sister of J. P. Morgan.

was in ruins. You probably remember how anxiously we waited for the news last July as to whether or not the Germans would be able to pull themselves out of the Château-Thierry salient, and what bitter fighting there was in this region. There are still many indications of a large amount of supplies which they were forced to leave behind, ammunition dumps, often made up of shells of very large caliber. This was the salient where the Americans had their first real taste of fighting.

Beyond Ville-en-Tardenois one mounts a height which is really a spur of the mountain of Rheims, from which one looks down on the plain of the Vesle, with Rheims in the far distance, clearly marked by the cathedral towers. As one approaches the city from the southwest, the road runs through the German trenches built last year in June and early July, when they were making desperate efforts to encircle Rheims; the trenches are battered and, from the number of shell-holes, it is obvious that desperate fighting went on in this region. We had stopped near Dormans on the Marne for a second breakfast, but found in Rheims a hotel which had reopened its restaurant; here we had a very fair lunch at prices which, while they were not cheap, did not equal those of Paris.

Rheims in broad daylight presents an even more pitiable aspect than it did last March at sunset. After lunch I walked through the streets over to the cathedral and was impressed by the completeness of the destruction, which one does not notice in simply riding through in an automobile; the walls of a great many houses are intact, and at a distance one would not notice that the interior of the house is completely gutted. Frequently you come to a street in which no walls whatever are standing, and in which the debris is piled high on the sidewalks. Of the larger buildings, such as the theaters and the Bourse, the steel framework has been twisted and is on the ground in a tangled mass resembling gigantic barbed wire.

The life of the town is beginning to revive in extraordinary fashion. I saw three or four places were one could get something to eat, generally in the ground floor of a building of which the walls were standing and where canvas formed temporary ceilings and oilpaper served for windows; life must be somewhat similar to that in San Francisco after the earthquake and fire. We spent some time going around the cathedral, but were unable to find an entrance. The stones which were weakened during the bombardment and fire are now being taken down by the German prisoners; from the noise of falling debris inside, it is unsafe to go in. My first visit had inured me to some extent to the damage done to the cathedral, and I was not so depressed by its sight as in March. The damage done to the northern tower, where a whole shaft has been shot away, certainly spoils the perfection of the west front.

The facade is unquestionably marred beyond repair by the statues which have been broken, but I think that the battered effect will pass away in time when the stone broken by shrapnel has lost its white color and takes on the same as that of the part of the cathedral which is untouched; from the side it looks certainly like a shell, for the roof is fallen in; but the flying buttresses are nearly all intact. Provided it is not restored, or is only restored slightly, I think that it will still be the most magnificent church in this part of the country, possibly in the world; but the absolute perfection which was one of its great characteristics is certainly gone.

We went out east from Rheims on the road to Suippes, passing through a myriad of trenches, some of which were knocked all to pieces, others being still in a state of excellent preservation, and therefore particularly interesting. We stopped near the fort of La Pompelle, where extremely heavy fighting had gone on last year; the fort itself is nothing but a mass of subsoil churned up; over the concrete foundations, some of which are still intact, a little further east, we came to the permanent German line as it was established after the great French offensive of September 1915. Many of these trenches were in concrete with elegantly fitted and very deep dugouts; others belonging to the same system were made only of sandbags; but the Germans had evidently left them in such haste last September that they were in the same condition as when the fighting was going on.

The wire has not yet been cleared from these fields, and there are masses and masses of it stretching across in long lines. In one place we could distinguish the front firing line of both the French and the Germeans about 500 yards apart, then the support trenches on both sides 5 or 6 deep, and behind them a series of dugouts fitted up with comparative luxury.

We wanted to spend more time in this region, but it was getting late in the afternoon, so we motored down to Chalons to see if we could get a hotel, planning to go out in the evening to the front again. Not the least interesting part of the ride was to pass through the series of camps behind the lines, the first aid stations, then more elaborate ambulance stations, and finally more to the rear an evacuation hospital; the open air stables for the horses, and the camps for camions well in the rear. Not far from Chalons was a large aviation field with 400 or 500 aeroplanes, and close to these a series of bombproof houses half underground, possibly one hundred of them, all of which were labeled for concentration of hand grenades. All along the road, of course, were enormous ammunition dumps, the shells still there rusting in the sun and rain.

At Chalons we found that there was no hotel accommodation, and we were urged by the lady who kept the hotel where we inquired to burn as much ground between us and Chalons as possible since there would be no chance of finding shelter even in the house of a private person. We had telegraphed for rooms to Bar-le-Duc, but feared that the wire had not gone through, and knew that it would be so late by the time we reached there that, unless we had a room, we should be in a bad fix. So we decided to go southeast to Vitry-le-François, a lovely ride up the Marne Valley. Here our chauffeur knew of a small hotel which, as it turned out, was glad to take us in.

Sunday morning we got started at 7 o'clock, going east from Vitry-le-François to Bar-le-Duc, over lovely rolling ground. We stopped at various villages, which had been occupied for a few days by the Germans during their first great advance in 1914, half a dozen of them,

I should think; four of these had been burnt to the ground by the Germans when they were forced to get out. Our chauffeur told us that the burning parties had as a matter of fact been captured in the French advance and had been shot immediately. In most of these no attempt has been made to rebuild, and the devastation is as complete or more so than that done by the shelling in the Soissons district; the foundations are all that remain and the sight is made more lugubrious by the weeds growing in the courtyards and over the stones. At Etrepy some rebuilding has been done in brick and is not very picturesque, but at least it offers shelter to the inhabitants who are coming back. I did not know that the Germans had come so far south in 1914 in that region and was appalled to see the signs of devastation still so manifest after nearly five years.

We got to Bar-le-Duc at about 9, left our bags at the hotel where we reserved rooms, and set out at once for St.-Mihiel. One goes up a gradual incline for about 15 kilometers, reaches the crest of a ridge and looks down on the Meuse Valley which, at this distance, is green and beautiful. The villages as one approaches the St.-Mihiel front are almost completely battered to pieces, and it is surprising that the farmers who are still obviously working their fields can find any shelter for themselves and their families. But they are full of people, in contradistinction to the villages which have been burnt or which were in the fighting area itself. Just before one descends to the valley of the Meuse, there is a fine view of the St.-Mihiel massif, which stands out like a great bastion.

The road comes down a slope to the river, passing through myriads of trenches, some of which have been filled up and the fields about them cultivated this spring; but most of which are still as they were when the Germans were driven out in September. I looked with a good deal of interest on the woods and villages along the road as I have talked with so many of our American soldiers who came up here before the attack of September. The German trenches cross the river one kilometer or so to the west, then curve around on the heights of

St.-Mihiel itself. The town is larger than I had supposed, and a good deal of life is going on there, although there are practically no houses which are not what we should call destroyed.

We motored south, just on the side of the hill which rises very steeply from the river, following the course of the German trenches which turn sharply to the east about four kilometers to the south of the town. At the apex of the salient we left the car and walked up to the top of the Fort des Romains, a superb position dominating the whole valley; there are about 15 German trenches, most of which are built in concrete, and the spaces between them filled up with tangled masses of barbed wire. Any direct assault on the position was obviously out of the question. Where we left the car, about a quarter of the way to the top of the hill, was a superb concrete dugout, extending about 40 feet underground. A platform runs along inside, upon which one could stand resting one's elbows on a slight concrete ledge and from which one could look out across the valley at least 20 kilometers to the southwest. It commands all the plain of the Meuse and the woods in which lay the French trenches; commands also the plain to the south and the whole valley of the Meuse to the northwest. A single lookout from this concrete bastion could immediately uncover any movements of troops over three-quarters of the horizon.

We walked up the hill back through one trench after another, the path following gaps in the barbed wire. Three-quarters of the way up there was a large flat plateau, about the size of a football field, surrounded by low concrete walls which were covered with sandbags and with sod on the top of these, and which, though badly mashed in, still offered great protection. Here were a couple of tennis courts; and close to the battlements outdoor pavilions where the German officers could take their ease. The dugouts themselves were fitted with an elegance which seemed to indicate that the place had been used as a sort of a rest area. The top of the hill was a mass of shell-holes and had evidently undergone very severe fire; but the various trenches and dugouts, the position of which could not possibly have been determined by their enemy, were in excellent condition.

From the top of the hill, one could look east all along the line of
the salient to Seicheprey and Pont-à-Mousson. The view of the whole
salient was so superb and the trenches so interesting that we stayed
here longer than we had intended and had to give up any ideas of
motoring further to the east. So we came back and went north on the
road from St.-Mihiel to Verdun again, passing through the line of
German and French trenches to the north of the town where the
salient curved east from the Meuse. At Troyon we went up from the
road to the Fort with its network of trenches, and had our lunch. This
fort has been held successfully by the French all through the war,
holding out in 1914 with a handful of men and machine guns.

Thence we went on the 15 kilometers to Verdun and out from the
town northeast to what had once been the original ring of forts. Verdun itself still preserves its very picturesque aspect, for the buildings
along the river have not suffered nearly so much as one might expect.
In the center of the town, however, there is nothing left but a mass
of stones and plaster. The roads taking us to Vaux and Douaumont
were in beautiful condition, being the strategic routes built during
1916 and afterwards. For the first few kilometers out of town, the
ground looks like the ordinary battle area; then one suddenly comes
up on the heights of Belleville, and gets a view of the whole ring of
hills. The first glance is not so appalling for, in the distance, the hills
look like Connecticut pasture land; then one suddenly realizes that
the whole landscape is nothing but a series of shell-holes, not one of
which is complete but is broken into on all sides by kindred shell-holes
filled with water and overgrown with weeds. Here and there rise on
the skyline a few black splinters, which is all that remains of the magnificent forest which once covered these hills.

The area is surprisingly large; we motored for 15 or 20 minutes
around these roads; always the same desolation intensified by the
thousands of crosses which stick up from the mud. At one point we
stopped and on consulting our map found that we ought to be at a
village called Fleury; we looked around and found as a matter of fact
a few bricks and stones, and realized that we were on the site of the

village, which had completely disappeared. Vaux and Douaumont can hardly be distinguished from the rest of the hills, so completely have the villages and the forests disappeared. The side of the hills is a mass of dugouts, some of them large, some of them very small, and badly battered; we went through a number of these, I taking the time to go far underground.

It is without question the most lugubrious sight I ever saw in my life, and it is impossible to imagine the impression made without getting it oneself. For large areas even the weeds are unable to grow, a whole side of the hill being absolutely white with the subsoil turned up by the shellfire. One of the most shocking experiences was to come out of a dugout and look at a bank about 20 yards square and suddenly to realize that it was plastered with hand grenades which were lying as thick as pebbles on the seashore. The sides of the hills are a network not of barbed wire, most of which has been cleared away, although along some lines it remains thick and tangled, but of telephone wires run about a foot above the ground and into the various dugouts.

As you may imagine, we spent some time here, then crossing over to the other bank of the river to see Mort'homme and Hill 304, then going south to Glorieux to visit the American cemetery outside the evacuation hospital. This is where Harold Hemingway was buried last October; we are the first of the friends to be able to come to Verdun, and I was very glad to be able to locate his grave. We had brought some flowers for it, and I made arrangements with the man in charge of the hospital to have it planted and looked after, and hope later on to have some kind of a monument put on it. The American graves are plainly marked and there should be no possible mistake. It was a great satisfaction to have seen it, and I know that the Hemingways at home will be much relieved.[21]

We had hoped to be able to go from Verdun to Montfaucon in the Argonne; but we had taken so much of the day that it seemed unwise,

21. Harold Hemingway was later reburied in Grove Street Cemetery in New Haven.

particularly as we had broken a spring, and the roads in the Argonne are said to be extremely rough. As a matter of fact we had already taken in about all that our imagination could hold, so we came back up the Meuse to St.-Mihiel and thence to Bar-le-Duc, which we reached at 8 in the evening. The trip from Verdun to St.-Mihiel on the west bank of the river was particularly interesting as showing us the arrangements made for the maintenance of troops in support, thousands of dugouts in the cliffs, footbridges built across the river, huge stables quarried out of the rock, hospitals, ammunition dumps, narrow gauge railways, and signs for the direction of the troops, the camions, and the wounded.

It was an extraordinary feeling motoring back to Bar-le-Duc to leave the signs of war and come into cultivated fields which for kilometers at a stretch look as though they might never have heard the sound of a gun. We finished the day with a really excellent dinner and a bottle of champagne.

I ought to have taken the train Sunday night for Paris, as my day on Tuesday was to be a very busy one, and I needed a good many hours to get ready for it; but I decided to forget my conscience and have a comfortable night and a pleasant motor trip back. We came back on the direct road through Chalons to Montmirail, riding very easily, getting coffee at Chalons and lunch at Montmirail at a hotel which I remembered perfectly from my trip in 1902. This direct road does not pass through very much of the present war; but it took us near the marsh of St.-Gond, from which Marshal Foch made his famous offensive in the battle of the Marne in 1914, and also where Napoleon fought his brilliant defensive campaign of 1814. It is curious and extraordinarily affecting to pass in the same field the monument of a soldier killed in the German invasion of 1814 and not 50 yards from it one of a soldier killed in the German invasion of 1914.

We got to Paris at 5 o'clock, thanks to the perfect weather and the comfortable car, by no means tired.

·   ·   ·

My work has taken on a sudden recrudescence, owing to the fact that, as always, many things have been forgotten which have to go into the treaties with Austria and Hungary, and we are working at feverish haste to get the treaties ready. The Austrians at St. Germain are having a very good time and evidently enjoying their food; so they are in no particular hurry to receive the treaty and have to work; but we had been hoping that things might be so fixed as to have it signed at the same time as that with the Germans. Our territorial commissions have been resuscitated to decide the various little points which come up at the last minute, and we have been meeting daily. I missed a Czech meeting on Saturday and a Rumanian and Jugoslav meeting on Monday, by reason of my trip, but it evidently didn't make much difference as there was no scrap on.

Yesterday morning we had to spend in hearing the claims of the Jugoslavs, who had told Clemenceau that we had not given them sufficient opportunity to make their demands understood. So, after discussing for two hours in the Czech Commission various clauses to go into the treaty with Austria which concern Czechoslovakia, I spent the rest of the morning listening to Vesnić, Trumbič, and Žolger, who represent the Kingdom of the Serbs, Croats, and Slovenes. Then from 2 until 5, Day, Johnson, and I discussed what attitude we should take toward their demands. It was rather a difficult situation, for while Clive and I are the official representatives on the Commission, Johnson and I have made the particular studies of the districts involved, and we disagree. Johnson, largely at the inspiration of Colonel House, is very anxious to satisfy the Jugoslavs, who are losing at the hand of Italy; he wanted to grant their claims at the expense of Austria. I, on the other hand, did not think it fair or wise to make Austria pay for the greediness of Italy; and I felt this the more strongly in that I have always supported the Jugoslavs against the Italians. We had a very hot discussion, and it was only with great difficulty that we finally reached a compromise which really met my point of view and refused the worst of Jugoslav demands.

Then at 5 Clive and I went into a Commission meeting to fight for my point of view. We could not get the Commission to accept it; but it has yet to go before the Council of Foreign Ministers [Council of Five], and then before the Council of Four and I may yet be able to put it over. It is one of the few points on which I know I am right; I am in an absolute minority; but I think that I can yet beat the others. It is a point which was settled according to my way of thinking six weeks ago, but the French and the British have wobbled. Tardieu and Crowe were genial but very sad over my obstinacy, Crowe making one of his affecting appeals, with tears in his voice and begging his "American colleagues to show once more that spirit of conciliation and compromise which had always characterized their actions." But we were adamant. De Martino, the Italian, was there and showed poor diplomacy, I thought. None of the questions involved Italy at all, and he might, by supporting Jugoslav claims, have put them under an obligation to Italy which would have been very useful to Italy in later negotiations. But instead of doing it gracefully, he bluntly said that he would support the Jugoslav claims only at a price.

The Italian diplomacy all through has been Prussian rather than Machiavellian, and by its bluntness has disgusted people. De Monthille, who is a skillful diplomat, said to me that he did not mind the Italians' crookedness, but he did object to the gaucherie. The Adriatic negotiations are coming along well although they are so delicate that anything may upset them. The Italians have apparently given up all hope of getting any sort of sovereignty over Fiume;[22] it looks now as if it would be an international free city but practically controlled by Jugoslavia. They are also backing down on Northern Dalmatia and most of the Islands. They will get something to save their face, which is more than they should have in strict justice; but the Adriatic question will apparently be settled with moderate fairness.

There is still much gossip as to whether or not the Germans will

22. This was a misjudgment. (C.S.) See Seymour, "The Struggle for the Adriatic," *Yale Review*, 9 (April 1920), 462–81.

sign, but the people that know most think that they will have to, although they may stall yet for some time. I do not think that I shall have to stay for the signing of the treaties and believe that we shall sail about June 7.

These days are so busy that we have not much social life. But yesterday Bill Warren[23] came in to lunch with Lester and George Abbott, Harvard baseball captain in 1916, and we had interesting tales of the front and of Poland; for Warren has been one of the American officers accompanying General Haller's army to Poland. He has made two trips across Germany and is just starting out on a third.[24] The Germans are rather nasty, he says. Last night we had dinner with the Days and heard about their trip to the Somme, which they took while we were at Verdun. Tonight we are going to Mlle. Turpin's;[25] she has asked us to come and hear some Chopin.

The weather is wonderful and I wish you could be here on our balcony. Paris looks and feels just as it was ten years ago, full of taxis and gaily dressed people. It is unbelievable that a year ago the country seemed on the brink of disaster.

(Later.)

I have just heard that the economic clauses are going to be softened for the Germans—this may hold things up, but we still expect to sail on June 7.

---

23. William C. Warren, Jr. (b. 1892), Yale '14, an artillery captain, saw action at Saint-Mihiel and was then placed on detached service convoying Polish troops from France back to their homeland. He returned to law practice and headed the New York State Dormitory Authority.

24. General Joseph Haller de Hallenburg (b. 1873) helped form the Polish Legion and fought against the Russians until the Treaty of Brest-Litovsk in 1918. Compelled to disarm his forces by the Germans, he fled to Paris to join the Allies. In 1919 be recrossed Germany to lead the continued Polish fight against the Bolsheviks. Later he served a brief term as head of the Polish government (1923–26). In 1940 he was imprisoned by the Russians and disappeared.

25. Mlle. Gabrielle Turpin, concert-pianist, was a friend of Mrs. Seymour.

⇢⇢9⇠⇠

THE TREATY OF VERSAILLES

May 28–July 2, 1919

THE FINAL DRAFTING of the peace terms to be imposed upon Germany continued to produce violent disagreements within the Council of Four. Already Wilson and Lloyd George had opposed any French annexations other than Alsace-Lorraine, but to appease French security demands the President agreed to a tripartite military guarantee treaty, which the Senate later rejected. Already they had locked horns on the reparations issue, never completely settled by the Conference itself but delegated to a successor commission. Already they had encountered Polish claims supported by France, Japanese claims opposed by China and Australia, Italian claims partially supported by Britain, and British claims in the Near East opposed by France. These had been the thorny questions settled by compromise in order to keep the Conference together and to preserve the League of Nations. Now, it seemed, the time for compromise was past, at least any compromise concerning Germany.

Neither German protests nor Lloyd George's second thoughts could move Wilson or Clemenceau. Orlando, having lost out on his own overextended demands, was no longer involved. In mid-June the Germans were given a few minor modifications and sternly told to sign at once. An acute crisis in the German government resulted. Prime Minister Philip Scheidemann refused and was replaced by a new ministry under Gustav Bauer who decided that further resistance was futile and that there was no alternative to signing, a decision echoed by a vote in the Weimar Assembly. Since the Socialists and Liberals controlled the Assembly they became the targets of Hitler's later nationalist resurgence.

While debating the German situation, the Council also attempted to iron out details of the treaty with Austria. The draft of this document was not formally presented until July 20, although the Austrians were told of its contents in late May. In the light of the German reaction, their own second thoughts, and Austria's plea that the new state should not even be considered the one that went to war in 1914, the Council spent much of June revising these proposals. The Treaty of St. Germain of September 1919 was the eventual result, followed by treaties with Bulgaria, Hungary, and Turkey (signed between November 1919 and August 1920).

But first there was Germany. On June 28 in the Galerie des Glaces of the royal palace the Treaty of Versailles was finally signed by all the Allied plenipotentiaries and two German underlings. Wilson and many of the Americans left for Brest at once and sailed on the following day. Crossing the Atlantic his party had moments for reflection. They knew it was a far from perfect treaty. They knew they had not measured up to their own high hopes and ambitions of seven months earlier. They could only argue that they had done their best under impossible circumstances, and they could point to the League of Nations—at first a "fantastic possibility," later a "desirability," and finally an "absolute necessity," in Seymour's phrases. But even this part of their answer was to be largely eliminated when, nine months later, the United States Senate rejected the Treaty and the League and, in effect, placed Wilson in the category of Clemenceau and Orlando—three of the Big Four who did not survive the political repercussions of their prolonged labors. Seymour felt that he had come home to find a "reverse Rip van Winkle." The country had "slept briefly but soundly," too soundly, for Harding's "normalcy" became the apostasy of Woodrow Wilson.

❦

American Commission to Negotiate Peace
4 Place de la Concorde, Paris

Tuesday, May 28, 1919

Our hopes of being able to finish up practically all the details necessary for the final draft of the Austrian treaty this week have been again deceived. The hope was to get the treaty for the Austrians completed by Friday of this week; but so many changes have been suggested and so many points hitherto not considered have arisen that this is going to be impossible. The Austrians have been getting rather uneasy despite their excellent food and comfortable quarters at Saint-Germain;[1] it is now planned to give them on Friday or Saturday the clauses which have been finished and to postpone until next week the unfinished economic and territorial questions. On the territorial side, the chief difficulty has been that the Jugoslavs have uttered strenuous protests against the findings of our territorial commission.

On that commission, Day and I consistently advocated a frontier which would give to Austria and to Hungary, so far as possible, natural boundaries; such a frontier, however, would include quite a large number of Jugoslavs, most of whom are Slovenes. Now as it happens the Slovenes are the weakest numerically of all the Jugoslavs, although they are the furthest advanced in civilization and, as we all feel, necessary to the success of a united Jugoslav state. Because of the Italian claims in the eastern Alps, a large number of Slovenes is going to be included in Italy. This is necessary; but the Jugoslavs claim that they ought not to lose any further number of Slovenes to Austria and Hungary, and therefore insist on a revision of the territorial commission's report. Vesnić protested strongly to Clemenceau last week and contended that Jugoslav claims had not been adequately heard. Clemenceau accordingly asked Tardieu to call our commission together again to listen to their claims. As a result of this meeting and hearing, the French and British delegations advocated changes in the recommended line.

The Italians also favored change, but naturally with the reservation that they could not approve it unless their own particular interests on the Jugoslav-Austrian frontier should be satisfied. Day and I opposed change on the ground that the frontier recommended had been carefully studied for several months and unanimously adopted by the Commission, that it was the frontier fairest both to Austria and to Jugoslavia, and that it was not right that because of the extent of Italian ambition the excessive losses to Jugoslavia should be compensated at the expense of Austria.

1. Like Versailles, a city with a famous royal château, close to Paris.

Our particular difficulty lay in the fact that Johnson, who has been working on this area with Day and myself, shared the point of view of the French and British. The three of us got together all last Friday and most of Monday to see if we could work out a compromise, but as each of us held to his opinions, we finally decided to send in separate memoranda to the President and Commissioners. Day's and my point of view is supported by Coolidge, who has been at the head of the mission at Vienna, and by Colonel Miles,[2] son of the general, who has made an investigation of conditions on the spot.

The Commissioners naturally have been confused at getting different advice from Johnson on the one hand, and from Day and myself on the other. Yesterday morning we all three had a long pow-wow with Lansing. I let Johnson explain his position to the Secretary first, inasmuch as Lansing's mind is naturally critical and tends invariably to be opposed to the point of view which is presented to him; and I thought Johnson might kill his own case by talking too much. This turned out to be correct; Lansing agreed with a good many of the points Johnson brought forward, but the latter talked a bit too long and too emphatically.

In the afternoon the question was discussed by the Council of Ten which met in the President's house at the Place des États-Unis. I had not talked personally to the President about the matter, having merely sent him memoranda, and did not know whether he would support Johnson or me. As it turned out, he had been strongly affected by Colonel Miles' memorandum and argued from my side of the case, endeavoring to persuade the British and the French not to change the frontier originally recommended. Lloyd George asked that the matter not be decided on the spot, and I do not know at the present moment how it will come out.

The Italians are slowly coming around to an acceptance of our point of view in the Adriatic. Tardieu told me yesterday that in a

2. Colonel Sherman Miles, an American liaison officer assigned to Coolidge's Vienna field office, investigated military activities in Carinthia and conditions along the Adriatic coast.

meeting of the Four the previous evening, Orlando agreed to give up Fiume, but asked for the integral carrying out of the Treaty of London. Wilson thereupon made what Tardieu described as a very strong speech, attacking the treaty as unjust and unlikely to prove a solid basis for future peace in the Adriatic and calling attention to the very wide concessions made to Italy in the Tyrol and to the northeast of Trieste. Clemenceau followed, affirming the readiness of France to maintain her engagements toward Italy, but advising Orlando in no uncertain words not to hold to the letter of the Treaty of London. He said that he could not understand how any wise statesman would want to carry back to Italy the empty honor of territorial acquisitions which meant isolation for Italy, since liberal opinion in France and England would be made hostile to Italy and it was improbable that the United States could sign any engagement containing execution of the Treaty of London.

Orlando, it appears, wilted and said that he would bring in a new proposition.[3] The evil results of Sonnino's policy are now becoming apparent. Italy is now apparently isolated; the Italian newspaper feeling is setting against the British and the French almost as strongly as it is against the United States. For myself, I believe that a new ministry in Italy is the only solution, and I hope that it will be sufficiently liberal to recognize the mistake of the Sonnino policy, and enter firmly and honestly into a policy of cooperation with France and England.

At the present time, however, Italy is doing all in her power to play a strong solitary game working for an understanding, if not an alliance, with Bulgaria; doing everything in her power also to come into close contact with Austria, demanding that Jugoslavia shall surrender to Austria a large block of pure Slovene territory in order that Trieste and Vienna shall have as effective railroad connections as possible.

Lansing is convinced that Austria cannot stand alone; he feels that

3. Orlando's eventual inability to acquire Fiume led to his being unseated and replaced by Nitti, who adopted an effective policy of procrastination.

it is merely a question of time to arrange an economic alliance be-tween Austria and Germany, or Austria and Italy, and that economic alliance in the case of Germany practically means political incorpora-tion. The best solution, naturally from our point of view, would be the confederation of Danubian states we worked so hard for last fall. But this seems to be impossible—both because Italy does not want it, and, primarily, because the Czechoslovaks, Rumanians, and Jugoslavs re-fuse absolutely to enter into such political arrangements.

While some days have been busy, pressure of work has been spasmodic, and we have been able to find a good deal of free time. Last week, we went out to Fontainebleau and Chartres with the Days and Hugh Bayne. We left Paris immediately after an early lunch, going up the Seine to Melun; motored then on in the forest to Fon-tainebleau, where we spent a couple of hours going through the palace. Elsie, when she found the crowd of visitors gathered at the door, characteristically let the guardian know that we were from the American Peace Commission; with the result that we were taken around in a party by ourselves, shown all the private staircases and back alleys which I had never seen, as well as an infinity of storerooms with treasures of furniture, statues, and tapestries from the towns of the devastated regions, which have not yet been returned. After tea we went through the forest to Barbizon, left our bags and motored for an hour, getting out to see the gorges and pick flowers.

Sunday morning we went on to Chartres where we had lunch and spent two hours in the cathedral; came back by Mainenon and Ram-bouillet, where we stopped to see the Chateau, and Versailles, where we hoped to see the Germans, but did not. With Bayne along it was a very merry party and a most complete rest.

This week we are comparatively gay. Monday night the Chris Her-ters had us to dinner and took us to Marigny where there is a gor-geous show, with decorations and costumes by the man who did the Russian Ballet; it was a composition of the most daring and vivid color that I have ever seen. Last night we had George Nettleton to dinner. Tonight we are going to *Pelléas* at the Opera. Tomorrow night to the Majestic with some British diplomats, and Friday to some reception or other, the name of which I forget, but which Gladys insists upon attending.

It looks now as though we should not be able to sail as early in June as we hoped. I sent in a request to the Commission to be released the first week of June which was refused. I was told that I ought to stay until the Austrian treaty was signed. This I hope will be certainly by the first of July, and my hope is that we shall be home by the first. It seems likely that the Commission will pack up when the German and Austrian treaties are signed inasmuch as we are not at war with Bulgaria and Turkey. Bliss and White consider that their mandate as Peace Commissioners ends when the Austrian and German treaties are signed, and Lansing says that if the United States is to help in the construction of the Bulgarian treaty, he can work as well or better in Washington, especially if the President is there. The President, I suppose, will sail the moment the German treaty is signed and it is possible that he may go sooner.

Friday, May 31, 1919

I failed to get this off when I meant to, so I will add a postscript. The question of the southern frontiers of Austria around Klagenfurt,[4] which gave rise to so much trouble, has been settled, and my point of view with slight modifications is accepted by the Big Four and will go into the treaty. It is a great satisfaction to me and a personal triumph, as I had the French, British, and Italian delegates on the territorial commission opposed to me as well as Johnson. But Wilson backed my point of view and persuaded Lloyd George and Clemenceau.

4. Klagenfurt was the capital city of the former duchy of Carinthia, located in a basin lying at the southeastern extremity of the Austrian Alps. The territory was divided ethnically between Austrians and Slovenes. Seymour's Commission recommended the basin be kept intact and left to Austria, but the Council of Four heeded a Yugoslav plea for a two-zone plebiscite, which eventually confirmed the original recommendation.

We learned of the decision Thursday morning when several of us were summoned to Wilson's house where the Council of Four was meeting. We sat around in the big room upstairs before the fireplace for half an hour, the Four being downstairs. Then Lloyd George came in and said: "Well we've settled it." Orlando came in with his impassive, expressionless face and Clemenceau in his grey gloves. Wilson appeared looking very brisk and smiling, and said: "Gentlemen, my colleagues have asked me to tell you of our decision. We are going to have a plebiscite."

We went into the next room where the floor was clear and Wilson spread out a big map (made in our office) on the floor and got down on his hands and knees behind it to show what had been done; most of us were also on our hands and knees. I was in the front row and felt someone pushing me, and looked around angrily to find that it was Orlando, on *his* hands and knees crawling like a bear toward the map. I gave way and he was soon in the front row. I wish that I could have had a picture of the most important men in the world on all fours over this map.

The Italians were not entirely satisfied with the decision and I was interested to see how Wilson parried their objections, very genial but understanding the significance of their points and not yielding. I was also interested that he should be the man of the Four to explain what had been done. More and more the feeling on the inside of the Conference is that he is the biggest man here. Lloyd George is strong by reason of his magnetism and his cleverness, but he lacks background —is really uneducated. Clemenceau is hampered by his old traditions from which he can never get away. Moreover he feels, I think, that his chief work is now done, when the frontiers of France are settled and the proportion of French drafts on the indemnities fixed. So he is content to be staying in the background. Naturally it has been to his advantage to keep in the background entirely so far as Adriatic questions are concerned.

As soon as we had received the decision of the Four we hurried around to the Foreign Office to draft the clauses for the treaty which was to have been handed to the Austrians the next day. We went over again in the afternoon and had a look in at the plenary session, which ended a few minutes after it was called when Bratianu demanded that time be given to the little powers concerned to look over the treaty. Clemenceau was rather peeved, but it was a reasonable request and had to be granted. So it is likely that the treaty will not get to the Austrians until Monday or Tuesday. In the meantime I have been working over the proofs of the treaty, checking up errors and alterations. The Italians are apt to slip something in at the last moment; had done that in at least one instance, hoping that it might not be noticed. They are slick!

Thursday evening we went out to dinner with Nicolson and Leeper at the Majestic, which the ladies enjoyed greatly. Last night I was to have gone to another dinner there, where Lord Robert Cecil was to have presented a scheme for an international institute for the study of international relations and publications of documents.[5] But I had come down with a mean cold and decided to give it up. I got my cold by having a fine game of golf at St. Cloud Wednesday afternoon and then rushing back to the Opera with Gladys and Lester, the Opera being very cold.

Paris, Monday June 3, 1919

We are very much disturbed because of an eleventh-hour loss of nerve on the part of the British, who are bringing up proposals for very serious changes in the German treaty. They had a Cabinet meeting yesterday, as a result of which Lloyd George wants to let up on the Germans and accept some of their counterpropositions. Doubtless by the time this reaches you, you will have it in the papers, though I

5. This was the origin of the Royal Institute of International Affairs, which first met in London in 1920, and its American counterpart, the Council on Foreign Relations. (Nicolson states that Lionel Curtis first conceived the plan.) One of the Institute's first projects was H. W. V. Temperley, ed., *A History of the Peace Conference of Paris* (6 vols. London, 1920).

presume it will be colored and denatured. I believe that the following is true. The British, and to some extent the French, have just come to realize how severe the terms given to Germany are, especially the economic clauses. For the first time they are appreciating what we told them six months ago, that they risked not getting anything from Germany by asking too much. They are also realizing that, especially in the east, they run the risk of raising up a truly national German movement by assigning too much purely German territory to Poland. They have also come to realize that the occupation of German territory on the Rhine is not for military purposes but in order to give France economic control of the Rhine and its tributary territory for 15 years.

This eleventh-hour realization combined with the pressure of liberal opinion in England which regards the terms of the treaty as too severe, and also combined with the fear that the present German government will not sign, has put them into a state of "funk." As a result they suggest a series of changes in favor of Germany, which would mean going over and refashioning the work of the last four months. The three changes they want consist of compromises in the matter of reparations, Polish frontiers, and period of occupation of German territories.[6]

Now the curious, the humorous, and the discouraging aspect of all this is that what they propose now we ourselves advocated at the beginning of the negotiations. We met the British and the French halfway, softening down their first demands but yielding on many points. We yielded because we felt that the first necessity was absolute unanimity among the Allies against Germany and also because we were honestly persuaded that on several points they were right. But having come around to an agreement, now we do not feel like saying that we will change back again, especially as it means the danger of splitting the Allies.

6. Seymour later attributed this change, in part at least, to the influence of Keynes, who convinced Lloyd George that the Treaty, if not immoral and impossible, was at least too punitive. Representatives of the Dominions, especially Smuts, also contributed to this change in attitude.

Naturally France does not agree with this new tack of Lloyd George, Clemenceau pointing out that all of the changes suggested involve sacrifices by France and not by England. France will modify the reparations clauses to some extent, so as to make it possible for Germany to pay; but she will not go as far as Lloyd George wants; and she will not lessen the period of occupation which, as written in the treaty, represented a compromise between Foch, who wanted 30 years, and the British, who wanted two to four years.

As a result of the crisis we had a grand meeting this morning of all the American delegates. It was the first time they had all been together and in many ways it was the most interesting morning I have had over here. It was in Lansing's study downstairs. Wilson, Lansing, White, Bliss, and House sat in big armchairs while the experts —territorial, financial, and economic—faced them, sitting in a semicircle. Wilson as usual was very genial and came around the small circle shaking hands with each of us and saying some words to everyone on his particular work.

He began by saying that it was time to decide how much the German counterpropositions were worth and explained the new attitude of Lloyd George who wanted to make big concessions. He said that he had his own opinion but wanted to know what we thought; he asked the persons chiefly concerned with the questions of reparations, Polish frontiers, and occupation of German territory (the three chief points raised by the British), to give their views. Lamont, Norman Davis,[7] Baruch, and McCormick spoke on reparations. They explained they had always regarded the hopes of the French and the British of getting their enormous indemnity as illusory; they felt that the German protest against a permanent reparations commission, empowered to take an indefinite amount of capital from Germany,

7. Norman Hezekiah Davis (1878–1944), banker and statesman, was the Treasury's Finance Commissioner to Europe in 1919, and became head of the Finance Section of the American delegation and a member of the reparations and finance commissions. He was in the van of the Americans contending for reasonable reparations. Later he worked for the League of Nations and became a roving ambassador for President Roosevelt.

was well founded. They thought that it would make it impossible to
revive German industry and therefore for Germany to pay its indemnity. Evidently the French and British had been under the impression that America would finance Germany, and it was only now that
the British realized that we would not, that they were drawing back.

We had always contended that a fixed indemnity should be established so that German industry could know exactly how much it was
to pay; unless it knew, there would be no chance of a revival of German industry and ability to pay. Germany was justified in protesting
against an all-powerful commission because of the way in which
French commissions during the last four months had consistently
violated all agreements of an economic nature.

Colonel House then spoke of his interview with Clemenceau and
Tardieu. Clemenceau had agreed that he would make some concessions in details but not in principle; Lamont thought that he would
consent to a fixed indemnity. It was agreed that our men should go
back to the French and British with the idea of establishing a fixed
indemnity. Apparently the Germans, they feel, will pay anything that
they can, if only they know how much it is going to be.

Then the question of Polish frontiers came up and Lord put up a
strong plea for the maintenance of the frontier as contained in the
treaty draft. He used arguments which I have used often myself,
namely that it is criminal weakness, after studying a problem for
months and arriving at the best solution, to get cold feet at the last
minute and make a snap judgment. After all, the German counterpropositions added nothing to our knowledge and it was wrong to be
affected by eleventh-hour emotion.

Then Bliss took up the question of the occupation of German territory, showing that it was useless from the military point of view
and was designed to give control of the Rhine from an economic
point of view. It was also wanted by the French as a means of paying
for their army, inasmuch as it is to be maintained by Germany. Of
course the cost of maintaining the army would be deducted from the

amount that Germany could pay. Many of the French themselves were convinced that it was an extravagant thing; but since they do not want to decrease the size of their army at once, this would enable them to maintain it without the French taxpayer realizing the cost of the military establishment.

House then brought up the question of admitting Germany at once into the League of Nations, which is one of the chief complaints of the Germans. He thought that if it were not for the question of occupation the French would consent to the immediate admission of Germany. Wilson answered that he was not himself in favor of immediate admission; that he thought that we must still wait some time to be certain that the change in Germany was definite and sincere; he was almost certain that the new Rhineland republic was camouflage. Germany could not be treated on a basis of equality until we were absolutely assured that the new Germany was a peaceful democracy. In this and in regard to a good many other points, I think that many of our friends at home would be surprised by Wilson; it was this which particularly interested me, for in the midst of his idealism, and I think he is an idealist, he showed himself very hardheaded.

When, for example, Lansing suggested that every delegate hand in a list of things which he thought could be conceded to Germany without serious effect and make it easier for her to sign, he argued strongly against it. "We ought not to be sentimental," he said. "Personally I do not want to soften the terms for Germany. I think that it is a good thing for the world and Germany that the terms should be so hard, so that Germany may know what an unjust war means. My concern is only to eliminate anything that is really unjust. I do not want to do anything simply to persuade Germany to sign. We did not write this treaty simply in order to have it signed. We must not give up the things we fought for now, even if we have to fight again."[8]

He went on to show the danger of trying to remodel the treaty en-

8. The author later used these words of the President to refute the charge that Wilson's concept of justice was flabby.

tirely at this moment and emphasized the necessity of maintaining absolute unity among the Allies and of getting the peace signed at once. "What is necessary," he said, "is to get out of this atmosphere. If the Germans won't sign the treaty as we have written it then we must renew the war; at all events we must not allow ourselves to flop and wobble trying to find something they will sign."

Altogether I was much pleased with his attitude, which is that of the statesman who has worked hard for months through conflicting interests and ideas and has finally come to an agreement as to what is the best arrangement, certainly not ideal, but the best in the circumstances, and who does not intend that everything shall be thrown back into the melting pot at the last moment. I am equally disappointed in Lloyd George. He made his great mistake last December, when in order to meet British opinion in the elections he promised impossible indemnities from Germany; because of his election pledges he advocated impossible terms. Now opinion in England has changed and he is changing with it, to the detriment of the international situation. He has kept his eye too much on home politics. I should not want to call him either weak or shifty, for we are too close to the event. But the last two days have raised Wilson, in my judgment, far above him. Of course great pressure has been brought on him by the British politicians. As Wilson said, the whole raft of politicos has been over here, from Winston Churchill to Fisher,[9] "from the bumptious to the prudent, from the pert to the priggish, from Kerr to Eustace Percy."

I think that our policy will be to urge upon the French certain key concessions, such as a fixed indemnity and, if possible, a shortening of the period of occupation; to urge the British not to press for large changes, and to get a definite ultimatum to the Germans as soon as feasible.

9. Admiral Lord John Fisher (1841–1920) was First Sea Lord, broght back to the Admiralty at age 74 by Churchill. It was he who first suggested the unsuccessful Dardanelles expedition.

Tuesday, June 4, 1919

No further news as to what is going on with the German counter-proposals. The papers hardly referred to the suggestions made by the British, which are evidently being kept a dark secret. I suppose that whatever concessions are made to Germany, Wilson and the American delegation will get the blame for. Wilson realized this yesterday, and laughed over it. "I shall have to take the responsibility for holding things up."

I have been busy over the Klagenfurt question again. It seems that after the Four approved the solution which I had fought for against Johnson and the other delegations, the Jugoslavs came in with a threat that they would not sign the treaty if this were not changed. They made it a part of the proposed Fiume dicker, saying that if they got part of the Klagenfurt Basin they would accept our proposal for Fiume, which the Italians have accepted in principle. As a result the clause about Klagenfurt was not handed to the Austrians on Monday, and I had a long pow-wow with Tardieu and the drafting committee at the Quai d'Orsay. Our representative on the drafting committee, James Brown Scott,[10] stood by his guns manfully; the decision of the Four was incorporated in an article and I hope will be handed to the Austrians with the other clauses. But the French and the British are doing everything to hinder it. You never know when anything is settled until it is in the treaty, and now it looks as if it wasn't settled then. Frankly speaking I think that we are the only people here who have the "guts" to stay by a decision once made.

Tuesday, June 11, 1919

We left Paris Saturday morning at 8 o'clock in the Express for Lille. There was a tremendous crowd at the station, train running in

10. James Brown Scott (1886–1943), Harvard-trained lawyer, educator, and internationalist, served as chairman of the Joint State and Navy Neutrality Board, 1914–17, and was a technical adviser in the International Law Section of the American Commission. In later years he was active in the disarmament and conciliation movements.

four sections; but we were able to get corner seats where we had a good view and it was really an excursion trip through the Somme. I should say that about two-thirds of the people in the train were persons living in the devastated regions going back to make their headquarters at Lille, which is the center of the work of reconstruction.

The line branches off from the main road to the coast just before Amiens and, shortly after Longeau, passes through the fighting area of about ten or fifteen kilometers. It is in the region immediately behind the French lines where the trenches were very hastily constructed. For a distance of five or ten kilometers west of the road these hastily made entrenchments seem to indicate that the French were getting ready for a still further retreat. Then the line goes into the fighting area of last spring after the German breakthrough, and near Albert, the territory for which the first drive on the Somme in 1916 was launched. The woods are absolutely destroyed by shellfire, and the ground is as thickly pitted with shell-holes as at Verdun. In some areas here it looks from the amount of subsoil thrown up as though there had been even more liberal use of high explosives. The ground is marshy and flooded although the weather has been very dry; some places entirely covered with water for areas of half an acre or more.

Albert itself is as badly knocked to pieces as the towns we saw along the Chemin-des-Dames. Except for the hastily constructed trenches, evidently made last year, there is no indication of the old lines along this part of the Somme, which were evidently knocked to bits. For a space of about ten or fifteen kilometers the country is pretty clear and prosperous looking, but near Arras, where the permanent line curved back, it is in as bad shape as further south. Arras itself is pretty well broken up although life has begun again. All along the line small patches have been reclaimed by the farmers and are being worked, and in a good many of the shell-marked fields they have been able to turn cattle out to graze.

There is evidence of a very well-organized movement for the reclamation of these territories, and according to conversation I had with the people of the district, there seem to be only two great difficulties to be encountered: first, financial arrangements, there being no spare capital in France for the backing of agricultural enterprises; second, the danger from grenades and duds scattered throughout the fields. Some way or another the money for the purchase of agricultural implements is being found and we saw huge quantities of plows on flat cars which are being distributed throughout the districts. The people are evidently simply blinking the danger that comes from the explosives lying around. They say the number of accidents is very high. I was surprised to find out how easily food-grazing ground can be found on fields that have been knocked to bits, and I should say the influence the churning up of the subsoil has on the value of the ground for grazing is rather exaggerated. One man told me that if they could train the cows not to kick the hand grenades around they could really turn these lands into pretty good grazing areas.

North of Arras we went through the Hindenburg line where for about a kilometer much of the ground is strongly entrenched. At this point in the line the trenches are of the regular concrete style with fine steps and entrances to what looked like very deep dugouts. Where the trenches had been badly battered to pieces there were pillboxes, but for most of the area it was the trench style of 1916 rather than 1917. Getting out of the real fighting areas and into the industrial regions of Douai and Lille it was obvious that the Germans in their retreat of last fall had done a good deal of damage in the way of blowing up factories, bridges, and railroads. Once in a while we went by a factory very much intact where they had evidently been pressed and had little time to do their dirty work. Douai itself is in better shape than Arras, but the factories, made of masonry, are in weak condition.

We got to Lille at 1 o'clock and were met by Perrin Galpin who, as head of the Commission of Relief of Belgium and Northern France at Lille,[11] got a car and papers to take us into Belgium. We

---

11. Perrin Galpin (b. 1889), Yale '10, a captain in the Field Artillery, also served overseas with the Committee for Relief in Belgium both before and after military duty. Later he became president of the Belgian-American Educational Foundation, executive director of the Grant Foundation, and trustee of the Institute for Advanced Study.

went up to his house for lunch and started out immediately afterwards with him and his wife. Lille has the outward appearance of being in very good condition, but he said that few factories had any machinery that could be used and transportation is difficult, as the Germans blew up all the bridges and spoiled all the railway lines when they got out. Just now the town is suffering from the influx of the returned refugees. We went north, crossing the Belgian border near Menin and then out on the Menin-Ypres road by which the Germans used to bring up all their stuff to the Ypres sector. Until within about ten kilometers of Ypres the country is like the rest of the battle area—the villages knocked to pieces by British shellfire. About five kilometers east of Ypres the aspect of the situation changes very abruptly.

When one gets on the ridge held by the Germans he has a superb view over the whole battlefield for about 40 kilometers. The ground is so flat that even a slight ridge gives a good view of the whole situation. To the south the skyline is marked by Messines Ridge, which does not look like anything more than a slight fold in the ground; then Mt. Kemmel which has a flat cone shape, and which looks important because it is the only thing that can be called a hill in the whole country. Then in the distance lies Ypres itself, which can be distinguished only because of a bit of masonry left standing from the old cloth mill, and farther to the north Passchendaele Ridge.

All this plain at one's feet is completely churned up and in many places absolutely barren even of weeds. There is practically no trace of any trench systems remaining but the line of German pillboxes, some of them shattered to pieces, but most of them in very good condition. They are concrete buildings about 20 feet square rising about 4 feet above the ground and going down very deep. The ground is so cut up with very deep shell-holes that I found it difficult to understand how a machine gunner could find any target with the enemy advancing, for the shell-holes are so thick that they seem to offer perfect cover.

We got out of the car and wandered around through some black sticks which were once Sanctuary Woods, came to a sign which marked the village of Hooge, which has completely disappared, and looked over the scattered remnants of one kind and another which have not yet been cleaned up. There are groups of British tanks stuck in the mud and every kind of British and German equipment. By stooping down anywhere you can pick up pieces of shrapnel or high explosive; in fact you are practically walking on iron. The thing that struck me particularly was the strength of the German positions, as they held to the high ground. A British officer, who was showing some people over the field, told us how he used to hear at night the German pumps going, and knew that every drop of water they pumped out of their trenches would necessarily run down into his. How it was that the Germans, after they had recaptured Messines Ridge and Kemmel Hill, were unable to get Ypres and drive on to the sea, I could not understand.

Farther on we went into the town of Ypres, which because of its size seems to me the most impressive and lugubrious of all the ruined cities I have seen. It is an absolute desert with no sign of life, and simply scattered bits of masonry sticking up. The British trenches run through the town and immediately outside it and are still in pretty fair condition. Outside of these trenches and near the German lines the British used shell-holes to develop a sort of pillbox system of their own, not made of concrete but of elephant iron.

We motored up the road to Poelcapelle with Passchendaele Ridge on our right. This gives about as good an idea, I imagine, of what no-man's-land looked like while fighting was on, for it is not cleaned up at all. We passed a large number of British tanks, some of them sunk in the mud, others knocked into bits as though they had been hit directly by a high explosive shell. There were lots of skeletons of aeroplanes. The riding was very slow inasmuch as the road was blown up at about every half kilometer. Vast craters about 25 feet across, all of them filled with water. In fact all of the shell craters of any size, although the weather has been very dry, are still full of water.

We went on north following the line to Dixmude where there are eight cafés running and not a single house standing. The thrifty Belgians are already preparing for the tourist trade, getting their trinkets ready for the traveler and selling postcards. Here we crossed the Yser, which is less of a stream than the Byram River,[12] but which formed no-man's-land in this sector for four years. The trenches here are redoubts above the ground; apparently as soon as a foot of earth is lifted there is nothing but water underneath. The Belgian trenches, which are very well preserved, and which we went through at some length, are built on the old railroad which evidently forms the only solid foundation. In front of the trenches is a strip of mud about a kilometer in width with a good deal of debris, fallen aeroplanes, etc. Then on the other side of the mud and the river, German pillboxes, for in this sector as well the Germans seemed to have given up the use of a single trench.

It looked as though the Belgians were taking life very easy and on the whole very comfortably in this quiet sector. The land is absolutely flat, so that everything is carefully camouflaged; there is not a fold of ground in which to hide. The villages are all destroyed, but on both sides wherever a chimney was left it had been lined with concrete, bombproof steel put on the inside, and turned into an observation post from which you could see five miles. At a distance of 50 yards it would be impossible to guess that this observation post was anything else except an unimportant piece of masonry which had not fallen down.

When we got to the coast at Nieuport we found that there were no bridges over the Yser, so we had to come back on our tracks nearly to Dixmude and cross over by the one road that has been repaired. The change, after we had crossed the German lines, from the absolute desolation of the fighting areas to the beautiful green and prosperous

12. A small stream near Rye, N.Y., where Mrs. Seymour's family was living.

territory occupied by the Germans was extraordinary. It was almost impossible to believe that the muddy desert we had just left had once been of the same character as the beautiful fields, well diked and drained, with white, red-roofed farmhouses and fields covered with cattle of all kinds. By this time it was half-past eight in the evening and although it was light we were getting hungry; so we put on all speed for the coast and got to Ostend by 9 o'clock. The town is about what it was in the old days before the war, although all the hotels are not yet open. We got good rooms on the sea front and had the best dinner I have had for five years, with perfect coffee, lots of butter and sugar.

Sunday morning, after driving around the town, which has its bathing crowds on the beach and Casino going, we went east along the coast back of the dikes which had all been fortified against an attack or landing party by the British. We got out several times to look into the very comfortable dugouts and to go up to the gun emplacements. Most of them are eight-inch guns with revolving turrets on heavy concrete foundations. The Germans tried to blow most of them up last fall but several of them are still in perfect condition. They have the range of all the points along the coast pointed on the insides of the turrets. Sleeping quarters are very comfortable and I imagine the German officers had a very good time, probably going into Ostend every night to dance and gamble. All along the coast for about half a kilometer inland the country is covered with barbed wire arranged in such a way that any landing party would be seriously handicapped.

We went on to Zeebrugge and walked out on the mole. The part that was blown up by the British submarines in their raid last year has been repaired so that it is possible to walk across, but they had done a thoroughly good job, about 30 yards having been blown away so that it was impossible for the Germans to bring up reinforcements. The mole is about a mile and a half long, and about half a mile from its end the British had drawn up their ladders and landed the party which put the guns on the end of the mole out of business. All the buildings on the mole are in a state of collapse; but it is hard to tell whether this was a result of the Germans blowing them up last fall or of the fighting on the mole. From the end of the mole we got a good view of the three ships which the British sank in the channel. The mole itself, where the British threw on their landing party, is about 40 feet above sea level, and one has to take off his hat to the nerve they showed in climbing up their ladders in the face of the machine-gun fire they must have had, for there are about 12 concrete turrets for machine guns along the mole.

We got lunch at Blankenberge and then motored down to Bruges where we had a fine concert by the chimes of the belfry; then on to Ghent where we got off and looked into the cathedral. We got to Brussels about half-past six, looked around the grand place, went to the arcades and had a better dinner even than that at Ostend the night before.

Brussels is the liveliest place I have seen for ten years. It is like the gayest of continental cities before the war. I never saw so many restaurants all brilliantly lighted, cafés of all kinds, dance halls, movie shows, and crowds of people in the street. The café next to our hotel must have had 500 people sitting at little tables out in front in the street, drinking and singing. Any kind of food or drink desired is brought at once. Prices for the most part are high, except for the dairy products such as eggs and butter. For breakfast Monday morning we had strawberries with an enormous bowl of thick whipped cream, an enormous omelet, crescent rolls, and all the butter and sugar we wanted for five francs. In fact, as I see it, the rule seems to be that the more a country suffered in the war the better food she now has and the gayer her spirits. It would be impossible to find a restaurant in Paris, and certainly none in England, where food and drink is so plentiful or spirits so high.

Galpin was in Brussels during 1915 as Hoover's assistant, and he told us that the country remained prosperous largely because the big businessmen and industrialists stayed in the country. The Germans obviously took pretty good care of the place, possibly because they meant to keep it for themselves. The Belgians, he said, were for the most part fairly docile to German rule and did not make very much trouble except for the gangs of apaches in the poorer quarters where the Germans never dared go. These apaches, he said, used to make open fun of the Germans and would get Derby hats, stick cabbages into their tops, and drill; "Nach Paris," they would cry, and then would all goosestep backwards.

Monday morning we spent looking around the town seeing the quarters where the German mutiny took place last fall, the churches and palaces; and after getting a delicious lunch we motored out to Waterloo where there is as big a crowd of tourists as though there had never been a war since 1815; then back to Lille through Ath and Tournai. We got there at quarter of five, just in time to catch the Express back to Paris.

It was a wonderful trip, not merely because of seeing the battlefront from Ypres northward to the sea (and in many ways this seems to me worse devastated even than the Chemin-des-Dames and Verdun sectors), but also because of the opportunity to see the reaction of Belgian life six months after the Germans got out.

I hope that Gladys has told you of our various gaieties, going to the theater last week, and up to the Lapin Agile.[13] Almost every day we get off for a walk, when it is not too hot, and stop for an ice or a drink at a café or terrasse. We have been having dinner parties up in our room for various people, and enjoying the long sunset from our balcony. Nothing new today on when we get off. I am trying, however, to make arrangements with Coolidge, who has returned from Vienna, to take over the details that crop up; if this arrangement goes through we may get off on June 21.

13. The Lapin Agile was a small restaurant in the Montmartre section, frequented largely by students and artists.

Tuesday, June 11, 1919
[Second letter of this date]

For the moment, work on the Austrian treaty had been held up because of the necessity of formulating the answer to the German counterproposals as quickly as possible. The attitude of the different governments remains unchanged from last week and it seems very questionable whether they can reach an agreement during the next four or five days. Lloyd George is still insisting on radical changes and concessions to the Germans. Wilson has agreed that so far as economic terms are concerned it would be most desirable to have a fixed indemnity set; but in this respect the French are holding out, fearing that the amount of the indemnity which seems large to us now would seem very small in a few years. I believe that the suggestion of our people in the Reparations Commission is that instead of postponing the fixing of a sum to be paid by Germany within two or three years, the sum should be fixed within two or three months, and that Germany will be given a representative on the Reparations Commission. What the Germans dislike most of all is that the future Reparations Commission, according to the terms of the draft treaty, is to have absolute powers; they fear, perhaps justifiably, that it will be dominated by the French who will use their power unfairly as in the case of the armistice commissions during the past few months.[14]

The reconsideration of the eastern frontier of Germany touching the new Poland has thus far lead to no definite result. The Americans (Bowman and Lord), who seem to me rather pro-Polish in their ideas, insist that Germany must surrender a large block of territory which is really German in character; this contains coal that the Poles maintain is necessary to their economic life. Wilson, on the whole, supports this point of view and works for it, I believe, on the Council of Four. But Lloyd George, on the other hand, is determined on im-

14. Ironically some of the Americans, mistakenly assuming that the United States would be represented on the future Reparations Commission, argued strongly for absolute powers, including the veto, which they could use to prevent actions they might consider excessive.

portant cessions to Germany in this quarter, although he is opposed by his own experts. He removed Sir Esme Howard from the Polish Commission because he was too pro-Polish, and replaced him by Sir Eyre Crowe; then he discovered that Crowe was anti-German; so he has replaced him by Headlam-Morley. The latter is a man, as I see him, of rather weak character and shifty ideas. He is described by Balfour as the "man who looks like a horse and talks like an ass." The probability of the immediate admission of Germany into the League of Nations is still being discussed with no result as yet.

Our point of view, as regards Austrian boundaries, suffered a serious setback last Friday when the Council of Four sent down a new decision with regard to the Klagenfurt Basin. The previous week they had accepted the principle that the basin should remain undivided and a plebiscite be taken of the whole area. This caused great discontent amongst the British and French, who told the Jugoslavs they ought not to submit to it. So Vesnić threatened the Four with the promise that Jugoslavia would refuse to sign the treaty and would not accept the American compromise on Fiume if they did not get a slice of the Klagenfurt Basin. Colonel House, who cares more about establishing a compromise between Italy and Jugoslavia than he does about a good frontier for Austria, must have talked to the President. The latter agreed on Sunday to a new arrangement by which the Klagenfurt Basin should be divided into two zones: if the southern votes for Jugoslavia, the northern will then have the chance to decide between Austria and Jugoslavia. The Jugoslavs will exercise provisional control pending the plebiscite. This promises disastrous incorporation of the entire basin into Jugoslavia, for Serb officials are just as good as any Prussians or Tammany Braves in getting people to vote the "right line."

The Austrian delegates are, of course, setting up a tremendous howl and if the Germans refuse to sign the treaty I think it quite possible that the Austrians will follow suit. In fact, everything that has been done in Paris has tended to force Austria into the arms of Germany. A little more tact and diplomatic skill and Austria could have been kept absolutely free from German influence and made a more effective barrier against the spread of German influence in the future toward the Adriatic. A really wise policy would have been to place German Austria on the same plane as Jugoslavia and Czechoslovakia—not regarding it as an enemy state—but this would have been policy demanding more foresight and intelligence than anybody connected with the French Foreign Office possesses.

Wednesday, June 12, 1919

The last two mornings I have spent at the Quai d'Orsay with the Council of Five who are considering the question of peace with Hungary. For a number of weeks the Belá Kun government seemed very weak and the Rumanians occupied a large part of eastern Hungary. But the Hungarians concentrated against the Czechs and have reoccupied a large district in the north. The powers now think that they will offer to invite the Hungarians here if they will retire. So yesterday the Five called in Bratianu, Beneš, and Kramář to tell them what boundaries we had decided upon between Rumania, Czechoslovakia, and Hungary. Of course they knew unofficially but they had never been officially informed.

It was interesting to see the difference between the Rumanians and the Czechs. Bratianu was very sulky and belligerent in his dissatisfaction with the proposed frontier; said that he could not possibly accept it without consultation with his people in Bucharest. Beneš, although he pretended to be bitterly disappointed, was as usual very smiling and said he and the Czechs would do everything to help things along. The result was that in today's meeting of the Five, the small additions that Beneš asked for were granted; while in answer to Bratianu's complaint the Five recommended that the suggested frontier be maintained.

Monday, June 17, 1919

This is very possibly the last of my letters, for after long delay we have received permission to leave at the end of the month. We are hoping to go on the *Savoie,* which sails on June 28. The ship is technically full up, as is every ship until September 1, but the government has a certain quota of reserved rooms on each and we hope to be able to get what we need. Clive, now a single man,[15] can certainly get accommodation, and they tell Gladys and me that they can fix us up, although they may not know until a day or so before sailing what we shall be given. I put in a memorandum asking for release at the end of last week, just at the moment when the reply to Germany was finally formulated, and put the necessity of my sailing on the ground of the lectures I was to give at Wilmington. Then I saw the secretary of the Commission[16] privately and explained to him. The Commissioners were very flattering, said that they let us go with great regret, but they must realize that there is little left to do except details which can be handled, or at least we think they ought to be, by regular State Department officials.

My work of the last few days has been sporadic. We have been working over the Austrian treaty, which when taken in all its provisions seems to us impossible. It attempts to treat German Austria, which is now a tiny state, with the same degree of severity as Germany. The Austrians say, and it is probably true, that if the proposed conditions are put into the treaty they will either be thrown into the arms of Hungary or of Germany. What is the most likely is that the different provinces will split away from Vienna, for nothing can stop them, and demand incorporation in Germany. Personally I see no way of preventing the union of these people with Germany except the creation of a Danubian confederation, and that is out of the question because of the hostility of the various component parts of the old

15. Mrs. Day left Europe earlier.
16. Joseph C. Grew. The lectures were to be delivered at the University of Delaware and dealt with the French Revolution and Napoleon.

Austro-Hungarian monarchy. It is just what we feared last summer when the breakup of the monarchy was foreseen. We have worked out some of the possible alleviations for Austria, which have been approved by the Commissioners and which are going to be studied by the President on his trip to Belgium. In the meantime the completion of the Austrian treaty is held up and we are still working over the southern boundaries in the Klagenfurt region. We have a meeting of the Jugoslav Commission tomorrow.

We have taken advantage of the lull in work to put in several small joy parties. Saturday we got a car (the best of the Commission with the best driver) and with Clive and Lester drove out through the Bois and St. Cloud to Malmaison, where there is an exposition of Napoleonic relics. I had never seen the château and was delighted with it and the gardens with their lovely roses. I was interested in our chauffeur whom we took in with us. He was an automobile mechanic before the war, had driven a camion at the front, and has been here since the Conference opened. He took the keenest interest in everything, brought his camera to get pictures, and listened with the greatest intelligence to everything that was said about Napoleon. Gladys and I translated for him. We went on from Malmaison to St. Germain, where we got out of the car and walked through the forest for a bit. They have quite an area roped off so that the Austrian delegates can get the air. We hoped to run into them but were disappointed. We are forbidden to have any intercourse with them, and I have not even seen them yet.

Sunday we got a car to go out to the races—the Prix du Jockey-Club which is the French Derby. We filled the car—Gladys and I, Clive and Lester, Captain George, and Kenneth Simpson, who is on his way home to be demobilized. The crowd was enormous and very gay. My judgment was, I may say, above reproach, when it came to picking good horseflesh. I was commissioned by the crowd to bet on the first race for them and chose a beast (properly named *l'Inconnu*) which no one had ever heard of and which after galloping well in the rear for the entire course put on a burst of speed at the final turn and won out. They all thought that my luck would end there; so for the next race they made their own choices, with the result that my horse again came to the front—a 15 to 1 chance! After that it was uncanny; I think I made something on four out of five. We came back to the Ambassadeurs and had tea on the terrace; everyone in very good spirits except Lester, who failed to pick winners and who had been short-changed! Last night the Galpins came to town and we had them to dinner and took them to Marigny, the color and costume show, which we had seen but which is unquestionably the best revue in Paris.

Wednesday, June 19, 1919

I have just come back from a meeting of the Commissioners to which Clive and I were called. It seems that they have got cold feet about letting us go and wanted to see if they could not persuade us to stay on. We were both very firm and said that we absolutely had to go and that we had left instructions for all the details that are as yet unfinished. Only the three were there, as House is in England and Wilson in Belgium. Lansing was genial, as he always is, except in conference; very flattering, expressing the greatest appreciation of the work we had done, saying that they could not hope to finish without expert help as they really knew nothing about the problems, etc. We pointed out what was left and the men who could carry it through. They said they would think it over again. I am sure that I can go, for my work is far nearer a finish than Clive's and there are better men in my area than in his to handle the details that are left. Moreover I have the lectures that I have promised to give for Dr. Odell.[17] But I think that Clive can get off also if he will only hold firm and say that he has got to go. He really ought to, for he needs a vacation and his health is not in good shape.

Yesterday we were busy all day at the Quai d'Orsay. In the morning our Jugoslav territorial commission met to consider propositions

17. Dr. Odell was a mutual friend of the writer and President Samuel C. Mitchell of the University of Delaware, who arranged for the former to deliver the lecture.

of the Serbs for the Klagenfurt Basin, and we were on the job until 1. Then in the afternoon the Council of Foreign Ministers met and I had to attend, sitting behind Lansing. It was complicated and funny. Sonnino had put through a proposition in the Council of Four ordering all troops, both Austrian and Jugoslav, out of the basin. This in itself was a good idea; but it had behind it the motive that when the troops were out, the Italians, taking advantage of disorders which they could create, would occupy it with their own troops.

The Four, instead of sending the telegram themselves, sent a letter through their secretary, Hankey,[18] to the Five, asking them to approve and send the telegram. Hankey's communication, like everything that he does, was vague, and the foreign ministers, seeing through the Italian plan, did not want to send the telegram. Also they were rather vexed at being made a telegraph office for the Four. Sonnino argued strongly for sending it, but the more Balfour and Lansing thought about the way they were being ordered about by the Four and the small amount of authority they, the foreign ministers, enjoyed in foreign affairs, the angrier they got. Finally Lansing said: "I wasn't brought over to Paris to send telegrams," picked up his papers and marched out, much to the delight of Balfour and Pichon who wanted to postpone the telegram, and the meeting ended there. It was very funny. As he put on his hat Balfour pointed out the wording of the message from the Four: "They say to send the order 'if we approve.' *Mais moi, je ne l'approuve pas*," dropping into French as he does in the case of a simple sentence and with a British West End accent.

Sonnino, who had certainly fooled the Four, was absolutely in the right in insisting that the telegram should be sent. He was very good-natured about the rebuff he got from Lansing and Balfour. I was sitting right next to him, a little behind, and he turned to fix me continually with his eye in the debate as I explained the American

18. Maurice Paschal Alers Hankey, 1st Baron Hankey (1877–1948) served as a Royal Marine and then became a career civil servant. At Paris he was head of the British Secretariat, as well as secretary to the Big Four, and was to specialize in this work for countless national and international conferences. Eventually he became Minister Without Portfolio in the War Cabinet (1939–40).

position, and it is a very hawklike, ferocious orb. Nothing was accomplished, of course, and the same matter is to come up again this afternoon. It all shows the futility of the organization which keeps the Four by themselves, separated from the foreign ministers and the other Commissioners. Actually things went more speedily in the old Council of Ten. I believe that the fault lies largely with Lloyd George who dislikes Lansing and doesn't get on with Balfour and insisted that the heads of governments must meet by themselves.

I am enclosing an article from the *Journal de Débats* which summarizes the coolest French opinion on the Senate and which may interest you. Over here the opinion that the League is a necessity and cannot be separated from the treaty is general now in all quarters; there is great confusion of ideas resulting from the Senate's attitude. It is often ascribed to the desire on the part of American industrialists to get in again with Germany and make a separate peace for the advantage of American trade; naturally this does not help our popularity. I can forgive most of the senators because I don't think they can understand conditions outside of the United States; but I find it hard to believe that Lodge doesn't realize what a dangerous game he is playing.[19]

People are not worrying very much about the Germans. The general belief is that they will not sign next week, alleging that they need a mandate from their people before they can suscribe to such hard terms. It seems clear that Brockdorff would have to resign before he could consent, for he has characterized them as impossible. The chances seem to be that they will play for time, that our troops will advance a short distance, occupying Essen and important points, and that we shall begin a blockade. Then they will come around to it, protesting that it is a treaty forced on them. But affairs are so confused in Germany that all our intelligence reports are contradictory and they may sign up at once.

19. Henry Cabot Lodge (1850–1924), Republican senator from Massachusetts and chairman of the Foreign Relations Committee after 1918, led the fight to reject the Treaty of Versailles.

Our perfect weather continues and I hope that we shall be able to get in at least one more trip into the country. Tuesday night we had Clive's and my cousin, Betty Andrews, to dinner. She had been over here since last October in the Y. Last night Mlle. Turpin came to dinner with us, Lester, and Clive.

I have just had another interview with the Commissioners over Klagenfurt. The three[20] are really rather pathetic. They are excluded from the decision of all points, except where the Council of Four lets the other Commissioners in; very often their decisions are turned down flat, and they must often ask themselves what they are doing here. In many matters the advice of the experts is asked when the matter is not even referred to the Commissioners. But they play the game, meet regularly by themselves to consider everything that comes up, and keep perfectly good-natured on the surface, though they must often be galled by their position. I am not sure but that their position is inevitable, but it is nonetheless difficult.

·   ·   ·

The letter of June 19 was the last sent from Paris. After all the uncertainty about returning, the Seymours, Day, and Westermann were able to secure passage on President Wilson's ship, which sailed from Brest on June 29 and landed in New York on July 8. The following memoranda were penned en route.

·   ·   ·

Aboard the S.S. *George Washington*

Tuesday, July 2, 1919

Not having written any letters for ten days I want to put down some diary jottings. I talked with Westermann this morning about the Near East. He is pessimistic—feels that the peace is an "old peace" and in the East is a prelude of war.

Constantinople is not yet decided. May go to Turkey; otherwise an international state.

20. Bliss, Lansing, and White.

Greece is to secure an area in western Asia Minor. This was opposed by Westermann, who thinks that it will lead to trouble. Inhabitants are opposing the entrance of Greek troops—will fight Greek control. British officers think the Greeks cannot hold it without the support of the League. Venizelos realizes the difficulty of the future but must go back from the Conference "with the bacon" in order to hold his position in Greece—where he has martial law and his monarchist enemies locked up. Westermann evidently looks upon Venizelos as a great statesman, but of the old type, using his position in the League merely for the advantage of Greece.

Turkey is presumably to be independent but confined to the Anatolian plain.

Armenia indeterminate. British very anxious to have the United States take the mandate. Hoover wants us to tell British that they should take Armenia if they take Mesopotamia; otherwise we should take both.

Syria and Mesopotamia to be mandates, probably the former of the French, the latter of the British. Westermann thinks that the French in Syria means war. Wilson is opposed to it.

Palestine to be free, a mandate under Britain.

Above are based on Wilson's reply to Westermann's questions. Talked about influence of Colonel House with Wilson. Westermann thinks that it began to wane in mid-May and became apparent in June. Called in the Crillon "Passing of the Third Floor Front." I put the wane a little earlier, possibly about the time of the Fiume incident.

Last night went to dinner given by Lamont in honor of his wife's birthday. At one table sat Clive, Vance McCormick, Gladys, Mr. Lamont, Miss Benham, Baruch; at the other Mrs. Lamont, myself, Norman Davis, Shotwell, Taussig,[21] R. S. Baker. Davis told us about the negotiations in the Reparations Commission: Lloyd George was

21. Miss Edith Benham was Mrs. Wilson's secretary. Frank William Taussig (1859–1940), Harvard-trained economist, served on the Harvard faculty from 1882 until 1935. From 1917 to 1919 he was chairman of the United States Tariff Commission, and at Paris he was a technical adviser in the Economic Section of the Peace Commission.

very shifty and clever, as Shotwell said, like the "bright boy that doesn't have to study." Lloyd George was in a bad position because in his election speech he had promised 24 billion pounds.[22] His good sense knew that he couldn't get it. When he meant to do business he brought along Montagu and Keynes;[23] when he was going to hedge he brought in Sumner and Cunliffe.[24] Once when the thing seemed fixed two months ago (Wilson being ill and House taking his place) Davis said, pointing to Lloyd George who had Summer and Cunliffe with him, "There's nothing doing—see whom he has got."

At Gladys' table they talked home politics, Lamont getting Baruch and McCormick to suggest presidential candidates. They spoke of Wood.[25] Baruch said that if Henry P. Davison had broken connection with Morgan when he went into the Red Cross nothing could stop him. We all went to the movies afterwards. Very interesting party.

Yesterday afternoon discussed Wilson with Westermann and Magie.[26] Former thinks that he is a man "without greatness who will go down in history as great." Great characteristic is his almost

---

22. $120,000,000,000.

23. Edwin Samuel Montagu (1879–1924), statesman and financier, was Financial Secretary to the British Treasury, 1914–16, and Minister of Munitions in 1916. From 1917 until 1922 he was Secretary of State for India. John Maynard Keynes, 1st Baron of Tifon (1883–1946), economist, statesman, and author, was the principle representative of the British Treasury at the Peace Conference. Thereafter he became one of the Treaty's harshest critics and wrote *The Economic Consequences of the Peace* (New York, 1919), which Seymour, in turn, criticized sharply. After World War II he became a governor of the International Bank for Reconstruction and Development. Montagu and Keynes agreed in principle with the Americans that the final reparations figure must be reasonable and within Germany's capacity to pay.

24. John Andrew Hamilton Sumner, 1st Viscount of Ibstone (1859–1934), lawyer and judge, was a member of the Reparations Commission. Walter Cunliffe, 1st Baron Cunliffe (1855–1920), was a financier and a governor of the Bank of England. Sumner and Cunliffe were labeled "the heavenly twins" because of the astronomically high reparations figures they advocated.

25. General Leonard Wood (1860–1927), physician, army officer, and colonial administrator, fought with Theodore Roosevelt's "Rough Riders" and served as military governor of Cuba, 1899–1902, then of Mindanao, 1903. He was Chief of Staff of the Army, 1910–14, and received frequent mention as a possible Republican presidential candidate in 1916 and again in 1920. In 1921 he became governor general of the Philippines and served in that post until 1927.

26. David Magie, German-trained professor of classics at Princeton, served with the Inquiry in connection with Syria and Lebanon.

feminine intuition in feeling what the people want and giving it expression in words. A perfect demagogue. Caught the idea of "self-determination" (stolen by the Bolshevists from the German Socialists) and made it popular. When it came to giving practical effect to the idea in the treaty, he failed.

Magie agreed with me that he had not failed, that he had put through a peace which marked a long step in advance, especially as it had written in it the Covenant of the League. Magie told of the ease with which Wilson threw off his worries. Agreed about his personal magnetism and his useless alienation of persons. Compared it to his fight for the quad system in Princeton—failed for the moment but will finally come.[27]

Aboard the S.S. *George Washington*

[Undated]

Economic difficulties are only the prelude to political conflicts between the different races who, as a natural result of the recent development of the nationalistic spirit, are mutually jealous and suspicious of each other. Never has racial hatred approached such a white heat of intemperance as in these last 14 months.

The Czechs and the Poles are at swords points over the coal mines in Teschen. More than once feeling has burst out into armed conflict. However the boundary is drawn, both sides will be discontented. In Galicia the handing over of the eastern part of the province to Poland has left a soreness which may at any moment fester into a political ulcer. In the Banat Rumanians and Serbs are at drawn daggers, and there is the pathetic spectacle of two nations, friends in the long days of oppression and prosecution, but who now in the moment of prosperity and freedom are brought by their dispute over a few square miles of territory into close proximity of war. It is natural, possibly inevitable, but pathetic.

27. While president of Princeton, Wilson tried to eliminate the social eating clubs and institute a system of residential quadrangles.

Hungary is complaining of the loss of her territory to Austria, Czechoslovakia, and Rumania; Austria is bewailing the aggressiveness of the Jugoslavs on her new southern boundary; and in the Tyrol 400,000 German Austrians[28] are vowing to provide all the trouble they can to the Italian government which has annexed them; and if we remember the rebellion led a century ago by the Tyrollese Andreas Hofer[29] against Napoleon we must admit they probably know how to make trouble.

In the Adriatic there is always dynamite. The Italians feel that their services in the war have not been recognized and that their just reward is being withheld from them and given to the enemies of the Allies who fought for four years under the Hapsburg standards. The Jugoslavs are convinced that, simply because Italy is a big power, justice is denied them and that territories inhabited by a majority of Jugoslavs and essential to the economic life of Jugoslavia are about to be given to Italy simply because England and France are afraid of making her sore.

· · ·

Nearly three months after his return to New Haven Charles Seymour received the following message, which was dated "Paris, June 28, 1919" but was not mailed from Washington until October 1.

· · ·

Dear Dr. Seymour:

With the completion of your work with the American Commission to Negotiate Peace, we, the Commissioners, desire to extend to you, on behalf of the Government which we represent, as well as personally, our warm thanks for the important services which you have rendered your country while on duty here. The task of making peace has been great and arduous and our country is indebted to those

28. The number later proved to be only 250,000.
29. Hofer (1767–1810) was a famed patriot who led the successful 1809 rebellion against the Bavarian government but was later defeated by combined French and Bavarian troops. He fled into hiding, was betrayed, captured, and shot.

who, like you, have rendered such valuable service to the Government.

You take with you the sincere wishes of the Commission for the future.

Faithfully yours,

s/ ROBERT LANSING
HENRY WHITE
E. M. HOUSE
TASKER H. BLISS

INDEX

Vosnjak, Bugumil, 66
Vreeland, Herbert Harold, Jr., 88–89

Walworth, Arthur C., xvii
Warren, William C., 242
Waters, William Otis, Jr., 96, 149–50
Watkins, Charles Law, 47, 64, 76, 140, 195
Westermann, William Linn, xxvii–xxviii, 7, 15, 22, 27, 39, 91, 186, 274–75
What Really Happened at Paris, xiv
White, Henry, xxxi, 279; Seymour's meeting with, 10; speaks about Algeciras Conference, 13; opposes elements of League of Nations restricting national sovereignty, 30–31; reminiscences about beginning of World War I, 30; on voyage to Conference, 32, 51; views on League of Nations compared with those of Bliss, 54, 62; Seymour to brief for interview, 122; meeting with Cellere, 126–29; excluded from decisions, 206–07; end of mandate as Peace Commissioner, 249
White, Mrs. Henry, 10
Widor, Charles Marie, 73
Wilhelm, Crown Prince of Germany, 14, 15
Wilson at Versailles, vii, xi
Wilson, Woodrow: as leader of delegates to Paris Peace Conference, vision of new world, viii; rejection of French proposals to renounce "secret treaties," ix; program a radical approach to national problems, ix; resurgence of international democratic idealism sparked by, x; plan impossible to ignore as basis for *1919* Versailles Treaty, price of obtaining League of Nations, x; conduct of Conference, xi; epitomized quarrel over isolation vs. involvement, xi; promised open meetings, discovery of impossibility in practice, xi–xii; use of scholars of the Inquiry, xiii, xxx; conviction of need

Wilson, Woodrow *(cont.)*
of League of Nations, xiii; estrangement from Col. House, xv; decision to go to Paris, xviii; illness and defeat, xviii; preparation for conference, xxi–xxii; relations with Military Intelligence Division, xxx–xxxi; voyage on *George Washington,* 6–7, 10, 12, 16, 21, 24, 28–29, 31; reversals in elections, problems of Conference, 34–35; arrival in Brest, 36–40; at opening of Conference, 114–15; accord with British on League of Nations and disposal of German colonies, 135–36; departure from Paris, 163; return to Paris, 183; opposes Orlando on Fiume, 191 n.; plans to leave Paris on *May 5, 1919,* on *George Washington,* 195; stand on Italian threat to League of Nations, 203; support from British and French press, 212; fear for U.S. support of League, 217; opposes French annexation of Alsace-Lorraine, 243; praises American delegates, 253; in Belgium on way to U.S., 271; sailed for U.S. from Brest, 274
Wilson, Mrs. Woodrow (Edith Bolling Galt), xviii, 10; Seymour's opinion of, 5–6, 30; arrival in Brest, 37, 104
Wiseman, Sir William, xvii
Woodrow Wilson, xvii
Woodrow Wilson, Life and Letters, xxiv
Woodrow Wilson and World Settlement, xxiv
Woodrow Wilson and the World War, xiv
Wood, General Leonard, 276
Wyeth, Mrs. John A., 60

Yale University, xii, xiv, xv, xvi–xvii, xix, xxiii, xxv, xxvi, 36, 104, 105
Young, Allyn A., 6, 30, 62, 204

Zolger, Ivan Ritter von, 120 n., 210 n., 240